UNITED STATES OF AMERICA VS. SEX

HOW THE MEESE COMMISSION LIED ABOUT PORNOGRAPHY

BY PH███ █████ AND ███ █████DLER

MINOTAUR PRESS, LTD.
A PENTHOUSE INTERNATIONAL COMPANY

Copyright © 1986 by Minotaur Press, Ltd.

All rights reserved

No portion of this book may be reproduced—mechanically, elec-
tronically or by any other means, including photocopying—without written permission of the publisher.

ISBN 0-89110-020-2

Library of Congress Catalog Card Number 86-61758

Unless otherwise specified, the authors have relied on official
transcripts of the Meese Commission and personal interviews
for the quotations in this book.

Interior designed by John Arocho

Minotaur Press, Ltd.
A Penthouse International Company
1965 Broadway
New York, NY 10023-5965

Manufactured in the United States of America

First printing: September 1986

10 9 8 7 6 5 4 3 2 1

THIS BOOK IS FOR

Rob Kenney
and
Emanuel Nadler

and for the American people
who take pleasure
in the First Amendment

CONTENTS

PREFACE

W hen Attorney General Edwin Meese announced the appointment of a new pornography commission in May of 1985, we took notice. As editors of *Forum* and journalists of sexual politics, we have observed the recent quarrels over erotica in America. We surmised that a conservative administration's foray into the erogenous zone would be a fascinating but scary enterprise in censorship.

We set out to follow the Meese commission around the nation and report on its theory and practice. What we discovered along the way in hearings, executive meetings and conversations with the commissioners themselves alarmed and ultimately dismayed us. While the panel's verdict was a foregone conclusion, owing to its mandate and membership, we could not have predicted the depth of its bias and the lack of its intellectual rigor.

Although the universality of sexual images in our culture offends many citizens on moral, political and aesthetic grounds, erotica stands for an idea. And when the government joins forces with special-interest groups to repress freedom of thought, it is time to protest their not-so-silent scream.

—*Philip Nobile and Eric Nadler*

New York, New York
June, 1986

"The increasing number of sex crimes is due precisely to sex literature madly presented in certain magazines. Filthy literature is the great moron maker. It is creating criminals faster than jails can be built."

—*J. Edgar Hoover*

CHRONOLOGY

September, 1970—Panel appointed by President Lyndon B. Johnson to investigate obscenity and pornography issues its final report. It urges repeal of virtually all obscenity laws.

May, 1984—President Reagan calls for the establishment of new commission.

May 20, 1985—Attorney General Edwin Meese announces the appointment of the new panel.

June 19–20, 1985—First public hearing, in Washington: Overview of pornography.

July 24–25, 1985—Second public hearing, in Chicago: Law Enforcement.

September 11–12, 1985—Third public hearing, in Houston: Social Science.

October 16–17, 1985—Fourth public hearing, in Los Angeles: Production and Distribution.

November 20–21, 1985—Fifth public hearing, in Miami: Child Pornography.

January 21–22, 1986—Sixth public hearing, in New York: Organized Crime.

February 11, 1986—Executive Director Alan Sears notifies RCA, CBS, Ramada Inns, Warner Communications and the Southland Corporation, among others, that they have been identified as pornography distributors and that, unless they prove otherwise in 30 days, they will be described as such in the commission's final report.

February 26–March 1, 1986—Work session in Scottsdale, Arizona.

February 28, 1986—Alan Sears, executive director of the panel, says documents will no longer be released to the public.

April 3, 1986—American Civil Liberties Union sues the commission for withholding draft report and working papers.

April 10, 1986—Justice Department settles case, agrees to release materials.

April 10, 1986—Southland Corporation announces it will no longer sell *Penthouse, Playboy* and *Forum* at its 7-Eleven outlets.

April 29, 1986–May 2, 1986—Final work session in Washington, D.C.

May 15, 1986—*Penthouse* sues the commission.

May 19, 1986—*Playboy* and the American Booksellers Association sue the commission.

June 30, 1986—*Playboy* announces future pictorial, "The Girls of 7-Eleven."

July 3, 1986—Federal court orders the commission to retract the Sears letter.

July 9, 1986—Release of the Final Report of the U.S. Attorney General's Commission on Pornography.

EROTIC NATION

On the morning of April 29, 1986, in a government annex building in Washington, D.C., 11 carefully chosen advisers to the United States Justice Department debated the pros and cons of a lesbian-orgy movie.

"Does it make any difference if the camera is five feet away or three inches away from a lady's vagina?" an ex-sheriff wondered.

"Can such a film depict truly loving, mutual and consensual sex?" a jittery law professor asked.

The seven men and four women soon moved on to other pressing topics.

"I've got a couple of questions about bestiality," said a former aide to Richard Nixon.

11

"What about a man having sex with a dog?" A medievalist who has never had sex with anybody scratched his bald head.

A radio evangelist asked the group to spend a few minutes thinking about the explicit details of "a woman masturbating with a bottle."

A women's-magazine editor was upset that some of her colleagues were confused about the actual degree of cunnilingus that Jon Voight performed on Jane Fonda in *Coming Home*.

And a psychiatrist with known FBI connections pointed out that François Truffaut may have padded the population of sex deviates by bringing a leg fetishist to the screen in *The Man Who Loved Women*.

After 10 months on the job, the Attorney General's Commission on Pornography—the F Troop of the Erogenous Zone—was still wandering in the briar patch of the bizarre during its climactic deliberations.

THE NEW AGE OF PORNOGRAPHY

Not so long ago pornography was thought of as something relatively shocking. In the late 50s, for instance, commerce in hard-core was generally confined to red-light districts, and romantic movies went all the way only in the seldom-seen "French version." *Playboy*, then the leader of the pack, still felt compelled to depilate the deltas of every girl-next-door.

The deluge originated in the cradle of modern erotica—Scandinavia. When Denmark dropped the legal fig leaf in the late 60s, real pornography began to flower as never before. Pictures of genitals in gridlock were openly displayed and hurriedly sold in special sex shops and even in neighborhood grocery stores.

The pornographic temptation was irresistible in the United States. The 1970 Presidential Commission on Obscenity and Pornography paved the road by recommending the abolition of obscenity laws. After two years of study, the 18-member panel (minus three dissenters) found that neither hard-core nor soft-core leads to antisocial behavior.

Although Richard Nixon and the Senate distanced themselves from the controversial report, the Scandinavianization of American sex gradually unfolded. Men's magazines got more explicit; porn movies rose from the tenderloin to the neighborhood Bijous; an actress known merely as a deep fellatrix became a household name. There was Jackie O. naked in *Screw,* pubic hair off-Broadway and off-the-street orgies at Plato's Retreat on Manhattan's West Side. Adult bookstores broke out of the inner city and popped up in shopping malls in suburbia. Live sex shows were winked at by world-weary cops. Soon a beauty queen would be stripped in shame. And then there came Prince, the Rock & Roll Rambo of self-stimulation.

But it was the rise of the videocassette that made every VCR owner his or her own maharaja of erotic delights. In 1984 the Video Software Dealers Association estimated that 54 million X-rated tapes were rented from 14,000 national outlets. Adult cassettes comprised approximately 20 percent of a $2 billion trade.

Apparently pornography, especially hard-core, recognizes no class distinctions. In the village of Scarsdale, a quintessential Eden in New York's Westchester County, the Video Ranger store does heavy traffic in hard-core—an estimated 35 percent of its rentals. Today more sexual materials are sold through regular retail establishments than in traditional peep emporiums. And for the first time in history, the United States has begun exporting more hard-core material than it imports.

By the 80s, Hollywood was thoroughly eroticized. Teenage summer movies like *Porky's, Caddyshack, Little Darlings, Sixteen Candles, Risky Business* and *Meatballs* were

13

studded with crowd-pleasing scenes of sexual initiation. Prime-time television turned pink thematically. Unwedded sex abounded in evening soaps. TV movies and miniseries were special realms of illicit behavior. On any given night during the sweeps, viewers could watch a priest sleep with his girlfriend in "The Thornbirds" and a father molest his daughter in "Something About Amelia."

The pornography revolution seemed almost invisible in satiation. As a measure of frustration, the Catholic Church's Legion of Decency changed its name and stopped condemning films with its once feared C-rating.

But not all citizens accepted the country's liberated state of affairs. Conservative activists from conservative churches kept porn and its pomps on the agenda. In their hearts they believe explicit sex is wrong and regard the report of the 1970 commission as the *Roe vs. Wade* of lust.

Outfits like the National Federation for Decency and Citizens for Decency Through Law sprang up with glossy newsletters and computerized mailing lists to do battle with purveyors. Reverend Jerry Falwell of the Moral Majority urged born-again citizens to march upon the gates of distributors. Local boycotts forced scores of small retailers to stop selling men's magazines.

The anti-porn movement cheered the election of Ronald Reagan and took their case directly to him.

In March of 1983, the president told a group of perturbed clergymen at a private White House meeting that his administration had "identified the worst hazardous waste sites in America. We have to do the same with the worst sources of pornography."

Two months later 100 Catholic bishops wrote to Reagan requesting a federal coordinator to monitor enforcement of obscenity laws. Reagan was sympathetic but noncommittal. Nonetheless, he soon sent congratulations to the Reverend John Berns of the Lima (Ohio) Rock Life Fellowship Church, who lugged a six-foot crucifix for 83 miles to protest pornography in his community.

Meanwhile support for censorship swelled among women. Some mainstream feminists, like *Ms.* editor Gloria Steinem, harking to a distinction between smooth erotica and hairy pornography, argued that pornography degraded women and hampered full emancipation. In a 1977 *Ms.* piece, Steinem declared civil war on everybody who so much as looks at porn or tolerates those who do. "We now have the courage to demonstrate publicly against pornography, to keep its magazines and films out of our houses, to boycott its purveyors, to treat even friends and family members who support it as seriously as we would treat someone who supported and enjoyed Nazi literature or the teachings of the Klan," she wrote.

The National Organization for Women passed a resolution against porn at its 1984 convention. On the radical feminist fringe, Women Against Pornography successfully introduced into political debate the notion of pornography as a violation of women's civil rights. (The Supreme Court eventually ruled that the ordinance passed in Indianapolis was unconstitutional.)

Even a few liberals became squeamish about the trend toward rousing explicitness. Sociologist David Reisman, author of *The Lonely Crowd,* moaned in an interview about the "lack of celibate role models for young women" and applauded the backlash: "It's an overreaction to be sure, but an overreaction to an overpermissive, overlascivious culture of hedonism."

By the second term of Ronald Reagan, it was time for grousers to have a pornography commission of their own.

The president made the announcement on the occasion of signing the Child Protection Act of 1984. At a Rose Garden ceremony, Reagan told an appreciative audience about his Sex War plans.

"In the last few months, we've seen news reports of cases involving child pornography and child abuse on a large scale. We've seen reports suggesting a link between child molesting and pornography. And academic studies have suggested a link between pornography and sexual violence toward women.

"Back in 1970, you may recall, a presidential commission studied the whole issue. And its famous conclusion was that pornography had no significant effect on behavior.

"I think the evidence that has come out since that time, plus the tendency of pornography to become increasingly more extreme, shows that it is time to take a new look at this conclusion, and it's time to stop pretending that extreme pornography is a victimless crime.

"And so I want to announce that the attorney general is setting up a new national commission to study the effects of pornography on our society. The commission will study the dimensions of the problem and what we can do about it . . . .

"We consider pornography to be a public problem, and we feel it is an issue that demands a second look."

Thus, mouthing the major clichés of the anti-erotica movement, an amiable president authorized his detectives to find the elusive smoking gun in the porn-crime connection. The move had political dividends for the Reagan Revolution. It was easier to blame pornographers for battered wives than it was to explain why his administration was closing shelters for such women. It was the sexual equivalent of blaming trees for pollution while gutting the Environmental Protection Agency.

PACKING THE COMMISSION

Inside the Justice Department, then-Attorney General William French Smith asked his chief aide, Harold "Tex" Lezar, to get the pornography project off the ground. He was the right man for the job. A Yale graduate (1970) with a

Chairman Henry Hudson: work-aholic prosecutor; bulldog style; an erotic illiterate; never read Ulysses, Lolita, *or* Lady Chatterley's Lover; *naked of own ideas; president nominated him for U.S. attorney for Eastern District of Virginia in March; effectively locked Commission into his law-and-order plans; favorite question of victim-witnesses: Is it your contention, then, that pornography contributed to your injuries?*

degree from the University of Texas Law School, Lezar was a familiar face in right-wing Republican circles.

He composed unsigned editorials at the *National Review* while serving as William F. Buckley's assistant in 1971 and 1972; wrote speeches for Richard Nixon into the final days; and toiled as special counsel to John Connally. Merrie Spaeth, a former child actress and Reagan assistant, was his second wife.

Lezar directed young Justice Department officers to cruise the nation in search of talent. The attorney general's men did not knock on the doors of the sex and civil liberties establishments. They talked, instead, to priests, child abuse experts, evangelists and criminologists.

The investigators took pains to weed out potential troublemakers. Prospective commissioner Lois Lee, the director of Children of the Night, an organization in Los Angeles that counsels young prostitutes, says she made the mistake of informing one of the feds that she accepted funds from The Playboy Foundation. "After that, things just died," she recalled.

The retirement of William French Smith delayed the

start-up for a few months. When he quit, Tex returned to his home on the range, signing on with the Dallas law firm of Carrington, Coleman, Solman, and Blumenthal.

But the new attorney general, Ed Meese, kept up the battle. No fan of explicit sex, he once backed a call to make selling minors a magazine with a naked female breast a federal crime.

He owed this lame-duck valentine to old friends. And after settling in, Meese delivered. The attorney general must have been tickled by the final picks:

Father Bruce Ritter, a stern Franciscan priest who rescues runaways in Times Square. The executive director of Covenant House thought pornography was immoral and worse. In a 1984 article, "The Sexual Exploitation of America," Father Ritter chided politicians who have "failed to recognize the role which *adult* pornography can play in harming our young." He even condemned Dr. Ruth Westheimer for extolling orgasms in premarital sex. In one bizarre ad pitch for Covenant House, Father Ritter charged that a "major Fortune 500 company" operated a sex ring providing young boys to their pedophile clients (the New York County district attorney's office reported that the priest had never referred the case to them).

Father Ritter was no stranger to Justice Department officials. They had given him $1.25 million in grants since 1982 for his operation.

Dr. James Dobson, the founder and president of Focus on the Family, a publishing and broadcast organization dedicated to the maintenance of "traditional values." Dr. Dobson, called the "Dr. Spock of the Right," was the author of the best-selling *Dare to Discipline*, which counseled spanking kids for their own good. The professional Christian from southern California could not cope with the sexual revolution. "The indiscriminate release of sexual energy

outside the boundaries of the family is potentially cata-
strophic,'' Dr. Dobson commented in another book. ''The
very force which binds a people together then becomes an
agent for its own destruction.''

Dr. Dobson was blessed with good government connections. He sat on the National Advisory Commission for the
Office of Juvenile Justice and Delinquency Prevention
(headquarters of the administration's other anti-porn initiatives) and was invited to the White House now and then to
talk about tax reform with the president. He also consulted
directly with a higher power, boasting of *two-way* conversations with the Greater Communicator. A gung-ho promot-
er, Dr. Dobson would soon be hawking audiotapes of his
porn commission ruminations at $5.00 a pop.

Frederick Schauer, a professor at the University of Michigan Law School. The bearded and brooding Schauer is
notorious in First Amendment circles for arguing that pornography is not constitutionally protected. In a 1979 volume of *The Georgetown Law Review*, Schauer observed
that a ''prototypical pornography item . . . shares more of
the characteristics of sexual activity than of communicative
processes.'' In plainer speech, the professor thinks that
Debbie Does Dallas is more dildo than movie. Consequently, on his appointment to the commission, he told a local
newspaper reporter ''some regulation of hard-core pornography is permissible.''

Dr. Park Elliot Dietz, a psychiatrist/sociologist at the University of Virginia. The 37-year-old criminologist special-
izes in violent crime and sexual disorders, and believes that
aberrations develop when young males masturbate to
images of deviant or criminal behavior. In *The American
Journal of Psychiatry*, Dietz remarked that ''sadism and
masochism, in the broadest sense, also play a role in all
pornography.'' The president's men knew him well: He was

not only an FBI consultant but an expert government witness at the trial of John Hinckley.

Edward Garcia, a Reagan-appointed federal judge in his late 50s, from Sacramento. Although Judge Garcia prosecuted obscenity cases while a young district attorney, he claimed no special expertise or even interest in the subject. Right connections landed him the job.

Diane Cusack, a councilwoman from Scottsdale, Arizona. She is the mother of three grown children and a community and parish activist of long standing. She admitted knowing very little about pornography, but promised to do her best. Such ignorance did not prevent her from supporting efforts—including restrictive zoning—to harass adult businesses in Scottsdale. Coincidentally or not, the national office of Citizens for Decency Through Law was located in her town; its leaders were active in local politics.

Dr. Judith Becker, a nationally recognized expert on the treatment of sex offenders and their victims and the director of the sexual behavior clinic at the New York State Psychiatric Institute. Dr. Dietz had suggested this front-line psychologist for the panel.

Deanne Tilton, the head of the California Consortium of Child Abuse Councils. The soft-spoken former social worker had recently testified before the White House's task force on family violence. Ursula (Mrs. Ed) Meese sat on that panel. Tilton had a special interest in child pornography.

The token media seat went to **Ellen Levine**, the editor of *Woman's Day*. Despite her association with the libertine *Cosmopolitan,* where she was decorating and food editor, nobody at Justice took her for a screwball or wrote off her vote. If balance demanded a representative of the press, then Levine was a safe choice. As the mother of two teen-age boys, she was personally concerned about Dial-a-Porn and cable erotica—mothers who read her magazine also expressed alarm. The attorney general could count on the author of *Children's Rooms, Waiting For Baby* and *Planning Your Wedding* not to make a big scene;

Tex Lezar, the commission's early architect, agreed to sign on as vice-chair.

Ed Meese could bet his badge on this all-white, middle-aged, upper-class and presumably heterosexual citizens' council, but he was not taking any chances. An independent chairman of uncertain sympathies might ruin the sting. What the attorney general required in order to lock up the case was an enforcer, preferably an ambitious Republican stiff. The ideal candidate would be a pale, balding, humor-less ex-deputy sheriff of narrow reading, tastes and interests who lusted after a U.S. attorney's post.

Henry Hudson was the Ace in the Hole. Known as "Hang 'em High Henry" for his obsessive pursuit of crime-doers, the 38-year-old commonwealth's attorney for Arlington County, Virginia, consistently refused to coddle offenses of the venereal type. "I live to put people in jail," he told the *Washington Post*. His campaigns against massage parlors, adult bookstores, prostitutes and merchants of X-rated vid-eotapes paid off with a White House commendation in 1983. He was a superstar among a tiny band of smut-busting commissars dotting the nation. He would give his soul brothers a platform on which to rap about the struggle.

As his executive director, Hudson selected **Alan Sears**, a 34-year-old federal prosecutor from Louisville. A carefully groomed man with Southern courtesy, the Kentuckian was one of the few U.S. attorneys in the nation to bring obscenity cases to trial in recent years. The boyish, bespectacled

21

Sears was first exposed to the trade when he indicted two 14-year-old boys whose exploding Coke bottle went off inside a 19-year-old actress while they were making a home porn movie. In his office, Sears proudly displayed a collection of baseball caps from federal law-enforcement agencies next to a framed copy of the Ten Commandments. And unbeknownst to the commissioners, he had a secret religious agenda.

To assist Sears, Hudson assembled a team of gun-toting cops from the FBI, the U.S. Postal Service, the Customs Service and D.C.-area police departments.

Legal backup was provided by David Cayer—a 34-year-old attorney who toiled as Hudson's assistant in Virginia for four years before moving on to a post at the Department of Agriculture. Cayer was aided by Genny McSweeny, a young California blonde fresh out of law school who scored points on the Reagan Inaugural Committee.

The anti-porn tilt of the commission was so obvious that the attorney general took heat from the press the moment he announced his appointments on May 20, 1985.

"Is there anyone on the lists that we are missing that does not have a background of having expressed an opinion or worked with the law, prosecuted, judged or crusaded for a particular position?" asked one reporter.

Meese didn't even blink: "I think it really is a very broad-based commission."

1970: THE ORIGINAL COMMISSION

The antipornography movement saw the new panel as the most effective way to discredit the devasting verdict of the 1970 presidential commission. For years, critics had wailed that the earlier jury was packed with card-carrying members of the ACLU who tripped out on the permissive karma of the 60s.

Its report, decried as a "magna carta for the pornographer," was actually a state-of-the-art study. The panelists appointed by Lyndon Johnson spent $2 million, hired a staff of 22 and sponsored two years' worth of pioneering research. They measured the blood flow in aroused penises, asked married couples how centerfolds affected their bedroom habits and interviewed patrons of peep shows. It was the most thorough investigation of erotica ever undertaken.

As a member of the "effects" panel, Dr. Morris A. Lipton, a research psychiatrist at the University of North Carolina Medical School, recalls devoting 1000-plus hours to the task.

His team tested the notion of satiation to pornography. He got 23 male undergraduates to spend time in a room, 90 minutes a day, five days a week, for three weeks. The students could do anything except homework or fall asleep. For their diversion, Dr. Lipton provided a filing cabinet with four drawers containing (1) porn movies, (2) porn still photos, (3) porn books and (4) old copies of popular magazines. Urine specimens were taken before and after each session and measured for a telltale enzyme in prostatic fluid that flows during sexual arousal.

"We found quick satiation," Dr. Lipton said during an interview in Chapel Hill. "After a day, they were looking at *Popular Mechanics*. The only antisocial effect was that they borrowed the movies to show back in their dorm rooms."

By the time the commissioners were ready to report their findings, Richard Nixon was president. They gave him news he did not want to hear: "If a case is to be made against pornography in 1970, it will have to be made on grounds other than demonstrated effects of a damaging personal or social nature. Empirical research designed to clarify the question has found no reliable evidence to date that exposure to explicit sexual materials plays a significant role in the causation of delinquent or criminal sexual behavior among youth or adults." Thus the panel went on to recommend that "federal, state and local legislation prohibiting the sale, exhibition or distribution of sexual materials to consenting adults be repealed."

In addition, the commission urged a "massive" sex-education effort: "Appropriate sex information provided openly and directly through legitimate channels and from reliable sources in healthy contexts can compete successfully with potentially distorted, warped, inaccurate and unreliable information from clandestine, illegitimate sources."

The commission asked citizens to organize themselves at "local, regional and national levels" to ensure that sex-ed programs became a reality.

Nixon became apoplectic. He blasted the panel's "morally bankrupt conclusions."

"So long as I am in the White House, there will be no relaxation of the national effort to control and eliminate smut from our national life . . . . I totally reject this report."

Nixon had company. Senate leaders in both parties condemned clear thinking on this volatile issue and refused, by a 60-5 vote, to accept it.

Senator Robert Byrd (D-West Virginia) called the sophisticated report "shameful" and criticized the majority of the commissioners as "malicious or misguided or both."

Yet the fairness of the panelists like Dr. Lipton is indisputable. Personally he would have preferred the disappearance of dirty pictures. In fact he expressed regret in the 1970 report that pornography was not nailed.

"We would have welcomed evidence relating exposure to erotica to delinquency, crime and antisocial behavior, for if such evidence existed we might have a simple solution to some of our most urgent problems," he wrote in a personal statement with fellow panelist Dr. Edward Greenwood.

"However, the work of the commission has failed to uncover such evidence. Although the many and various studies contracted for the commission may have flaws, they

24

are remarkably uniform in the direction in which they point. This direction fails to establish a meaningful causal relationship or even a significant correlation between exposure to erotica and immediate or delayed antisocial behavior among adults. To assert the contrary from the available evidence is not only to deny the fact, but also to delude the public by offering a spurious and simplistic answer to highly complex problems.''

Not all of Dr. Lipton's colleagues were persuaded by the evidence. Three dissenters kicked and screamed about the majority report. Morton Hill, S.J., of Morality in Media and Reverend Methodist minister Winfrey Link lambasted the panel in a minority report of their own for not putting God above all.

"The government interest in regulating pornography has always been related primarily to the prevention of moral corruption and *not* to the prevention of overt criminal acts and conduct, or the protection of persons from being shocked or offended,'' they howled.

Commissioner Charles Keating, Jr., a wealthy real-estate developer from Cincinnati who was appointed by Nixon to fill a vacant seat, wanted to know what the majority had been smoking for the last 24 months.

"For a presidential commission to have labored for two years at the expense to the taxpayers of almost two million dollars and arrive at the conclusion that pornography is harmless must strike the average American as the epitome of government gone berserk,'' he said in his separate statement. "Credit the American public with enough common sense to know that one who wallows in filth is going to get dirty.''

He listed a few things that a saner porn commission would have recommended—a federal assault against porn to be launched by a Justice Department task force and a comprehensive data bank on the pornographers. He also called for close monitoring of obscene rock lyrics.

Despite the fulminations of the dissenters, the majority's findings were corroborated by two other government commissions.

The Williams Committee of England and Wales declared in 1979 that "Given the amount of explicit sexual material in circulation and the allegations often made about its effects, it is striking that one can study case after case of sex crimes and murder without finding any hint at all that pornography was present in the background."

And in 1984, Canada's Fraser Committee made the case against linking pornography with decline in the quality of life. "The Committee is not prepared to state, solely on the basis of the evidence and research it has seen, that pornography is a significant causal factor in the commission of some forms of violent crime, in the sexual abuse of children, or the disintegration of communities and society."

This surprising unanimity, coming as it did from three separate bodies studying three separate cultures, was powerful proof that pornography, when considered dispassionately in a climate free from political pressure, is not judged to be a destructive force in society.

But the Meese panel, Charles Keating's dream commission, was not free from political influence. It was born of such pressure.

INSIDE JOB

The 1970 report did not prompt any state to repeal its obscenity laws. But overworked cops and prosecutors now had powerful justification to look the other way.

Although the Meese commission was formed to turn the tide of apathy—cheaply and quickly—it was not a top priority for the administration. The attorney general gave the panel only 12 months and $400,000 to do the job. His orders were direct. "The objectives of the Commission are to determine the nature, extent and impact on society of

26

pornography in the United States," read the charter of the Commission, *"and to make specific recommendations to the Attorney General concerning more effective ways in which the spread of pornography could be contained, consistent with constitutional guarantees"* (emphasis added).

"We won't be contracting out research," Dee Kuhn, the panel's press liaison, explained. "We are hoping that knowledgeable individuals and groups will share their expertise with us."

The accommodating "public hearing" forum was dusted off for that purpose. The Justice Department scheduled six of them over eight months in every region of the country. This tactic was inexpensive, dramatic and promised a few good photo opportunities. Unfortunately hearings were totally ineffective for fact-finding purposes. As the 1970 panel noted, views of most witnesses were predictable.

The decision to go public this time was made by the Justice Department before the commissioners ever met. Hearing agendas and witness lists were likewise drawn up.

Hudson and Sears, also without input from the commissioners, sent their investigators around the country in search of "victims" of pornography. They followed leads suggested by vice cops and the Reverend Donald Wildmon's National Federation for Decency. Hudson's men were helpful sorts; they agreed to write bathos-bathed testimonials against porn for a few of the less literate pornoplegics.

Lois Lee, the jilted prospective commissioner who aids teen hookers, remembered a visit from the victim-seekers. "Ed Chapman came to me and asked to see teenagers who started turning tricks after their fathers showed them *Playboy* and *Penthouse*," she said. "I told him, 'Look, *none* of our kids got into their situations that way.' He said, 'I don't think we're going to want your kids.' The conversation was over."

In effect, Meese's panelists were prisoners of a shrewdly crafted process that lifted the debate out of the labs and into the back alleys, where allegedly porn-crazed men raped America's daughters. Current obscenity laws permit suppression of material simply because it is offensive. The Meese Commission wanted to go further by showing that dirty pictures are demonstrably harmful, and it relied on anecdotes, not science, to make the case.

The Justice Department invited the commissioners to a lynching. An army of vice cops, zealous D.A.'s, worked-up clergymen, man-hating feminists and anonymous "victims" brought the rope. Hudson made sure there was practically no room for those who wanted to cut porn down.

Of the 208 witnesses who addressed the commission, almost four out of five urged tighter controls over sexually explicit material. This included 68 cops, eight elected officials (not one pol spoke in defense of the explicit), 30 victims and 14 representatives of antipornography organizations. Fewer than one in five witnesses dared to suggest that no *new* censorship efforts be undertaken.

Fairness was as lewd to the engineers of the Meese commission as *Ozark Virgin*.

2

FIRST BLOOD

The cavernous Great Hall of the Department of Justice in Washington, D.C., was nearly empty on June 19, 1985, when Henry Hudson opened the government's inquiry into un-American sex. Sitting on a long raised platform, the 11 panelists fingered pens and pencils and prepared for their imminent voyage into the nation's bedrooms and back rooms.

The Justice Department did not delay in setting the tone of the proceedings. The first witness was one of its own—Meese aide Lois Herrington. The heavyset assistant attorney general did not suppress her revulsion for the subject matter.

"Pornography has many facets," she read from a text. "It can be the record of a crime being committed against

29

children. It can be the depiction of women as sexual objects to be used, abused and tossed aside. It can be an anaesthetic desensitizing people to the violence and sexual deviates in society, and it is a source of a multibillion-dollar industry.''

Hewing to the Justice Department's line, she said succinctly, "Pornography victimizes both those whose abuse it depicts, and those whose abuse it provokes.''

Herrington, who coordinates Justice Department symposia on sexual assault and child abuse, cited vice cop claims that sex crimes rise with the availability of hard-core.

She quoted a Michigan police survey indicating that "in at least 41 percent of sexual assaults, pornography was used or imitated just prior to or during the act.'' For her haymaker, Herrington noted that 29 of 36 serial killers studied by the FBI "were attracted to pornography and reenacted its lessons in their pattern of serial rape, mutilation and murder.'' Herrington failed to mention that these men were obviously psychotic (as serial killers tend to be), with histories of alcoholism, drug abuse and sexually abusive parents.

Herrington even linked naughty pictures of consenting adults to the horror of child molestation: "The Family Violence Task Force found that parents and other trusted adults who wanted to cultivate sexual relations with children often leave pornography many times in their own home, exposing their children to preconditioned behavior.

"One," she emphasized, "kept the material in his son's toy drawer.''

Herrington then turned to the tragic and sensational issue of kiddie porn: "[Child pornography] is a photographic record of a crime in progress and that crime can devastate the life of a child. We heard of a 14-year-old girl who was taken to Children's Hospital National Medical Center (in D.C.) for attempting to commit suicide. She had been continually truant from school as well and when teachers asked her why, she revealed that her mother had forced her into pornography to supplement the family income.

"That child," she said, pausing for maximum effect, "is now institutionalized."

Herrington advised the panel to brace itself for the testimony to come. "You will hear of these cases and they will stir you. They will outrage you and they will surely compel you to action."

Finally, Ed Meese's assistant gave the commission its marching orders: "It is your mission to open the public's eyes to a problem that many people have preferred not to see, but see it we must. Pornography is not a victimless crime."

A solemn Chairman Hudson let that sink in for a moment. "We appreciate your insight," he said, breaking the silence in the auditorium.

WITNESSES FOR THE PROSECUTION

What followed in Washington, and to a remarkable degree at the hearings in Chicago, Houston, Los Angeles, Miami and New York, was mere piling-on. Over and over again, the commission heard that porn was "filth," a "killer of souls," an "addiction" and an "insidious cancer."

The second witness on opening day was FBI special agent Kenneth Lanning. The bald G-man was famous in law-enforcement circles for his eye-opening "Overview of Pornography" slide show. Never really off-duty, the agent lugged his prize collection to various religious anti-porn confabs in his spare time. For such good work, Lanning was recruited by the commission's staff and allotted a prime chunk of hearing time.

His presentation in the dimmed hall began innocently with color slides of bare-breasted native women from *National Geographic*. But in no time, agent Lanning had some in the audience wincing with snapshots of babies with

Vice-Chairman Harold "Tex" Lezar: Yale ('70); beefy law-and-order Republican arriviste; second marriage to a former Reagan assistant; friend of recent Attorneys General; architect of Commission while at Justice Department; inspired tough laws recommended in final report; most unforgettable moment at business meeting: when he said to stress the negatives in talking to children about sex.

penises stuffed in their mouths.

"Here we have *Erotica Grotesque* [magazine]," Lanning said, advancing the carousel. "What kind of stuff is in it? We will look through here. (click) Teach you how to drive a nail through the foreskin of your penis. (click) Here is someone urinating in the mouth of his sexual partner. (click) Here is an individual having sex with a dog. A lot of people have seen pictures of women having sex with a dog, but here is one with a man having sex with a dog."

At this point, a wholesome all-American tourist family made the mistake of wandering into the Great Hall. The father ordered little Emily and Stefan to "get up here and watch what the men are doing." Mom and Pop were aghast when Lanning flashed on a man-chicken coupling. The family fled for the exit. But the kids will probably never forget their glimpse of Our Government at Work.

"Here is another publication—*PHQ*," Lanning droned on. "This is designed for a particular audience, those interested in pinning and piercing. There are articles, one using the Indian ritual, in this case, of showing a man having hooks through the skin of his chest being suspended in the air. (click) There is another article that tells you how to impale your penis, giving you step-by-step instructions if you want to drive a nail or bolt through your penis, this is how to do it. (click)

"How to pierce your nipples. (click) Here is one that says if your nipples are pierced and you have rings through your nipples, can you still breast-feed your baby? The article assures you you can and then shows you in pictures that you can still breast-feed your baby. (click)

"Here is one that shows how to stick all these pins and needles in your scrotum and spread it out, 'tacking' as it is sometimes referred to. Pinning and piercing. That is what is portrayed in the magazine. Later on, when the police came, one of these groups—you can't see it very clearly—but there is an actual photograph taken from these individuals. This is a homemade photograph where they are doing exactly what is portrayed in the magazine. In this case the individual has his genitals inserted through a board, but he is having his scrotum tacked out on the other side by his assistant, his partner. Here you can see another view. It would be just as well if you can't see it too clearly."

Like Herrington, Lanning drove home the horrors of kiddie porn. He screened a page from the Sears Roebuck catalog featuring young boys and girls in their underwear and a picture of actress Jessica Lange with her naked baby. "Is this pornography?" agent Lanning asked the panel with a straight face.

"Here you can see an example of another kind of publication. Here a little boy in this is quoted as saying, 'Everyone else has done it, Mr. Brown, please do it. Please fuck me.' "

Lanning finished with an ugly flourish: "This girl here was a young girl, abducted, somebody murdered her, stuck the hand up her vagina and ripped out her intestines. When they went to the subject's house after he left, he had this material, individuals sticking hands in different body parts

33

of people. 'Fist-fucking' as it is called.''

The special agent did not ask for any particular legislation or make any specific recommendations. His slide show was designed solely to supercharge the anti-porn batteries of the commission. Just one hour into the investigation, commissioners were steeped in mutilation, bestiality and murder.

J. Edgar Hoover smiled down from heaven. He hated erotica and all it stood for.

''The circulation of periodicals containing salacious material, and highly suggestive and offensive motion pictures and television, play an important part in the development of crime among our youth,'' he said back in the 60s.

Writing in *This Week,* the director was even more emphatic: ''[T]he flood of pornography that has been circulating among our young people for the past ten years is a major factor in today's rapidly rising rate of sex crime . . . .''

Dorchen Leidholdt, a founder of Women Against Pornography, shuttled down to D.C. with her own slide show. Her presentation, featuring the now famous meat-grinding *Hustler* cover, usually brought gasps to feminists' lips. Next to Lanning's effort, however, Leidholdt's was strictly PG.

Leidholdt told the panel that the 1975 presidential panel was ''blind'' to the reality of porn's effect on women. ''They failed to see that pornography perpetuates the devaluation of women—that it sexualizes bigotry, promotes rape, battery and incest and threatens women's safety and self-esteem.''

Dr. Morris Lipton and his effects panel ''didn't see the married woman whose husband collects bondage pornography, forces it on her and demands that she enact scenarios. They didn't see the girl whose father eyes her developing body in the same way he eyes Penthouse Pets. They didn't see the secretary whose boss subscribes to *Playboy*'s philosophy.''

A few Capitol Hill lightweights appeared at the two-day hearing to score some political points. Six senators—five Republicans and Arizona Democrat Dennis DeConcini urged the passage of their pet censorship bills. Alabama Senator Jeremiah Denton—who linked porn to divorce and the decline of the West—pushed a ban on Dial-a-Porn. Senator Paul Trible (R-Virginia) wanted to give the FBI a green light to tap into computer "bulletin boards" in a search for child molesters.

Surgeon General Everett C. Koop, America's doctor, strolled in to do battle on day two of the hearings. Looking almost fit in his pressed Navy whites, Dr. Koop started by trashing the findings of the 1970 commission, which were supposedly based on a "very limited universe of scientific literature and experience."

"Porn," he said, "is a clear and present danger to American public health." This remark captured the attention of the chairman:

"How do you know porn affects public health?" he asked during the question-and-answer session. The government's physician replied that it was his "intuitive reaction."

But Dr. Koop could not promise any magic bullet: "As much as we might wish for it, we will never come up with a vaccine or a medication that will cure anyone of engaging in pornography."

In closing, he vowed to do all he could to assist the commission. Hudson told him the panel would be in touch.

In this anti-porn circus, Barry Lynn, the wry legislative counsel of the ACLU, took the microphone to offer the best liberal response. The lanky lawyer dismissed as irrelevant the guilt-by-association smear used by porn-haters: "Pedophiles, child molesters, who have been arrested are often found to have in their homes not simply commercial child pornography, but scrapbooks containing department-store underwear advertisements . . . If the measure of suppression was what material caused one person to do, we would all be reduced to sitting in darkened rooms to prevent some errant image from crossing the eye or the mind of someone who would react in an antisocial manner."

He likewise ridiculed the serial-killer connection: "The presence of two phenomena, criminal activity and pornography, does not necessarily demonstrate a causal connection between them. It is at least as likely to demonstrate that people with certain abusive personalities are attracted to both crimes and use for pornography. The fact that most people die in bed should not lead to the conclusion that mattresses are lethal."

That brought Lynn to his coup de grace—the catharsis theory. He quoted Edward Donnerstein of the University of Wisconsin, whose work is often cited by the other camp: "A good amount of research strongly supports the position that exposure to certain types of erotica can reduce aggressive responses in people who are predisposed to aggression."

How did the panel react to the ACLU's defense? Chairman Hudson went right for the jugular. "To what extent has the financial support of your program over the years by The Playboy Foundation had any effect on your views?" he asked Lynn's colleague. Lynn accused Hudson of implying that the ACLU could be "bought off" by *Playboy.* "If that was your intention, it was wholly inappropriate."

Hudson coolly responded: "Your observations have been noted."

Barry Lynn was the Inspector Javert of the pornography commission. He followed it around the nation, debated its executive director, briefed the press on its sins and took to the airwaves to defend the sexually explicit. The media-genic 37-year-old minister and lawyer did his best to lampoon the operation. He took no prisoners, even slapping around the more liberal members for their docility in the face of an aggressive chairman and his closed-minded disciples. By the end of the year-long journey, the dogged Lynn would be dreaming regularly about the Meese Commission members.

THE PORNOPLEGICS: VICTIMS ON PARADE

Meese's men had special shock treatments in store for the public hearings—the lurid, unsubstantiated and unverifiable testimony of victims of sex crimes, drug abuse and alcoholism. Henry Hudson misnamed them "victims of pornography," when it was evident that centerfolds were the least of this sad bunch's problems. Early on the first hearing day in Washington, the Commissioners watched the shadow of a short, skinny male sit down behind a backlighted white curtain.

"My name is David," said a low, almost inaudible voice. "I am seventeen years old. I was born in Massachusetts and I lived there for fourteen years. Then I moved to California. I ran away a lot in my early teenage years and I was moving between my aunt and uncle, with whom I was residing at that time.

"When I was young, my uncle sexually molested me. He introduced me to alcohol and drugs. He took nude photographs of me with body paint and took me to bars and introduced me to some of his friends. My aunt and uncle separated and I was moved to California to live with him.

"I spent a lot of time in Las Vegas with him when he worked as a dealer. I stayed with my aunt until I started to get in trouble. So I moved to California to escape the trouble I had gotten into with drugs.

"The sexual abuse by my uncle continued and I ran away from home.

"I used to travel back and forth from California to Massachusetts. Occasionally I would baby-sit with other relatives when they went to church. One particular occasion, I

37

was baby-sitting and I felt a girl on many occasions. I felt this girl and did sexual things to her—well, after reading *Penthouse* magazines or whatever—to arouse me. I ran away a lot. On one occasion, I was living on a beach and a man approached me and asked me if I had smoked pot. He was about thirty or forty. I told him yes and suggested that maybe we could go to his apartment and get high. He bought clothes for me, fed me and gave me a lot of money and drugs.

"I was sixteen and he offered—he had a lot of sex, he took pictures of me in the nude, also brought in another man who he used to operate a video camera. I lived with him for a while, for about, I'd say, a week, and I was filmed on four occasions. I don't know what happened to these films. He told me they were for him and his friends to view.

"It was a difficult situation for me. And afterwards, I attempted suicide several times. I don't know if I really wanted to kill myself, but I think I wanted attention from people. I felt pretty worthless.

"The sexual abuse that was afflicted on me lowered my self-esteem and the films reminded me of that. I was afraid that this would be shown to the world.

"The drugs helped me escape reality with my sexual degradation, but that added to my depreciation. Since coming to Straight, Inc. [one of Nancy Reagan's pet antidrug clinics], I have been able to regain my feelings of self-importance and self-worth and changed my way of living. I see myself now as a victim, not a participant, someone who used to be abused or was abused. I feel like I can go forward now and create a new life for myself. I hope to return to school and get my diploma and maybe go into law.

"I have set high goals for myself. I want to accomplish these goals and really make something out of my life.

"By coming here today, I am hoping I can help other teenagers and adults understand that not only did I face many obstacles, not only do they have to work on grades and friends, but also they have to fight against the temptation of drugs and alcohol, and their own sexual gratification. That's about all.''

"Do any of the commission members have any questions for David?," asked Chairman Hudson. None had.

The confessions of the pornography victims were controversial from the start. They *were* truly pathetic glimpses of lives lost—drug abuse, bad marriages, child molestation, beatings, forced sex and incest. But each individual dragged the devil of porn into the etiology. It was a cause, not merely an accessory, to their depravity. After the sordid testimony of a father who fondled his daughter's friends and who happened to mention his sizable collection of men's magazines, Father Ritter seized the moment and inquired: "Was pornography the spark that lit the fuse?"

The panel also heard from "Bonnie," now 31, who was sexually and physically abused by her first husband, Leon, a homosexual, and by her second husband. "Pornography," she said, "both hard-core adult and child pornography, appears to have played a significant role in the prolonged period of sexual abuse and resulting family trauma." However, she failed to criticize her poor taste in men.

"Susan" recalled being drugged and "used in group demonstrations" on how to sexually desensitize young girls. Commissioners did not seize the opportunity to ask Susan who did this to her. And poor "Susan" was not terribly clear on the point.

Perhaps the most moving testimony came from Valerie Heller, a New York victims' advocate who eschewed the anonymity of the white curtains to expose her dreadful childhood ordeal of sexual assault by family members, fueled, of course, by their obsession with porn. Her later exploitation coincided with a voracious appetite for angel dust and LSD, but pictures seemed to be the biggest problem. Her self-styled porn crucifixion has left her with sexual stigmata. Apparently, she is still lashed by the unexplained recurrence of "somatic lesions." "They resemble actual attacks or beatings or rapes I have endured."

In Miami, five months later, the commission's most bizarre victim told his sad tale.

Dr. Simon Miranda, a clinical and child psychologist from Miami, counseled many patients troubled by porn. He brought along one of them—Larry Madigan, a frail, neatly dressed Bible-clutcher who spoke without camouflage.

"I am a victim of pornography," he began. "At age twelve, I was a typically normal healthy boy. My life was filled with normal activities and hobbies. All that changed the following summer when I went to visit relatives, a married couple, who decided to teach me about sex. Other than an embarrassing recipe of facts and jokes, the only other recollection pertinent to that memory was that I saw a *Playboy* magazine for the first time in my life.

"All the trouble began a few months later, back at my mother's home. The house we rented had a shed out back, and there's where I found a hidden deck of cards. All fifty-two cards depicted hard-core pornography, penetration, fellatio and cunnilingus. These porno cards highly aroused me and gave me a desire I never had before. My reaction was an obsession to steal *Playboy* magazines at the local grocery and get my hands on any other pornography I could steal. I had never shoplifted before in my whole life.

"About the same time a friend of mine who was thirteen years old would stay overnight at my house occasionally, and he taught me how to masturbate.

"Later, when I showed him the deck of cards, our reaction was to look through a keyhole late at night, after we were supposed to go to bed, to watch my mother undressing.

"I don't know where we got the condoms, but we tried reciprocal anal sexual intercourse. This proved to be painful and we didn't continue. He probably got scared and didn't come back to my house anymore.

"My preoccupation with the pictures escalated, and I drilled some holes in the bathroom ceiling to look at the twenty-five-year-old woman who lived with us. I watched her bathe and also tried to view other women who came to our house. Also, from the pictures, I was stimulated to practice oral and finger stimulation on my parents' dogs. They were females and too small for sexual intercourse. Later, I masturbated with bigger dogs.

"I also went into the room of the woman who lived with us and went through her intimate things and masturbated on her bed. Later on in my life, I would go through other people's things looking for intimate objects, pornography and porno objects. That's where I learned how to masturbate with a vibrator in my rectum.

"By the age of sixteen, after a diet of *Playboy, Penthouse, Scandinavian Children,* perverted paperback books and sexology magazines, I had to see a doctor for neuralgia of the prostate. Later on in my life, after learning so many different ways to masturbate over the years, I caused myself to bleed a number of times, endured painful urination and eventually got a urinary-tract infection. With all the guilt, loneliness and isolation, I turned to drugs for escape and also to heighten the sexual feeling and arousal.

"I used to read Hugh Hefner's Playboy Philosophy, and I am sure through his help I bought the program of the sixties hook, line and sinker. If it feels good, do it.

"I proceeded again to sidetrack my Catholic upbringing about promiscuous sex and, at the age of nineteen and twenty, had sex with two different women, but I was unable to open up emotionally to a woman, so I went back to my perversions.

"Later in life, when I needed a sex escape, I would get aroused by watching R-rated movies on HBO and Showtime cable. I would get off on that and then masturbate.

"In closing, I am thirty-eight years old, unmarried and

41

under the care of Dr. Miranda. I strongly believe and feel that all that has happened to me can be traced back to the finding of those porno cards. If it weren't for my faith in God, and the forgiveness of Jesus Christ, I would now possibly be a pervert, an alcoholic or dead. I am a victim of pornography. Yes, I am a victim, and also totally assuming free will, for I am responsible for my actions.

"But the Bible says, 'I will sprinkle clean water upon you to cleanse you from all your impurities and your idols, I will cleanse you, I will give you a new heart and place a new spirit within you, taking from your bodies your stony hearts and giving you natural hearts. I will put my spirit within you and make you live by my statutes, careful to observe my decrees.''

"Thank you very much."

This was sick theater. Some of the sharper commissioners thought these performances were embarrassing and worthless.

"If I never heard another victim, I would be perfectly happy," Ellen Levine said at an early business meeting. "I felt much of it [their testimony] had been written and structured for them." Hudson admitted it had: his detectives helped pen many of the statements. Judge Garcia pointed out another problem. "I have a tendency to give too little credibility to someone who is not subjected to cross-examination, and who hides his identity."

And even Father Ritter, who purports to know a thing or two about porn victims because of his work with kiddie porn stars in Times Square, called their "emotionally charged" testimony "irrelevant to our central concerns."

Dr. Becker longed to question them closer, but as a clinician with experience working with victims of sexual assault, she knew that she had to tread lightly. But other commissioners thought the awkward tales were important. Arizona's Diane Cusack candidly acknowledged the propaganda value of such testimony: "I see part of our mission as

42

that of bringing this whole issue to the perception of the public at large. And they tend to view things through the eyes of victims far more readily than they do through the eyes of social scientists and research papers.''

Henry Hudson and his oblong staff loved the sad songs of the victims. Based on these informants, Sears dutifully drew up a long bill of indictment against porn. With grim glee the staff typed up the most outrageous allegations. Victims had fiscal problems: Three reported their financial resources being sapped by a relative's addiction to pornography. ''Linda'' lost her home because of her mate's illness; ''Dan'' blew 50 grand on his habit; and ''Sharon'' spent $40,000 in legal fees when she moved against her junkie husband in court.

Hudson and Sears reached back to the nineteenth century to drag another victim into the hearing room. Mary Steinman was a little old lady with a heavy past. At the Chicago hearings she recalled her truly horrible sexual abuse from years past, during the French-postcard era of porn:

''I was sexually abused as a child in my own home. My abuse started at the age of three. My father kept suitcases full of pornography pictures and magazines. From the earliest years he would have me perform oral sex on him. He would hang me upside down in a closet and push objects like screwdrivers or table knives inside me. Sometimes he would heat them first. All the while he would have me perform oral sex on him. He would look at his porno pictures almost every day, using them to get ideas of what to do to me or my siblings. I have had my hands tied, my feet tied, my mouth taped to teach me big girls don't cry. He would tell me I was very fortunate to have a father that would teach me the facts of life. Because of my sexual abuse as a child, I am extremely against pornography, and because of pornography I cannot enjoy sex. The word 'love' is very painful to me. My father said he loved me, and his love hurt me. The mere mention of the word sometimes gives me flashbacks to

43

the abuse I endured as a child.''

What was Mary doing at a 1986 commission on pornography? None of the panelists asked. But Mary told them—she was a professional on the anti-porn circuit.

"I have appeared on numerous radio and television shows, both national and local, in an effort to help other victims of child sexual abuse and to inform listening audiences of the dangers of the use of pornography. I testified in Madison, Wisconsin, in 1984, before the Wisconsin House of Representatives concerning the absence of obscenity laws in that state and to help them formulate new laws regarding obscenity. I also testified in Indianapolis, Indiana, concerning obscenity laws under consideration there.''

The more sophisticated commissioners never took these witnesses seriously. When the staff eventually proposed that states provide financial aid to those afflicted with "pornography-related injuries," Ellen Levine cynically inquired, "What's a porn-related injury?"

"Cigarette burns," suggested Tex Lezar earnestly.

"How about a paper cut when turning the pages?" cracked Dr. Becker. Several commissioners laughed, but the chairman did not even bother to force a smile.

BEHIND THE SCENES: RAPPING WHITE SLAVERY

The Meese Commission could not perform behind closed doors. Unlike the 1970 operation, its executive deliberations were open to the public. The Sunshine Act illuminated the odd quirks, biases and banalities in the minds of 11 citizens sitting around talking about sex on government time. The policy also threw light on ways in which Meese's men successfully coerced the panelists into a rendezvous with censorship.

Unlike the 1970 probers, some of whom took long sabbaticals to investigate the subject in depth, these commissioners treated their work as a part-time hobby. According to the instructions of the Justice Department, they never met privately to discuss the subject and could not even speak to each other over the phone. Their deliberations were confined to business meetings which framed the exhausting public hearings. This arrangement was so confining that 10 days of work sessions were eventually added to the end of the schedule. The agenda was always controlled by the staff.

Hudson ran the panel his way. Before the commission had even begun to discuss whether pornography was harmful, Hudson urged the adoption of a tidal wave of anti-porn measures drafted by Tex Lezar. The first official vote concerned an amendment to the White Slavery Trafficking Act of 1910.

At the first such conclave in Washington, commissioners introduced themselves and related short biographies. Father Ritter was absent because the First Lady was in New York that day touring his Covenant House. And Dr. Dobson was detained because he was visiting his president at the White House.

Chairman Hudson told the panel that his "primary interest" in the venture was to discover "what, if any, relationship there is between the consumption of pornography and the incidence of violent crime in the United States":

"And if we determine that there is a relationship between the two, I am very concerned about trying to develop law-enforcement initiatives that try to curb the flow of pornography. I am also very concerned about the possible impact that pornography may have on children, particularly what, if any, impact it may have on potential child molesters."

Hudson's mind did not appear to be totally open on the key question. "From what I have heard from law-enforcement people and investigators throughout the United States," he said, "I have had enough evidence presented to

45

me that I am very concerned about the possible relationship between porn and sexually violent crime.''

Dr. Dietz suggested hearing from ''individuals who believed they have been helped in some way by pornography.''

Hudson said he had already extended invitations to behavioral scientists who ''believe pornography has a remedial effect on their patients.'' . . . ''Everyone will have an opportunity to testify. I assure you we will have balanced evidence.'' But this assurance proved worthless.

The staff outlined the hearings to come. There would be ''Law Enforcement'' in Chicago; ''Social Science'' in Houston; ''Child Pornography'' in Los Angeles; ''Production and Distribution'' in Miami and ''Organized Crime'' in New York. (The commission swapped the topics in Miami and L.A. when they discovered Los Angeles was the adult-entertainment capital of the world.)

Hudson opened the floor. Was there anything they wanted to discuss?

Dr. Dobson, just back from his White House visit, raised his hand. ''I live in a clean, middle-class neighborhood and there is a very nice mall close to us. A year ago, there was a Hispanic ring . . . and when a girl would be walking alone through the mall, they would walk past her and stick her with a hypodermic needle. She would instantly be out. They would bend over her and say, 'This is my sister and she is having seizures.' And they would bundle her up and take her out. It's my understanding that they were taking them right to Tijuana. They were caught by two girls [who were] together but separate for that moment, and one of them saw what happened and screamed and they caught them.

''I would like at some time to know how widespread abductions are into white slavery.''

Chairman Hudson was willing to explore the troublesome question. ''I think to the extent that it relates to pornography

46

[it] certainly should be relevant.''

Deanne Tilton and Tex Lezar wanted to be sure that the commission would take up feminist concerns. ''This whole question of female subjugation and depiction of male dominance,'' said Tilton. ''That is the woman issue, how women are portrayed, not just in the sense of your normal pornographies, but in submissive roles, and that certainly is an issue.''

''I would like to be sure we were at some point talking about it,'' said Lezar, a John Connally feminist.

Ellen Levine then asked the $400,000 question: ''When are we going to get around to discussing what is going to be considered pornography?''

Hudson replied, ''I appreciate your bringing it up, but I don't know [if] that's within our province.''

''I think you need a common language here,'' Levine insisted.

Dr. Becker agreed. ''I think, as a researcher, the first thing that everybody does is define one's terms.''

Hudson begged off. ''I think these definitions are going to have to just evolve as the commission hears evidence,'' he said. ''We may or may not elect to come up with a definition of pornography.''

3

THE LONG BLUE LINE

Vice cop Mike Berish sipped black coffee in a booth at the Bushwacker Lounge near Miami and asked another customer, "What's the difference between erotic and kinky?"

"It is 'erotic' when you stroke a woman's naked body with a feather" he answered. "And it is 'kinky' when you rub her with the whole chicken."

When not telling jokes, Sergeant Berish, known on the street as "the Peeper," wages a one-man war against Miami's pornographic film and book outlets.

"I'm a man with his finger in the dike," the nattily dressed detective likes to say. A lone operator given wide latitude by supervisors, Berish claims credit for shutting down 15 porn emporiums on his beat.

This nine-year vet boasts a perfect conviction record. But he ruefully concedes that none of his collars ever went all the way to jail. His felony busts are always bargained down to misdemeanors, and the perpetrators walk after paying small fines.

"Judges and prosecutors don't think this is a high priority," he sighed.

Berish is a frustrated soul. His bosses have turned down three of his requests for transfer; and his only assistant quit after just 15 months. Even so, he does his best. The intrepid cop harasses porn merchants relentlessly. His photo, with a caption reading "Do Not Admit This Guy," is posted in cashiers' cages along Miami's sinful Biscayne Boulevard.

But Berish merely grows stubble on his chin, puts on new sunglasses and chases after fresh foes. While other viewers surrender to the special charms of the sexually explicit, Berish rushes into action—reciting a rapid-fire narration of felonious fellations and other on-screen offenses into a hand-held microphone connected to a tape recorder.

"At one show I looked over to my right and there was a guy jerking off, and I looked over to my left and the same thing," he recalls. "They must have figured, 'Big deal. He gets off talking into his hand.' "

Berish leaned forward in the darkness of the Bushwacker and assumed his best smut-busting posture. Eyes wide and unblinking, he began to speak into the invisible mike cradled in the palm of his right hand.

"Couple number one: a blonde female, hair parted in the middle. She's wearing a green dress. She sits down on a brown couch. There's a yellow rug. Enter male number one, he's got a mustache, a blue shirt, a tie . . . they engage in sexual intercourse. She performs fellatio on him. He performs cunnilingus on her. In walks another unknown male. He's got sandy hair . . .

"Get the idea?" Berish asked, snapping out of his trance.

"And that's before the obligatory orgy scene. With six men and six women, it's like calling a horse race."

Berish has viewed more than 1000 adult features with this modus operandi.

"Some people say, 'You watch dirty movies, oh, wow!' But to me, it's just a job. I wouldn't mind getting into narcotics, to be honest . . . but as long as I'm doing what I'm doing, I'm going to be the best at it."

THE PEEPERS: VICE COP CONFIDENTIAL

Berish and his beleaguered brethren saw the Meese commission as their Woodstock Festival. Organized by prosecutors for prosecutors, the hearings had the feel of a police precinct. The cops, resplendent in polyester, holstered handguns and closely cropped hair, wandered the corridors of the federal buildings where the commission pitched tent as if it were Hill Street.

The vice squad fraternity dominated the second session in Chicago on "Law Enforcement." Smut-busting dicks from around the nation—including one from Buffalo's crack Salacious Literature Unit—flew into the sweltering heartland in mid-July to whine about uncaring judges, uninformed juries, and legal technicalities that made their jobs a living hell.

These Dirty Harry's of dirty movies told the commission that every day the body count was rising and that organized crime's coffers got fatter off porn's decadent allure. They wanted more weapons to sanitize the commonwealth—tougher minimum sentences, heavier fines, federal task forces, a broader definition as to what was prosecutable.

Sergeant Don Smith of the LAPD Vice Squad was an impressive witness from an impressive porn center. In his best Joe Friday monotone, Smith told the panel about the town he lives in: "In Los Angeles we have 49 adult book stores, 49 hotels which show hard-core movies, 38 bookstores, 25 adult arcades and 27 prostitution-related massage parlors."

The balding, mustachioed sergeant brought good news from Sin City—details of a new anti-porn strategy that knowledgeable vice-squaders were hailing as "innovative"—translation: probably unconstitutional, but worth testing. Cops from a dozen Midwest PDs leaned forward in the courtroom of the Everett Dirksen Federal Building as the Californian outlined this new Magnum Force of the Porn Battle: Pandering.

Investigators received information from a reliable source that Hal Freeman, a major producer of adult movies, was going to shoot a hard-core film in Los Angeles, Smith testified. "A detailed surveillance of Freeman led officers to a market parking lot in an exclusive beach community. Investigators observed a number of young females and males arriving at the parking lot and entering two vans. The two vans and Freeman's vehicle left the parking lot and caravanned to an exclusive residence overlooking the Pacific Ocean. Investigators observed filmmaking equipment being taken into the residence."

After three days of moviemaking, the cops fanned out to interview the young starlets at their homes. All five said Freeman paid them $350 per day to commit sex acts including "sodomy, oral copulation and sexual intercourse."

Here came the new twist. The unfortunate pornographer was charged with five counts of "pandering": Section 266i of the California penal code states that any person who procures another person for the purpose of prostitution is guilty of a felony and is subject to imprisonment for three, four or six years. Serving time is mandatory.

At his trial Freeman said that *Caught From Behind II*, which unreeled 15 instances of oral copulation, 10 scenes of anal intercourse and six episodes of other coital play, was an art film and thus he was not guilty of pandering. The prosecution looked askance at the art defense and argued that the filming was merely an "overt act" to "substantiate" the sex-for-pay pleasure scheme.

The jury convicted Freeman on all five counts. The precedent-setting prosecution lifted the spirits of Sarge and his cohorts. But their satisfaction was tempered by the judge, who imposed the lightest sentence possible (three years in jail) and called the punishment "cruel and unusual." The case is making its way to the U.S. Supreme Court.

The cops from Milwaukee, rural Illinois and Iowa nodded, "Right on," as Smith left the lectern. Chairman Hudson could hardly contain himself: "Thank you very much, Sergeant Smith. We appreciate your testimony this morning."

The adult-film industry has lost more than a few erections over the new pandering strategy. "I'm not shooting anything," said Richard Aldrich, a producer of adult films and president of the West Coast Productions Association, an organization that represents about 40 makers of adult films.

"Unequivocally it has put a chill on the Los Angeles industry," noted Les Baker, the president of the Association of Adult Films. "No sensible person would stick his head into that meat grinder."

The guys in L.A. Vice reportedly play rough. A few X-rated starlets complained of blackmail: Cops allegedly threatened them with arrest if they did not rat.

One performer in the Freeman case stated in a court affidavit: "I was told by the investigating officer that if I did not cooperate, I would be arrested for prostitution." But, of course, commissioners heard none of that.

Though the L.A. vice unit is considered the nation's most elite, the Delta Force of the Obscenity Wars, even they had to admit that, yes, they were losing the campaign.

"Southern California has the dubious honor of being the

pornography capital of the world," remarked Captain James Dougherty at a later hearing in L.A. "Over $550 million is generated annually . . . and at least 80 percent of the sexually explicit videotapes, 8-millimeter films and adult novelties are produced and distributed within the county of Los Angeles."

The commissioners listened respectfully to this self-inflated expert whose handout billed him as a recognized authority figure in his field. He was a prince of Porn City, working both sides of the street.

Moonlighting in Hollywood, the Captain coauthored the screenplay of *Vice Squad*, a 1983 R-rated movie featuring nudity, violence and explicit language. This poor man's Joseph Wambaugh also scripted a sequel titled *Hollywood Vice Squad* (R) starring Carrie Fisher and plenty of sex and violence. *Vice Squad* was so sexually violent that Dr. Edward Donnerstein of the University of Wisconsin used the film—along with *Tool Box Murders, I Spit on Your Grave*, and *Texas Chain-Saw Massacre*—to test the effects of exposure to what he called "aggressive pornography." Thus the commander of the country's leading anti-porn police unit created a movie that most other witnesses thought moved men to rape.

Captain Dougherty even trained his men in mise-en-scène. Detective William Roberts read his paper "The Making of a Porno Movie A-Z" to the commissioners. His commentary revealed a lot of inside dope: "Sex scenes are usually shot in one take. Male models and the director communicate as to the timing of the ejaculation scene, the most important part of the film . . . off-screen stimulation is often necessary to complete the ejaculation scene or scenes."

The gracious LAPD also provided the anonymous victims for their hometown hearings—several ex-adult performers who now regret their early career choice.

Commissioner Schauer probed the mind of another L.A.

vice cop—Detective William Peters. The professor asked the 18-year veteran about his feelings toward photos of heterosexual intercourse without sadomasochism, excretion, urination, bondage "or anything of that sort." In other words, what did he think of the clean stuff?

Detective Peters thought for a moment and then offered the vice cop's anthem: "I believe sexual activity between a man and a woman is a private thing. Anytime we start projecting these images on the screen and degrade the female or turn a beautiful thing into an animal sex activity for photographing, then I think it's time for prosecution."

With that, members of the audience—mostly fellow vice cops—broke into applause.

In Chicago a lieutenant from Cincinnati Vice described the road to Utopia. "A few short years ago, [the city of Cincinnati] was, like most other Ohio cities, a haven for pornography," Lieutenant Harold Mills observed. "Cincinnati today has no X-rated bookstores, no X-rated movies, no massage parlors, no adult movies on cable television and no go-go dancers."

The constabulary of Pete Rose's turf even went after the Warner-Amex Corporation for distributing the Playboy Channel locally. A grand jury actually indicted Warner-Amex, but the case was settled when the company withdrew its video centerfold service from town. A TV station was charged with pandering for the crime of airing sexually explicit films late at night. Under such pressure, the station changed its fare.

Lieutenant Mills, a large, gray-bearded man, painted a picture of an Orwellian apparatus hard at work in his community.

For example, if a merchant places lusty material in a display window, it is standard police practice in Cincinnati to institute immediate surveillance, including the videotaping of all patrons. And if a minor goes into the store, the cops inform the parents. The cops go even further—supplying anti-porn community groups with the latest information on local smut-peddlers.

If a dirty film is screened, the police will bring a judge into the movie house and sit with him as he watches every orgasmic twist.

"The community, the prosecutor, the judge and the police are vital ingredients in any successful effort to eliminate or reduce pornography," according to Lt. Mills. "As a police officer, I believe *the police must take the lead*" (his emphasis).

Mills finished by noting that successful smut-busting would have been impossible without the help of organized legions from local antipornography groups including Citizens for Decency Through Law, the National Coalition Against Pornography, and Citizens Concerned for Community Values.

Hudson did not bother to invite any civil libertarians from Cincinnati, any forlorn consumers who missed their adult bookstores or any merchant who may have felt the chill of the cops.

Joe Haggerty, a commission investigator on loan from the D.C. vice squad, warned that pictures were not the only things the panel should worry about. "The next magazine is called *B & D Sex Devices*," he testified. "It features a new line of abusive furniture."

Cops lament that not many prosecutors have it in for vice. The U.S. attorney in New York, who patrols Times Square, has not made a case against adult porn in years.

The handful of uptight government lawyers who enjoy warring on porn came to the commission to praise their own vigilance.

Robert Showers, a young, blow-dried assistant U.S. attorney from North Carolina, urged an all-out "war on pornography." He recommended tougher federal laws, forfeiture provisions against porn merchants (i.e., the seizing of an entire convenience store if it were found to be hawking proscribed materials) and making some hard-core material obscene per se—bestiality, child porn and S&M love sets.

Showers had an impressive feather in his cap. As chairman of the North Carolina Law Enforcement Coordination Committee on Pornography, Organized Crime and Child Abuse, he was instrumental in declaring porn outlets off-limits to soldiers at Fort Bragg. The unhappy dogfaces saw 50 outlets close in nearby Jacksonville.

The intrepid prosecutor was also the primary author of his state's tough new obscenity law. Because of that measure, *Playboy, Penthouse* and *Hustler* were now sold only in adult bookstores in Jesse Helms country. And many such outlets had closed.

Showers told how undercover cops bought X-rated tapes at neighborhood video stores; most of the busted owners entered into immunity agreements and were going to testify against the shippers and producers of hard-core.

Some of the video outlets were now not selling or even renting R-rated materials.

Professor Schauer wondered where Showers drew the line. The law professor pointedly asked him about a drawing in *The Joy of Sex* featuring a heterosexual coupling. Showers said it was the burden of the purveyors of the volume to declare why it was not obscene. He would prosecute.

Larry Parrish, a legendary figure from the anti-porn movement, was the Robert Showers of his day. As a federal prosecutor in Memphis between 1972 and 1976, Parrish indicted 60 defendants for obscenity, including megastars Harry Reams and Georgina Spevlin. Now in private practice, Parrish still had a thing about erotica. He asked the panel to help "wipe pornography off the face of the earth." In a long rant, he went around the bend calling for mandatory jail time for hard-core porn *users*!

This apocalypticism was received with a raised eyebrow

only by commissioner Ellen Levine. "Are you suggesting that somebody who has bought an issue of a hard-core magazine go to jail for six months?"

Parrish didn't back down: "I am suggesting that if users understood that they could go to jail for six months, that there are not going to be any users to be prosecuted . . . . The users have got to know that this is an illegal thing."

He did show a little Solomonic compassion: "Maybe some exception should be made for users as far as mandatory incarceration . . . . If you can dry up the market, you don't have anybody to produce it. They are not going to be making it for nobody."

This amazing statement was left to hang in the air. The next interrogator, Dr. Dobson, merely wanted to inquire whether Parrish thought U.S. attorneys were doing a vigorous enough job.

Parrish, predictably, said that more had to be done.

During a colloquy with a stern U.S. attorney from North Carolina, Dr. Dietz brought up a fascinating tid-bit about the demographics of that state's pornography consumers.

"We have had testimony that 80 to 90 percent of North Carolinians are churchgoing people who hold to traditional conservative values. We have also heard testimony that North Carolina has the largest number of pornography outlets.

"Is it the churchgoers who are creating the market or is it the other 20 percent?"

Prosecutor Sam Currin got folksy.

"You know, we also have this saying in North Carolina that we will all vote dry as long as we can stagger to the polls."

He conceded that some peep-show fans probably went to church, as well.

"Where"—Dr. Dietz smiled—"they can repent for what they have done."

TWO KINDS OF FEMINISTS:
SOME LIKE IT HOT

The second day of the Chicago session belonged to the feminists. Women Against Pornography sent up their MVP, Catharine MacKinnon, an itinerant law professor then teaching at UCLA Law School. Along with radical activist Andrea Dworkin, she crafted a model city ordinance giving women the right to sue pornographers for violating their civil rights. This approach has caused a severe cleavage in feminist ranks. Nan Hunter, an ACLU attorney from New York as well as a leading light of the Feminist Anti-Censorship Taskforce (FACT), came to Chicago to defend pornography.

Hunter spoke first, dressed in a pants suit, her short grey hair cropped close. MacKinnon sat but a few feet away, furiously making notes on a yellow legal pad. With local FACT members in attendance, Hunter made her points authoritatively: "The problem with pornography, in our view, lies in the extent to which it reflects and glorifies male supremacy. Unfortunately, the indicia of male supremacy are found throughout society, not just in pornography. Pornography is not the cause of oppression in women nor is it even the primary channel in which that supremacy is reflected, validated and glorified. Other much more powerful, established and legitimate institutions contribute far more than does the pornography industry to the second-class status of women. Thus we and many other feminists believe that targeting pornography in a civil-rights law, as has been attempted by the ordinance in question, is a fundamentally misguided attempt to get at the root causes of an ideology which tells us that women are inferior and incompetent." Hunter argued forcefully against all obscenity laws because they drive porn underground, thereby creating rotten labor conditions for prostitutes and X-rated movie actresses (mostly poor women); she urged the decriminalization of prostitution and better sex-ed programs.

Hunter finished with a dig at the panel's boss—Attorney General Ed Meese—for cutting back funds to clinics for battered women. It was a solid, workmanlike performance. Dull with no surprises.

After lunch, MacKinnon rose to the occasion. Her greying hair tied in a bun on top of her head and her flowered jacket unbuttoned, she took command of the room. She was fierce, animated, a skilled and daring polemicist.

She read her soliloquy from a text, though it was clear she knew most of it by heart. "Pornographers, who are pimps, take the already powerless—the poor, the young, the innocent, the used, the desperate, the female—and deepen their invisibility and their silence." She linked porn to rape, child abuse, even murder. She pointed to studies that say pornography leads to "attitudes and behaviors of aggression and discrimination specifically by men against women" and heightened "desensitization" to "sexual force." (This controversial psychological point is gaining adherents among the zealots. Steve Goldsmith, a young and ambitious district attorney from Indianapolis, where city fathers and mothers passed the MacKinnon-Dworkin legislation, testified that porn causing "callousness" should be prosecutable.)

MacKinnon brushed aside all First Amendment concerns with disdain, insisting that victims are not obligated to respect their oppressors' laws.

She denounced women who opposed her ordinance "and who dare to call themselves feminists." This insult incited buzzing among WAP and FACT galleries. Several panelists looked lost during MacKinnon's more obscure rhetorical pirouettes. But she aroused slumbering Chairman Hudson when she linked FACT to the ACLU, which "is fronting for the pornographers."

For her finish, she roused the group with an absolute either/or: "Many people want the problem of pornography solved. It is our view that if you want it solved, you will recommend [our civil rights approach], and if you do not, you will not."

The room fell silent. MacKinnon's dramatics had stirred the commissioners like no other witness. Diane Cusack, the councilwoman from Scottsdale, complimented the lawyer for being "so articulate" and paused a second before asking her to "define sexuality."

Chairman Hudson mercifully cut MacKinnon's response off before too long and thanked her for her time.

MacKinnon's sexual politics have led her far out to sea. At first she and her sisters tied the tin can of harm on images that glorified violence against women and female subjugation. But now MacKinnon believes that virtually all sexually explicit images in our culture hurt women.

This riles a growing cadre of lesbian eroticists who, in recent years, have begun to print their own pornography. Magazines like *On Our Backs,* published in San Francisco, celebrate sapphist sex and even carry photos of dildo-equipped top-women. For this they get called "heterosexual lesbians" by authoritarians like MacKinnon.

At a debate in October 1985 over her civil-rights legislation in Cambridge, MacKinnon was asked by a female artist if paintings of female nudes would be banned. MacKinnon said yes, if they reinforced "male supremacist sexuality."

And what about women who happen to *enjoy* hard-core? "If pornography is part of your sexuality," she told a lesbian critic, "then you have no right to your sexuality."

BEHIND THE SCENES: DIRTY TRICKS

At the executive deliberations in Chicago, commissioners began to get cranky. Several chafed at what they correctly perceived as the hurried and ill-planned deliberative process. "Do you think we have allocated enough discussion time among ourselves to pull together and synthesize impressions and considerations?'' asked Father Ritter. "I'm really concerned that I'm beginning to feel isolated . . . . I have no relationship at all to other members of the commission in terms of digesting this enormous bulk of material.''

Ritter thought the staff was getting ahead of the commission. "The type of materials [the staff is sending out] presumes that we have already decided what the questions are, and perhaps really what the issues are, and maybe even what the answers are.''

Professor Schauer, who would come to dominate the commission in due time, also had criticism of the staff. "The packet [on First Amendment considerations] that was sent out consisted primarily of my work and some of Louis Revere's and Judge Bork's. In my judgment . . . [it] emphasizes too much a particular point of view . . . . I don't think the package is representative of academic opinion . . . . I like the publicity, but there are views other than mine and I'm not necessarily right.

"We talk a fair amount about the importance of appearing objective. Let me just add that I think it is equally important to *be* objective,'' he said, glaring at Sears.

The staff began playing dirty tricks early on. In a holding room prior to the first hearing in Washington, Dr. Dietz noticed a man handing commissioners a piece of paper with questions for witness Dr. Ann Burgess. Dr. Dietz asked Alan Sears who the fellow was and what he was doing. The executive director said the man—David Alexander Scott— was serving the commission in a "voluntary capacity.''

Scott *did* have a special interest in the subject. He had just authored an anti-porn polemic which was published by the radical right-wing Free Congress Foundation headed by Paul Weyrich. In his monograph, Scott relied on newspaper clips and a misreading of social-science data to conclude that "pornography is addictive and can cause sexual deviance in those using it for harmless enjoyment." Dr. Dietz went public with the shenanigans, asking Dr. Burgess at the hearing if she had conferred with a "Mr. Scott" prior to her testimony. The witness said she hadn't, and the matter was officially dropped.

But the damage was done. Scott was booted from the commission's back rooms for the rest of the year. The zealot, who hailed from Toronto, tailed the attorney general's panel for seven months. He insisted that he be allowed to testify. But once burned, Meese's agents wanted no part of Scott, and they refused to give him the podium.

4

THE SEX PROFESSORS

S ocial scientists held the keys to the kingdom. Ultra-feminists and the religious Right needed the professorial leg of the triad to cinch the case against pornography. Despite years of flame-throwing rhetoric, the combined powers of women and clergy concerned had hardly nicked the nation. In 1986 things still went as far as they could go, only more so. Science, however, just might help turn the momentum in the court of public opinion. As the Great Anti-Porn Communicator said in the Rose Garden, "Academic studies have suggested a link between pornography and sexual violence."

The showdown with the sex professors in Houston was

the franchise. Perennial anti-pornography opinions meant little without incriminating facts. Although higher-ups in the Justice Department knew that the evidence was less than circumstantial, they allowed the commission to proceed.

"This may be the first significant discussion by this commission," predicted Chairman Hudson of the Houston meeting, the only stop in the Bible Belt. In September of 1985, the city was in a state of excitement over a recently staged live sex show. The police raided the performance and promised further harassment. Even Mayor Katherine J. Whitmire, who supported gay rights in an acrimonious political battle in 1984, turned tough on venereal actors. Foes of sexual freedom packed the hearings and watched the duel. After the scientists spent their contradictory findings and feelings, the chairman went away frustrated. He did not get the expected charge.

Actually, many of the best and brightest sexologists were no-shows. For example, none of Kinsey's living coauthors—Dr. Paul Gebhard, Dr. Wardell Pomeroy and Dr. Ralph Martin—was heard. The current head of the Kinsey Institute, Dr. June Reinisch, offered to acquaint the panel with the largest pornography collection in the world, but she was turned down.

In contrast, the 1970 panel held its first official meeting in Bloomington. Dr. Gebhard, now retired from the Institute, remembers the approach. "Bill Lockhart [the 1970 chairman] said to me, 'Look, I'm discovering that the commission members don't know what to discuss. Some of them think *Playboy* is hard-core.' So Lockhart wanted us to give them a survey of our erotica. We spent a whole day on it and we had many contacts after that."

Masters and Johnson, who have probably filmed more orgasms than Gerard Damiano, never appeared. Likewise the biggest names in sex therapy: psychiatrist Helen Singer Kaplan, founder and director of the human sexuality program at New York Hospital-Cornell Medical Center; Dr.

66

Bernard Apfelbaum, director of the Berkeley Sex Therapy Group; Dr. Lonnie Barbach, an expert in female erotica; and Dr. Michael Carrera, past president of the American Association of Sex Educators, Counselors and Therapists, who has recommended the joys of light bondage, group scenes and anal and video stimulation in his *Glamour* column, "Sex and Health".

Two prominent Harvard professors—child psychiatrist Robert Coles and sociobiologist James Q. Wilson— declined invitations to testify. So did psychiatrist Bruno Bettelheim, historian Christopher Lasch and conservative commentator Ernest Van Den Haag. Even the popularizers of sexual health shunned the proceedings. No Dr. Ruth Westheimer, Dr. Alex Comfort, or Nancy Friday.

Although the marquee lacked name recognition in spots, all the major arguments were stated by 20 researchers. The chimes rang for both sides.

THE ANTI-PORN SCIENTISTS

The overtly anti-porn witnesses were right in the chairman's ballpark. One of the most intriguing characters was globe-trotting psychologist Dr. John Court, who flew in from his native Australia the day before. Although Dr. Court pleaded jet lag, he looked fit and handsome in a tight white suit. He started off by lambasting Dr. Richard Green, a psychiatrist who edits the journal *Archives of Sexual Behavior*. At the previous day's session, Dr. Green had argued that sex crimes had decreased in Denmark and West Germany, where hard-core pornography is legal. But Dr. Court accused him of improper statistics and insisted that the best evidence proved that proliferation leads to waves of offenses. One of the major controversialists in the field, Dr. Court himself was roundly criticized by the British commission for his "totally unsubstantiated surmise."

With absolute moral certainty he endorsed the domino theory of porn: Lowered taboos against explicit sex caused a change in attitude and desensitization toward women that inevitably incites rape and molestation.

"While husbands think it [porn] is a great idea," he said, "wives don't like being treated in a less than human way."

Expressing personal distaste for his line of work, Dr. Court labeled pornography "psychological AIDS." Refusing to become the Karen Silkwood of explicit images, he announced that he had stopped his studies as "prophylaxis for my own marriage."

For Dr. Court, pornography was an international crime, and he blamed the 1970 presidential panel for the tide of tolerance in his own country. For example, the Aussat satellite launched in America was beaming TV signals into "media-naive" towns in the Australian outback. "It is my hope that the commission will recognize that recommendations made here affect not only the psychological laboratories of the United States but also vulnerable individuals around the world," he implored.

Hudson raised his favorite query in the question-and-answer session. "Have you ever observed documented instances where individuals may be psychologically predisposed to commit certain violent criminal acts, and because they actually consumed and viewed pornography, that it caused them to actuate those fantasies?"

Dr. Court referred the chairman to his egocentric 240-page response to the British commission; it was titled *Pornography and the Harm Condition* and contained 30 pages of such histories.

Indeed, in his own practice dirty pictures seemed to trigger human tragedy—*including eating disorders*. "It will only be a matter of time before a proportion of those presenting with anorexia nervosa will be shown to be the indirect victims of exposure to pornography," claimed Dr.

68

Court. "I have a number of indirect cases in the area."

Despite his academic status, this psychologist seemed more Christian scientist than a social scientist. His travel expenses were picked up in part by a church group in California. Which group? "Christians like to keep their charity private," he said in the corridor, failing to name his Good Samaritan.

Dr. Victor Cline, a professor of clinical psychology from the University of Utah and the most venerated critic of the 1970 report, upped the ante by calling pornography *physically* addictive. His spectacular claim rested on the treatment of 225 male sex offenders over the past 16 years. Dr. Cline has not published his results, but he related that addiction was nearly universal among the offenders. After getting hooked, they *escalated* their demands for harder stuff, became *desensitized* to taboo and then *acted out* their fantasies.

"This involved sexual acts including seduction of women in a few cases, sexual aggression against women and activities in the bedroom with one's current partner," Dr. Cline said. "Group sex and partner-switching were other outcomes. Voyeurism, exhibitionism, fetishism and necrophilia were other examples of acting-out behavior."

Assured of the toxic effects of pornography, Dr. Cline concluded that burden of proof ought to be on the defenders. Only Dr. Becker questioned the psychologist's views. Oddly, none of the panelists followed up the fascinating addiction theory or even the necrophile citation, two astonishing bombshells that should have rocked the courtroom.

If these claims came anywhere near the truth, the United States was headed for a calamity unparalleled in the annals of sex history. Dr. Cline supposedly had 225 cases of corpse-snatching, women-beating, cock-flashing porn addicts. There must be several thousand others in the 50 states, but he could not get anybody's attention.

Dr. Diane Russell, a sociologist from Mills College in California, is a specialist in rape and a major activist against pornography. She told the commission about the impact of this material on women based on her 1978 survey of 930 in San Francisco. Only 389 (40 percent) admitted any familiarity with the material, but almost half of those (44 percent) said that pornography had upset them. (Of course, Dr. Russell failed to ask any of her subjects about pleasurable responses.) One in seven women in the survey reported that they had been asked to pose, and one in 10 had been displeased by being asked to imitate a scene from a pornographic movie, picture or book. Dr. Russell, author of the eclectic *Sexual Exploitation, Rape, Child Sexual Abuse and Workplace Harassment*, coined a new pejorative in the ultra-feminist lexicon to describe such requests: "pornography-related experiences of victimization."

She quoted a few of the "victims":

"He read something in a pornographic book, and then he wanted to live it out. It was too violent for me to do something like that. It was basically getting dressed up and spanking, him spanking me."

"This person showed me a porno magazine with a picture of two women. He said he would like to see two women doing that, me being one of them. That upset me."

"Seeing pictures and reading about oral sex makes you feel your marriage might be shaky if you don't do it."

"Always I was upset about his idea of putting objects in my vagina until I learned it is not as deviant as I used to think."

Dr. Russell found that 15 women, or 1.6 percent of her entire sample, suffered a pornography-related rape or attempted rape. Since a whopping 44 percent said that they had been attacked at least once, pictures seemed to be a minuscule factor in sexual violence against women. But not on Dr. Russell's calculator: "One and six tenths of a percent may sound like a very low percentage, however, it represents 16,000 rapes per one million women.''

In closing, she cited the country's pornographic "reign of terror" and encouraged the commission to consider the civil-rights approach of Dworkin-MacKinnon.

Chairman Hudson was charmed by the accounting, but Dr. Dietz scented a rodent. He pointed out to Dr. Russell that her 1.6 percent really added up to 1.6 million porn-related rapes for the nation as a whole, yet "it would take about twenty years for reported rapes to get that many.''

The rape expert was undaunted, replying that almost half the women surveyed were victims of rape or attempted rape anyway and that younger groups of women were assaulted at even higher rates.

Instead of asking her to explain the extrapolation to 50 million American rape victims, Dr. Dietz turned to Dr. Russell's understanding of victimization, noting that she failed to distinguish between "reasonable requests" and "degenerate requests" in the male's post-porn state.

"There is some conflict between what men seem to seek out and what women seem to find repulsive," he said.

Dr. Russell backed down. She admitted that she had recorded the women's viewpoint uncritically and that some instances would allow a different opinion.

The chairman was still curious. Before letting the witness off, he underlined the 10 percent stat.

"Am I correct that approximately 100,000 out of every one million women would have some kind of negative response as a result of their being exposed to pornography?" inquired Hudson.

"Yes," the witness replied.

"Thank you very much," said Hudson.

"Thank you," said the witness.

Dr. William Marshall, a Canadian psychologist, flew down to Texas from Queens University in Ontario. A pioneer in the treatment of sex offenders, Dr. Marshall investigated the relationship between pornography and sex offenders for the Canadian government.

In a study of 89 rapists and child molesters, he found that offenders experienced greater exposure to hard-core during pubescence and use it more now than did a comparison control group of 29 non-offenders. Thirty-seven percent of the molesters and 35 percent of the rapists said that pornography was involved in the instigation of their crimes.

Running behind schedule, Hudson said goodbye to the Canadian without further questioning. This appeared to be another missed opportunity. Almost all offender research going back to Kinsey leaned the other way. Reverend Jerry Falwell touted Dr. Marshall's miracle on television, but the panel let him walk offstage without a word of explanation.

Dr. Diane Scully, a sociologist from Virginia Commonwealth University, interviewed 115 rapists in prison and 75 other non-offending felons. Sixty-five percent of the former, compared to 57 percent of the latter, "used pornography or sexually explicit magazines, books or movies." The rapist, Dr. Scully explained, drew on rape myths (e.g., women mean "yes" when they say "no" and victims get what they deserve).

However, she disappointed the chairman by not going all the way in her conclusion.

"The research I have presented is not intended to be evidence of a direct causal relationship between rape and violent pornography," she said. "Nor do I think that violent pornography is the only vehicle by which rape-compatible values are transmitted and perpetuated. Nonetheless, there is good reason to be concerned about the proliferation of violent pornography."

Rape was also on the mind of Dr. Wendy Stock, a young

sex therapist and psychologist from Texas A & M. She loathed violent pornography too and saw it as a precursor of aggression against women. She touched all the usual bases: *Hustler*'s connection to the notorious pool-table gang job in New Bedford, Massachusetts; Susan Brownmiller's *Against Our Will;* the FBI Uniform Crime Reports; Donnerstein and Malamuth; Zillman and Bryant; Steinem and Leidholdt; Hitler and the Holocaust.

And then, unexpectedly, she rolled a hand grenade into the zeitgeist by relating her original inquiry into the effect of violent pornography on women. Despite a decade of raised consciousness on matters of rape, Dr. Stock revealed, even her sex was greatly aroused by the "myth."

Her experiment, the basis for her doctorate, involved 75 undergraduate females who agreed to the insertion of a vaginal photometer which measured "vaginal congestion which is the equivalent to male erection." The subjects were divided into five groups. Each was exposed to one of five audiotapes of five-minute duration. Two tapes had neutral content—a man and a woman conversing about jazz. The other three tapes contained different versions of the same scenario, which was adapted from a letter printed in *Variations* (August 1981), a digest-size magazine published by Penthouse. According to the letter (originally titled "Trapped"), a woman meets a man in a bar, he drags her into the men's room, pulls off her clothes, ties her up and rapes her. But the woman has a pretty good time in the end, climaxes repeatedly and looks forward to her next encounter with the attacker.

Dr. Stock called the first version the "rape myth"— woman resists but says "yes" with her body. The second version was "mutual consent"—the woman goes to the men's room voluntarily and has sex without coercion. The third version was called "rape empathy"—the woman resists all the way with fear and pain and does not have multiple orgasms.

Guess which tape almost broke the needle on the photo-meter? The "rape myth"; and not far behind was "mutual consent"; and, lagging in third place, just ahead of the jazz talk, was "rape empathy."

Similar results obtained in subjective reports. The "rape myth" finished even with "mutual consent," while the jazz and painful "rape empathy" registered hardly any excitement.

Obviously Dr. Stock was embarrassed by her experiment. The "rape myth" she so strongly denounced in men turned out to be very exciting to women. Surely there must be a good feminist explanation, and she groped for one.

"In general, these findings indicate that women are not aroused and do not feel positively towards realistic depictions of rape which describe victim pain," she informed the panel. "With respect to fantasy of rape, which women so frequently engage in, reportedly, the one eighteen-year-old in this study addresses this issue eloquently, in terms which perhaps describe what many women are truly desirous of in their sexual interaction. In response to the question, 'What did you learn from this experiment?' she wrote: 'That a woman can be turned on to sex when it's done with affection and enjoy it. How she might not be turned on if sex is done with force, and if she is turned on, it may be only because such sexual acts remind her of the times she had sex with passionate affection, not with force.' "

Dr. Stock did not extend the same courtesy to men, who might also be reminded of "passionate affection" with their girlfriends in moments of frenzied fantasy.

RAPE AND MEN'S MAGAZINES

Dr. Larry Baron, a lecturer in sociology at Yale, seemed to be a welcome presence in the pile-up on porn. He had recently uncovered a symmetrical connection between sex-magazine circulation and rape rates in the 50 states. This dream correlation appeared heaven-sent. If explicit stills degraded women as much as Andrea Dworkin and Reverend Jerry Falwell prayed, then there should be such a correlation. But, just as in the case of Dr. Stock, the left hand took away what the right hand placed in the chairman's lap.

Dr. Baron and his collaborator, Dr. Murray Straus of the University of New Hampshire, are mainly interested in the causes of rape. For the past three years they have been looking into various explanatory hypotheses behind the variance in rape rates among the 50 states. They tested four possibilities: (1) sex magazine circulation (*Playboy, Penthouse, Hustler, Oui, Chic, Club, Genesis, Gallery*), (2) the level of social disorganization (unemployment, divorce, immigration), (3) the status of women and (4) legitimate violence (TV, hunting, corporal punishment).

What precisely did they find? That magazines and social disorganization had positive effects on the rape rate. For example, the greater the circulation of *Playboy* et al and the more social disarray, so too the higher incidence of rape across the country. The status of women, in contrast, had an inverse effect. In those states where women were on top, they were least likely to be attacked, and vice versa. Legitimate violence yielded no link at all.

The Baron-Straus discovery was the best news for the anti-porn movement since the defection of Linda Lovelace.

"In fact," Dr. Baron told the commission, "of all the independent variables used in the analysis, the sex-magazine-circulation index has the strongest association with the rape rate."

Even so, the sociologist argued against the temptation to jump from correlation to cause. "It is quite plausible that the findings could reflect state-to-state differences in a hypermasculated or macho culture pattern," he remarked. "Such a pattern could include norms and values that pro-

75

mote male interest and involvement with pornography, sexual aggression, the perception of women as objects and the belief in rape myths. If such a macho culture pattern does independently influence the purchase of sex magazines and the incidence of rape, the original association between sex-magazine circulation and the rape rate would be an artifact of the relationship to this macho culture pattern."

Then he closed with a caveat that no ultra-feminist or religious scourge wished to hear: "It should be clear at this point in our research: The nature of the relationship between pornography and rape is somewhat ambiguous and does not warrant the interpretation that pornography causes rape.

"In my opinion censorship would be a mistake because censorship threatens the freedom of all citizens, and feminists in particular.

"Additionally, if the relationship between pornography and rape is spurious and due to some common underlying factor, then the censorship of pornography would simply address the symptom of the underlying problem, rather than addressing the real causes of rape in the United States. Thank you."

Dr. Baron was a great sociological hope, but he refused to go with the flow of his own data. The chairman obviously preferred less contrary testimony, especially when it went in his direction. An expert in leading friendly witnesses, the prosecutor also knew how to neutralize inimical assertions. If Hudson could demonstrate the Yale lecturer's primal bias against censorship, then he could taint his liberal plea for pornographic tolerance.

"Doctor, do I understand your testimony to be that even if this commission, from the research presented to us, were to find that there was a positive linkage between pornography and some type of harmful sexual deviance, you would not be in favor of any type of governmental controls on those materials?"

Dr. Baron rejected the assumption. "I know the research

76

pretty well at this point, and that research shows that the link does not exist, at least not very clearly," he replied.

"Even if [the research] were to establish it [the link] to the satisfaction of a majority of scientists, you still don't know whether or not you would be in favor of control," Hudson pressed.

"Right, right, I am wobbling on that," Dr. Baron replied.

A few months after Dr. Baron's appearance in Houston, he came to doubt his statistical correlation. When he and Dr. Straus ran ten years of survey data (1973-1983), according to a "violent attitude index" of Dr. Straus' devising, sex magazines dropped out of sight. There was no correlation between such circulation and rape rates on the state level. However, these data were available for only 40 states, not the 50 in the original experiment. "I'm a rape researcher," said Dr. Baron in a telephone interview. "I don't see the pornography issue as that important. I believe the relationship is spurious."

THE UNREQUITED SEX EDUCATORS

At 82, Mary Calderone, M.D., is the grand old dame of sex education. Back in the 40s, she was the medical director of Planned Parenthood and went on to found the venerable Sex Education and Information Council of the United States (SIECUS). Advanced in years and honors, she spoke boldly about illiteracy in the erogenous zone. To dramatize her point, she showed the panel a specimen of prenatal porn— an ultrasound photograph of the erection of a fetus at 29 weeks. Apparently teeny-weeny tumescence occurs every 90 minutes *in utero*.

Armed with this confirmation of sexual response in the unborn, Dr. Calderone pleaded for teaching kids the right messages about their bodies. "We are not doing that with our children because we have not recognized as yet that human sexuality is an endowment, part of the divine plan, nature's plan, to carry on," said the devout Quaker. "And we need to socialize the sexuality of our children towards responsibility, towards caring, towards tenderness, towards a future of forming a family. We need to socialize this, in order to get away from the pathology that rears the addiction of pornography."

Only Commissioner Tilton asked a question, seeking clarification about abuse in the childhoods of adult abusers. "If you will go to any of the sex-offender prisons, like the one in New Jersey, there are two facts that stand out," Dr. Calderone explained. "Kinsey found, for instance, in his book on sex offenders, that the men who were in prison for sex offenses had had less exposure to pornography than the men who were in prison for other non-sex-related crimes, and that speaks to me of the hunger we have for good, accurate knowledge, early enough to take effect, about ourselves as sexual beings. That's why I am in sex education of adults, not of children. I don't believe a school could provide what parents don't do or fail to do.

"The other tendency, the finding of studies of sex offenders, of abused sex abusers, who have actually abused children: that they, themselves, very often—not often, very often—were abused."

Dr. Ann Welbourne-Moglia, executive director of SIECUS, followed Dr. Calderone with the same pitch. "We have a sexual-ignorance epidemic in our country," she said. "Most of our young people, parents, adults and health professionals are not prepared to take care of sexual-health issues . . . . Children and families need to know that the leaders of our country care about this problem."

Father Ritter cared. But he told the witness that sex education was a beam in the eyes of some biblicists. "I would suspect that most people with a fundamentalist, conservative religious orientation would not at all agree with the principles espoused by SIECUS in terms of the content of sex education," he lamented. "We all agree that it is absolutely necessary. *I personally think that it is probably the single thing most necessary in order to help combat the use and abuse of pornography* [emphasis added]. But I am genuinely puzzled by the difficulty with which we can find solutions here."

Unfortunately, Father Ritter, along with the majority of his colleagues, caved in to the fundamentalist smear.

THE EROTIC FILM FESTIVAL

The views of social scientists counted less than their data, and some data seemed harder than others. The most important body of evidence for the commission, the sine qua non of the entire investigation, came from the Ebert-and-Siskel professors, who screened porn for their student subjects and assiduously recorded their reactions. On the right were Dr. Jennings Bryant of the University of Houston and Dr. Dolf Zillman of Indiana University. And somewhere in the middle were Dr. Edward Donnerstein of the University of Wisconsin and Dr. Neil Malamuth of UCLA. None was a genuine sex researcher; their zone of expertise was fantasy-on-film. Yet they were the ones the panel held in thrall.

Dr. Bryant and Dr. Zillman collaborated in their studies and appeared in Houston as a team. "Massive" exposure of nonviolent porn was their forte. Dr. Bryant told the panel about the results obtained from saturating his sample with three hours of modern stag films for five consecutive days. During the same time period, a control group was dosed with an orgy of vanilla sitcoms like "Benson," "Diff'rent Strokes" and "Family Ties" (Ronald Reagan's favorite).

For three days, the subjects watched 14 brief scenes from television shows like "Dynasty" and "Hotel" highlighting either nonsexual transgressions or sexual improprieties. Then the kids rendered their moral judgments in response to

79

the suggestive question: "How *bad,* morally speaking, is the indiscretion, impropriety, transgression or crime that was perpetrated?" What did Dr. Bryant discover? Apparently, the porn-washed group found the TV sex scenes "less *bad,* morally speaking," than the "Diff'rent Strokes" controls.

Dr. Bryant asked the same kids to calculate their moral judgments on 24 hypothetical sexual or criminal situations (e.g., "A husband has an extramarital affair with a woman. How *bad,* morally speaking, is this indiscretion, impropriety, transgression or crime?"). The results were similar. The "Diff'rent Strokes" crowd was more offended than the stag film-goers.

Therefore Dr. Bryant concluded without qualification that porn is no good for civilization: "Overall, massive exposure to hard-core pornography made sexual improprieties and transgressions seem less *bad,* and the victims of the transgressions were perceived to suffer less and to be less severely wronged. It seems clear that the value systems of hard-core pornography can generalize to everyday moral judgment assessment."

Dr. Zillman described a joint study performed with his colleague from Houston in which they showed student and nonstudent subjects a variety of nonviolent erotica including fellatio, cunnilingus, consenting S/M and bestiality for six consecutive weeks. The controls saw merely innocuous movies. Afterward the professors tested both groups on their attitudes toward various sexual situations.

For example, they wanted to learn whether exposure to pornography correlated with liberal ideas regarding marriage. Indeed, they found exactly what they were looking for. The porn-watchers were (1) less repulsed by uncommon coital unions, (2) more tolerant of premarital and extramarital sex, (3) less concerned about the impact of pornography on society and (4) less accepting of sexual repression.

As usual, the chairman attempted to push the witness farther.

"Dr. Zillman, based upon your research and your readings in the field, do you feel that certain forms of violent pornography may well trigger individuals to commit violent crimes?

"Maybe I should disqualify myself. I'm not an authority on this," he replied.

Dr. Zillman was being modest or just unforthcoming. In fact, he was an amateur expert on the eroticization of pain. This professor, who has spent much of his career in the service of humanity's highest ideals of love and marriage and to the defeat of callous attitudes toward women, is an *ardent advocate of sadomasochism*. For him, pain, not porn, is the ultimate marriage-saver.

Consider the following passages from Dr. Zillman's *Connections Between Sex and Aggression*, which was published by Lawrence Erlbaum Associates in 1984:

"As the arousing capacity of novel partners is likely to fade and acute emotional reactions such as fear and guilt are improbable accompaniments of sexual activity, what can be done to combat the drabness of routine sexual engagements that is expected to result from excitatory habituation? *Roughhousing, pinching, biting and beating* emerge as viable answers. In terms of a theory it is the controlled engagement of pain that holds promise of reliably producing excitatory reactions for transfer into sexual behavior and experience. The excitatory capacity of acute pain is not in doubt. Moreover, pain is extremely resistant to habituation . . . . Acute pain then always can be counted on to stir up excitement. It is the habituation fighter par excellence . . . .

"It appears that there is no substitute for pain as a reliable standby for the creation of excitement, in case it is lacking. *Pinching, scratching, sucking, biting, squeezing, pulling, shoving and hitting* constitute the bulk of the arsenal of aggression-related arousers that can be exploited for the enhancement of drab sexual endeavors. And in exploiting these means receiving tends to work better than giving" [emphasis added].

Unfortunately, the commission never got to meet the Marquis de Zillman.

The oeuvre of Dr. Donnerstein and Dr. Malamuth is more liberal and sophisticated, but they share much of the Bryant-Zillman pornview. (The former included the latter in their recent $78 anthology *Sex and Aggression*). Their major concern is the mixture of sex and violence in the media.

The prolific Dr. Donnerstein has emerged as the pivotal figure in the school of slasher criticism. An ambitious social psychologist on and off campus, he has written 49 journal articles, 23 book chapters and 84 conference papers on the media. His manifold shock-box experiments at the University of Wisconsin, where he is a professor of both communications and women's studies, lends support to both sides. A smooth and good-looking man of 41, he spoke eloquently to the panel without referring to his written testimony.

For a recent study, Donnerstein explained, he screened four different films for college boys and then measured their attitudes toward women and their willingness to commit rape. The first film was vintage violent porn; the second was X-rated but contained no sexual coercion or rape-ecstatic victims; the third featured aggression toward women without sexual content; and the fourth was positively neutral.

The results exonerated sex and convicted violence. For example, the sex-only film aroused no more ill feeling toward the second sex than did the neutral film. Furthermore, the violence-only movie incited more viewer aggression toward women than did the X-rated one. In other words, violence, not explicitness, seemed to be more important in inciting male desensitization. "The most calloused attitudes and the highest percentage indicating some likelihood to rape were found in the aggression-only condition," Dr. Donnerstein observed. "The X-rated, sex-only film was the lowest. The research thus suggests that violence against women need not occur in a pornographic or sexually explicit context for the depictions to have an impact both on attitudes and behavior."

This brand of science is ridiculed by sexologists who believe that immersing college sophomores in reels of *Texas Chainsaw Massacre*, *I Spit on Your Grave*, *Vice Squad*, *The Getaway* and *Swept Away* is academic alchemy. The Evel Knievel jump from campus hard-ons to actual antisocial behavior is so broad that such casuistic calculations appear far removed from reality.

Dr. Donnerstein's chief critic on the left is Dr. Augustine Brannigan, a clever-minded Canadian sociologist from the University of Calgary who reviewed *Pornography and Sexual Aggression* with coauthor Dr. Sheldon Goldenberg. They violently disagree with his methods in testing the effects of sexually violent films. For example, Dr. Donnerstein has female "testers" insult and provoke male and female students. The subjects are then dosed with violent porn, and asked to administer shock treatments to their tormentors. "In our view, Donnerstein's design is contrived to guarantee what he dubs as 'aggression,'" Dr. Brannigan said in an interview. "And his interpretations are stacked to dismiss the relevance of the provocation which instigates the aggression in the laboratory. We mean the deliberate angering and insulting of the subjects at the beginning of the experiment, prior to exposure to pornography. Indeed, most people who cite his work in the advocacy of censorship are unaware of the conditions which produce the 'bad' reaction. Donnerstein himself is very selective in how he interprets the results.

"His work is premised on the porn-rape link. And so he ignores aggression by female subjects on female testers. Is this indication of rape proclivity among female consumers of porn? He also ignores factors like noise, drugs and exercise, which are known to enhance aggression too. Does this require censorship of jogging and noise bans to prevent sexual abuse to women? And is 'aggression' the right word for what the psychologists tell the subject that it is okay to do? Without a shred of plausible corroboration, Donnerstein equates the just, legitimate and modest retaliation of insulted and injured undergraduate students with the most reprehensible and unprovoked forms of sexual aggression.

"The leap from this type of lab contrivance to vicious rape boggles the imagination. On the same logic, we'll all become blithering idiots from watching 'Monty Python,' adulterers from 'Dynasty' and drug addicts from 'Miami Vice.' "

Dr. Brannigan and Dr. Goldenberg are not the only scholars from the North who scorn American pornoscience. "We would be seriously remiss if we failed to emphasize our level of astonishment at some of the nonsense going on and worse still being treated seriously in this research . . . ." wrote two of their fellow countrymen in a review of the American literature for the Canadian pornography commission in 1985.

On the other hand, Dr. Donnerstein is a useful citation for many varieties of anti-porn fauna. The concept of movie-induced desensitization plays into the hands of feminists and Republican prudes who are desperate for convincing refutations of the no-harm-done theory. Although frequently vulgarized by these interest groups, Dr. Donnerstein provides the intellectual framework for the censorial impulses.

Nevertheless, he is not a Christian scientist and does not tailor his research to satisfy moral tradition or feminist dogma. Herewith the hedged conclusion to his testimony in Texas:

"If one were to raise the question of whether or not pornography influences behaviors and attitudes toward women, the answer would be difficult. The problem, we believe, centers on what we mean by pornography. Are we talking about sexually explicit materials? If we are, then one would have to conclude that there is no evidence for any 'harm'-related effects. Are we talking about aggressive materials? In this case the research might be more supportive of a potential 'harm'-effect conclusion. The problem, however, is that aggressive images are the issue, not the sexual, in this type of material.

"In fact, more important here is the message about violence and the sexualized nature of violence, which is crucial. The problem, as we have tried to point out, is that while these types of messages may be part of some forms of pornography, they are also very pervasive of the media in general—from prime-time TV to popular films. Do males in our society have callous attitudes toward rape? Research would suggest that some do possess such attitudes. But where do they come from? Is the media, and in particular pornography, the cause? We would be hard-pressed to place the blame on the media. If anything, the media acts as a reinforcer for already existing attitudes and values regarding women and violence. In that sense they are a contributor . . . but only one of many contributors. Furthermore, it is all types of media, from violent pornography to daytime soap operas . . . .

"The issue of pornography and its relationship to violence will continue for years, perhaps without any definitive answers. We may never know if there is any real causal influence. We do know however that rape and other forms of violence against women do exist. How we change this situation is of crucial importance and our efforts need to be directed to this end."

His soft-core scientific analysis was easily the best evidence against violent pornography presented to the commission.

But the chairman was not fulfilled. The witness backed away from censorship, and that riled him. Two other commissioners embarrassed themselves when they challenged Dr. Donnerstein's integrity. In his most boorish moment at the hearings, commissioner Schauer inquired into the professor's bona fides.

"Finally, Dr. Donnerstein, you recently did a feature interview with *Penthouse* magazine. Were you paid for doing that interview?"

"No, I do not get paid for doing interviews," Dr. Donnerstein replied. "I freely give interviews to anybody."

Then it was Dr. Dietz's turn: "I would like to ask whether there has been any point at which the pornography industry or the manufacturers of materials that might be construed as pornography have tried to influence your work, either through financial support of research or travel or other professional activities or through intimidation, threats or any other effort of that sort."

"No," said the witness. "Well, let me step back. About, going back eight years, maybe nine years, I think maybe about nine years ago, *Playboy* did a number of articles about our research, particularly studies in which we find reduction in aggressive behavior. Somewhat tongue in cheek, I wrote a letter saying if you are so interested in the research, why don't you, in essence, give some money for equipment or something. Lo and behold, we got a check for $2000, I think, for video equipment.

"We were kind of surprised, because most people felt that given the nature of the newer research we had, they wouldn't touch us with a ten-foot pole. But that, basically, is the only time . . . .

"In fact, if one ever has listened to my lectures, as I know you have, Professor Dietz—I do about seventy to eighty a year—they rarely change; so the same message is there, whether it's for a church-related group or whether it's for a group of people who happen to be in the industry.

"What I have found interesting, however, is that the industry seems to want to know more about the research and within the last year, at least, I have personally been asked to talk about the research, either in terms of their conferences or from *Penthouse* as an interview; since I have never taken sides in this issue, and have tried to stay as objective as possible, we will go to those conferences and talk and will do the interviews, but no intimidation at all."

Why did the professor get this third degree? Probably because of rumors from Women Against Pornography and the religious Right that he was holding back research on nonviolent sex.

Patrick Fagan, a thug from the right-wing Free Congress Research and Education Foundation, dared to suggest at the New York hearings that Dr. Donnerstein was "in the pay of the pornography industry." But his bogus evidence was rejected by the commission.

As Dr. Donnerstein returned to the gallery in Houston, he leaned into the second row to shake the hand of arch anti-porn feminist Catharine MacKinnon, who had warned him in correspondence against lending his research to the bad guys. It was a gesture that chilled the hearts of the few libertarians in the courtroom. The professor from Wisconsin seemed too content to be some things to all people.

Dr. Malamuth, chairman of communications at UCLA, bolstered the positions of his colleague from Madison. He, too, had a large heart when it came to depictions of violence against women. However, despite myriad movie experiments showing misogynist twists in the minds of young men, he still could not confirm media-cause and brutal-effect.

Dr. Dietz, who argued that covers of detective magazines played a part in serial murders, desired more from Dr. Malamuth.

"Is there any reason to doubt that such [bad] effects occur?" Dr. Dietz wondered.

"On theoretical grounds, it's certainly a serious possibility," the witness replied. "But I think that social scientists, as of course you know, want to be cautious. Unless there is data to show it does occur, we won't accept a novel hypothesis at this point."

"Sometimes a decision has to be made when all the facts aren't in," the commissioner-criminologist continued. "Let me ask you a speculative question in that sense. It has seemed to me, based on the kinds of research that you have done and Dr. Donnerstein has done, that if a mad scientist wanted to take his best shot at creating a generation in which at least the males were likely to be sexually responsive to violence and to think that it was sexually gratifying to harm women, about the best thing a mad scientist could do would be to try to see that all the adolescents saw plenty of slasher films. Would you disagree with the statement, or do you know a better technique that a mad scientist could use?"

"I would have to say I haven't spent too much time in thinking about how mad scientists might go about doing that," the witness stated with amusement.

Next, Father Ritter took his shot.

"Dr. Malamuth, this question, I am sure, may seem to appear simplistic to many, but do you consider violent pornography harmful to the average citizen?"

"I really would feel more comfortable in terms of answering questions on a research basis and what the data shows."

The friar seemed to lose his Assisi cool.

"I am asking you as a father of children, as a husband, as a citizen of this country," he said. "Do you think that violent pornography is harmful to the average citizen?"

"I think that, yes, violent pornography is, to look at it in and of itself, harmful," said the witness. "There are many other elements in the society I find harmful as well. I personally find a lot of television programs, I think, harmful. I find a lot of other things that are part of our social environment harmful. I would say that I think, just as we have some concern about the air that we breathe, just as we have some concern about the food that we take in, I think we have to have some concern about the social environment we live in, as part of that mass media, as part of that violent pornography, as something we really need to have some concerns about."

When the joust was finished, Dr. Donnerstein and Dr. Malamuth had resisted subverting their data to please the censors on the panel.

THE PRO-CHOICE PROFESSORS

From Henry Hudson's vantage point, Dr. Richard Green was the George McGovern of sexology. As the founding president of the International Academy of Sexual Research, the founding editor of *Archives of Sexual Behavior* and the former president of the Society for the Scientific Study of Sex, Dr. Green never met a paraphilia he did not like.

Confident of his opinions and skeptical of the commission, the fortyish psychiatrist compressed his defense of pornography into four main arguments:

First, he cited the cross-cultural evidence indicating that certain sex crimes have decreased when sales of erotica increased. Child molestation dropped 67 percent in Denmark between 1967 and 1973 after pornography, including kiddie porn, was legalized. Between 1972 and 1980, the total number of reported sex crimes fell 11 percent in the liberalized Federal Republic of Germany—while nonsexual violent offenses rose 125 percent. The usual explanation for these changes is the catharsis theory.

"The common male reaction to pornographic pictures is masturbation," Dr. Green commented. "The availability of portrayals of a forbidden activity, accompanied by autoerotic behavior, or masturbation, may provide an outlet for antisocial sexual impulses. It may permit the person to experience vicariously or in fantasy what would otherwise have been acted out in a crime with a victim.''

Second, laboratory studies (e.g., Bryant & Zillman & Donnerstein & Malamuth) are not reliable predictors of actual behavior. Student guinea pigs are not naive subjects, because they know what the professors are looking for; they are totally unlike sex offenders, and the artificial setting of the laboratory affects the credibility of the experiment. ''A typical laboratory model has a male student view a sexually explicit film just after a female has attempted to provoke him to anger,'' he observed. ''He is now permitted to punish the female by delivering a mock shock believed to be real. The tether to street sexual assault here is tenuous. Other studies assess attitudes towards sexual assault after the subject views sexually violent films. Attitude assessment is usually very shortly after exposure to the erotic materials. Extending these findings to long-term attitudinal change is problematic. Extending attitudinal change to behavioral change is even more problematic.''

Third, prison research demonstrates that explicit materials hold no unusual fascination for sex offenders. ''A study in which I was coinvestigator assessed the experience with pornography of convicted rapists and pedophiles. Their experience was compared with normal males. The sex offender's experience with pornography, both in adolescence and in the year prior to incarceration, was lower.''

Fourth, pornography is both an educational and a therapeutic tool. Dr. Green told the panel that he has used commercial adult films in course work at the State University of New York at Stony Brook and at UCLA. Over 4000 institutions as well as 8000 individual practitioners have likewise utilized graphic sexual material.

This ultraliberal lecture, regarded as common sexological sense, ended with an ultraliberal put-down: ''Some will believe that pornography, however defined, should be banned or censored. Others will respond that there are many things in our society that are believed to cause more social harm than good but are not banned. In some cases these things are made available to consenting adults. At the same time educational efforts are mounted to make these things less attractive. It will be argued that more Americans will die this year because they were allowed to purchase cigarettes or alcohol than because they watched a pornographic film.''

Provoked by the witness's statistical data, the chairman attempted to squeeze an admission that rape rates in the United States have risen along with the pornographic surge.

Dr. Green toyed with the prosecutor. ''We must never forget that correlation has never proved causality . . . all that correlation will ever show in science is that they are moving in the same direction. But the classic of correlation fallacy was the Scandinavian studies, many years back, of the increase in number of stork sightings, which rose in relationship to the birth rate. And at least those of us who have gone through medical school don't believe that storks deliver babies.'' Hudson was not amused.

Occasionally possessed by the ghost of his forensic idol, Krafft-Ebing, Dr. Dietz brought up nutty deviations. In response to Dr. Green's denial of paraphilic formation resulting from simple masturbation fantasies, the criminologist posed an arresting question: ''Well, how do people learn to have [weird] preferences? How is that in England there are gas-mask fetishists?''

The witness topped the commissioner with an even odder turn-on.

''My colleague [Dr. Joseph Piccolo] once had a patient here in Texas who was aroused primarily by the handlebars of twelve-speed English racing bicycles. It's just a bit of a mystery how those fetishes evolve, though Piccolo is an experienced sex therapist, spent a lot of hours with this patient, went through a lot of aspects of this person's life, to get a sense, or a handle, on handlebars . . . and he couldn't . . . .

"So we really don't know where some really unusual sexual behaviors come from. But the evidence that they come from an immediate linking during adolescent adulthood, with what would have been a neutral stimulus, doesn't seem to hold up."

Dr. Donald Mosher was a voice from the past, and the chairman did not relish his message. A psychologist from the University of Connecticut, he contributed three research studies for the 1970 commission, and now he was returning to haunt the reprise.

"Although the president's commission of the 1970s has often been criticized as a social-science effort, it was a far more sophisticated and far more organized approach to the effects of pornography than this commission's approach," he commented. "You simply are underfunded. They simply were able to support three reviews of the literature, to hire a series of investigators to research specific questions. In this instance, you call together scientists and ask them to review their own research; and this isn't the best sort of review process to undertake."

The real problem, according to Dr. Mosher, was lack of good data on the effects of pornography. This failing has created the current predicament, wherein ideology has supplanted evidence. "If you are talking about a scientific knowledge based on a consensus, then the consensus which is required to form a public policy requires that the evidence be most clear-cut and that there really be agreement on the nature of the evidence and on the interpretation of the evidence," he said.

"In the area of pornography, I would submit from the testimony that you are hearing here, and from my knowledge of the field and going over a number of years, that such consensus does not exist; that what you are hearing is that either scientists are excessively cautious, not wanting to commit themselves when they don't think their data warrants firm convictions, or that they are forming particular convictions which are in part based on the evidence and in part a particular aspect of their ideology."

Given this confused state of affairs, Dr. Mosher called for education rather than censorship.

"If you go back to the recommendations of the President's Commission on Obscenity and Pornography, their argument 'that accurate, appropriate sex information provided openly and directly through legitimate channels and from reliable sources and healthy contexts can compete successfully with potentially distorted or inaccurate and unreliable information from clandestine and illegitimate sources' still seems compelling. We simply haven't done research in the last fifteen years."

How did the chairman react to this liberal high-mindedness? He went immediately to nipple-piercing and dog-fucking.

"Dr. Mosher, are you also suggesting to us that you do not think that publications that depict sado-masochistic acts, and publications that depict bestiality, you don't think they are harmful to anybody?"

"Let's take bestiality," replied the witness calmly. "I really don't believe, if you showed people films of bestiality, that they would engage in bestiality. I think you could show those films every night on public media and they won't engage in bestiality. That simply doesn't appeal to many people.

"The issue of sadomasochism is a bit more complex. Sadomasochistics, the people who one would identify as in a sadomasochistic culture, mainly engage in ritualized role-playing, in which there is much less emphasis on pain and there are careful controls over who's going to be in charge of the sexual interaction . . . . To other people, it doesn't have the same sort of appeal. There are also individuals, though, rapists or people of other sorts, who might have a very different reaction to the form of pornography.

"But the problem is, we have all sorts of portrayals on television which fall short of portraying X-rated levels of sexual intimacy but certainly which portray rape themes in a way which is indeed very suggestive."

The chairman continued to parry. "Dr. Mosher, let's assume, for the sake of discussion, that the type of research that you have suggested to us is properly conducted and that the majority of respected social scientists in your field agree that there is a definite correlation between sexual violence and the consumption of pornography: Would you change your view with respect to the governmental interest in controlling pornography?

"Yes, I would change my view; if that was what the scientific consensus showed."

"Because there is not consensus, you believe there should be no governmental control of adult pornography; isn't that right?" Hudson asked.

"I believe, because there is no consensus, there is nothing on which to base policy. As a civil libertarian I would say no control on pornography, but as a scientist I am saying if you are using scientific evidence, the scientific evidence isn't there. There is no consensus that people can take this piece of evidence and support this, and I have ideological biases like everyone else."

"I was going to point that out," said Hudson, summing up his contempt for the professors who would not spread their brains for the Meese commission. "You seem to have the same type of ideological bias that other social scientists are having."

The promise of the sex professors remained unconsummated. The link between pornography and crime was still missing. But the majority of Ed Meese's panel would not permit this intellectual interruptus to spoil their hanging party.

VISIT TO AN
ADULT BOOKSTORE:
THINGS GET STICKY

On the evening of the first day's hearings, the commissioners took a field trip. Accompanied by Sergeant Bill Brown of the Houston City Police Department, the panelists went to Mr. Peeper's, Arcade News and Talk of the Town adult bookstores.

"There is really no concern as far as your safety," the tour sergeant said before the jaunt. "These people are not violent. They know who we are and we know who they are. We deal with them every day, so it should go rather smoothly. Any questions?"

Commissioners had none. The group, including the press and a handful of commission groupies (e.g., Barry Lynn of the ACLU) jumped into two U.S. government vans. A police department station wagon cleared the route downtown.

The entourage walked into each establishment and encountered the wide-eyed stares of clerks and customers.

Vice cops, who led the way, discovered two male clients engaged in sex behind the unlocked door of one video booth. They scampered to safety. And the cops let them go.

Commissioners looked at the explicitly wrapped video selections available behind the magazine racks, and members purchased a booklet for $5 at Talk of the Town featuring a girl bound and gagged on its full-color cover.

"I've seen this all before," said steely-eyed Father Bruce Ritter, who works in Times Square. "But many of the other commissioners have not. We want to convince the public that we're not just an ivory-tower commission."

Some of them grimaced at S&M and practically held their noses when walking near gay porn. Deanne Tilton played her disapproval for the minicams that followed the group into the porn emporiums. "I'm a little queasy," she said.

Diane Cusack gulped: "It's very important that we see this in the context it's marketed."

BEHIND THE SCENES: MERELY SCIENTIFIC EVIDENCE

At the first business meeting in the Lone Star State, Hudson distributed proposed recommendations based on the Washington hearings. He wanted to make the Mann Act gender-neutral and do something about sexy rock-music lyrics.

This slavish devotion to arcana caused Father Ritter to explode. "We are not getting off the ground . . . . We have no way right now of understanding what the broad range of issues before this commission are or will be or of prioritizing them."

Hudson promised things would pick up.

The discussion soon wandered over to the "harm" of pornography. Sears wondered if it would be helpful to prepare a list "of every harm that's been brought to our attention," even including those that "would not be considered harmful by various groups."

Tex Lezar agreed immediately. And Professor Schauer said that it would be useful because "ultimately the question is not only social science, it is philosophy, it is religion, it is politics, it is everything we are all about. So hopefully it will be a long list."

Father Ritter wanted to know "just how much weight in the overall concern of the commission do we give to—may I say—*merely scientific evidence*?" (emphasis added)

Ellen Levine did not like the drift of things. "Are we also going to discuss the people who find pornography a benefit? We still have heard very little about that in the testimony."

Hudson turned to Sears, who soothingly told the editor that a "number of people who claim to be beneficiaries of

96

Father Bruce Ritter: doctorate in medieval dogma; priest for 30 years; smart, president of Covenant House; all sex outside marriage forbidden, and a lot within; late 50s; pet peeves—group sex and Dr. Ruth Westheimer; zinged Commission for overdoing kiddie porn and fringe fetishes; accepted $100,000 for Covenant House from leading anti-porn lobby while sitting on panel; swing liberal on two key votes.

pornography'' will testify at the next hearing in Los Angeles.

Levine was still testy. "Whenever I see the word 'pornography,' I am still confused. We have not had a working definition here." She also complained about the loose usage of the term "sexually oriented media." "I am not sure if that now means advertisements in *Better Homes and Gardens* or are we talking about pictures in *Hustler*. I think we need to have a working language at this table before we can digest those things."

Hudson rubbed his temple and suggested that between now and the next meeting, why didn't everyone go home and write their best definition of pornography, and they would be discussed at the next session.

Dr. Dobson, the dollar-conscious evangelist, then brought up the budget. "T[he] first commission on porn was given $2 million in 1968 dollars, and we were given . . . under $400,000 in 1985 dollars," he protested, referring to the presidential panel. "That doesn't seem adequate for the assignment." Against Hudson's wishes, Dr. Dobson put on the table an official request for more money. Professor Schauer said the problem wasn't really money but lack of deliberative time.

Levine said, "I think we need more money and more time."

Dobson kept pushing. "We were given a small amount of money to do a massive job, and to have to nickel and dime and piecemeal and perhaps do without staff that is needed, and have people travel on their own money, when you consider the billions of dollars wasted on government, this is a worthy cause. I don't think we ought to do it without yelling about it." The chairman promised to see what he could do.

5

THE INDUSTRY STRIKES BACK

At several stops along the route, the chairman met the local press. Although his commission had failed even to define the subject under investigation after three public hearings, Hudson was beyond embarrassment. At a press conference the day before the Los Angeles hearings in October, he fended off questions about the high and low hypocrisy of his commision.

One reporter mentioned the obvious anti-porn tilt of the panel—citing Hudson's background as a prosecutor; Dr. James Dobson, whose family-oriented cassettes are pitched on Jerry Falwell's TV show; and the Franciscan friar who believes that all arousal outside marriage is sinful. "Could you point to anyone on your commission, which you say is broad-minded and unbiased, who has expressed a different point of view about pornography?'' asked the reporter.

Hudson ducked. ''The problem that I have, sir,'' he replied, ''is that I cannot warrant to you that I have gone back and reviewed every public statement, every article published, every book, every interview of every commissioner.''

''Could you tell me,'' the reporter followed up, ''whether President Reagan makes your job more difficult when he has a son who writes regularly for the largest so-called pornographic magazine in the world? I'm referring to Ronald Reagan, Jr., who writes for *Playboy*. And the fact that Ronald Reagan invited porn star Sylvester Stallone to the White House in the same month his porn pictures are published in *Playgirl*.''

''That doesn't make my job more difficult,'' Hudson said icily. ''President Reagan makes his own decisions and our commission makes ours.''

At the end of the conference, this same reporter hoisted Hudson on the petard of fairness: ''Are you saying that you wouldn't be surprised if the majority of this commission, weighing the evidence, comes to the conclusion that pornography is harmless and that this commission's work may have been a waste of taxpayers' money?''

''I would withhold any type of judgment until I hear the evidence in the case and hear the debate that the commissioners took,'' he replied.

''So it could be that the majority will decide that porn is harmless?''

Said the chairman: ''It certainly is possible.''

SCREWING THE COMMISSION

America's porn purveyors did not believe him. They sent their counselors to the hearing in Los Angeles, knowing the fix was in. Since the commission lacked the authority to immunize witnesses from criminal prosecution, the porno kings themselves stayed home. The hearing room was filled with Los Angeles vice cops who were already on a "pandering" rampage. They would be more than happy to read Miranda rights to the producer of *Black Beaver Fever*.

Some of these entrepreneurs were sharing lucrative profits—the direct result of the videocassette boom. Adult films comprise 8 percent of this corner of the industry. But the heat kept coming. They were especially worried about a California law, effective January 1, 1986, allowing confiscation of the profits of second-obscenity offenders. (A salivating L.A. vice squad Sergeant Don Smith told *Daily Variety* a week before the commission hit down in October, "We're talking about multimillion-dollar companies.")

Beverly Hills lawyer John Weston, the garrulous and golden-tongued attorney for the Adult Film Association, unleashed a two-hour polemic in which he accurately assessed the commission's raison d'être. "Today's governmental antieroticism campaign," he charged, "is . . . not based upon a national consensus . . . Rather it seems to represent a shameless, undisguised political payoff for a small segment of the President's constituency—the fundamentalist religious Right."

Noting that 54 million X-rated videotapes were rented in 1984 and that Ronald Reagan garnered 52 million votes that same year, the clever Weston suggested "that there were many more adult decisions for sexually oriented materials in 1984 than voted for Mr. Reagan." This was a landslide for freedom: "I would suggest to you that the mandate that we have seen demonstrated is a mandate for choice in terms of sexually oriented materials and for adults to be able to make up their own minds."

Weston did his best to demolish one of the biggest smears against porn—its special allure for vicious sex criminals: "It seems, if one analyzes it, that most of the serial killers in the United States come from rather rural, right-wing fundamentalist Protestant backgrounds, where much of their reading matter was limited to the Bible as they grew up and in their formative years. Would one literally extrapolate from that the undeniable fact that somehow the Bible or formal fundamentalist Protestant theology inculcates within its adherents the desire or necessity of serial killing? I think not." The Adult Film Association had a clever mouthpiece.

William Margold, a thick-bodied jack-of-all-trades in the XXX-rated world, climbed out of the trenches to spit in the panel's face. "Welcome to Salem by the Pacific," his spirited, deep voice echoed through the nearly empty auditorium. For 13 years he toiled as an actor, agent, critic, director, publicist and scriptwriter, and he loved the life. Margold said that working on films like *Lust Inferno,* enriched his existence: "My multifaceted participation has been tremendously rewarding—creatively, mentally and physically."

In a rap he must use while scouting talent, Margold described the adult-film world as an "entertainment training ground, and an innovative force that is dedicated to enlightening, arousing and fulfilling its audience." He begged commissioners not to bomb his trade back into the Stone Age of grainy blue movies. "Forcing it underground would only result in encouraging factions to spuriously create and unpalatably supply lesser materials of a far more objectionable nature."

Margold said that any more censorship was intolerable, complaining that the reactionary social climate had already forced producers to inhibit artists at work. "The 'young look' is passé. Anal sex is out right now. It used to be in. Now it's out."

Chuck Dawson, founder and chairman of the Fun Unrestricted Network (FUN) available via satellite, shamelessly brought up his World War II military service in defense of the Constitution. He pleaded with commissioners not to trample on his right—won with blood, sweat and tears—to beam intercourse through outer space.

Commissioner Dietz grilled Brenda L. Fox, vice president and general counsel of the National Cable TV Association. "Are you familiar with a series called *The Hitchhiker*?" he asked. "Would it surprise you to know that in *The Hitchhiker* there are scenes in which women undress at least partially, and in the course of lovemaking are murdered?

"Does MTV not show scenes where women are bound, raped, caged, gagged?

"What percentage of cable subscriptions are from households with more than one person living there?" The startled Ms. Fox said that no survey like that had been performed. Dr. Dietz kept on: "In homes that have more than one person, would you still say there is individual choice about the materials that are broadcast into the home. . . ?"

Fox replied that parents could decide what their children should not watch. As far as adults living together, they would "make their decisions in whatever nature those adults would normally make their decisions."

Dr. Dietz had a darker scenario. "For men to control their wives through coercion and force, it's likely that those men are making the decision about the individual choice of the household."

Fox parried: "If the wife is that much under the thumb of the husband, I think she has got more problems than simply what television program is coming into the home."

Dr. Dietz smiled broadly. "I wouldn't disagree with you there."

Several East Coast porn-backers flew out West to bolster the arguments of their brethren.

Dennis Sobin, a trim, smooth-talking lobbyist from Washington, testified on behalf of an outfit called the First Amendment Consumer and Trade Society, which, he said, represents "1200 organizations ranging from international

103

magazines to mom-and-pop bookstores."

Sobin pulled up the window shades of his bedroom for commissioners. "Currently my wife and I use erotic materials to assist us in keeping our sex life fresh and innovative," he confessed. "When either of us is away from the other . . . the partner left at home will often go to our local neighborhood video store to rent an X-rated tape for late-night viewing while performing an act that statistics show 98 percent of us do—masturbate."

Screw publisher Al Goldstein jetted in from New York with his attorney and a female companion stuffed into tight black pants. The man behind "Midnight Blue" was uncharacteristically low-key and even polite during his brief remarks. What was slippery Al up to? Actually, he had a few surprises up his sleeve for the anticipated colloquy with commissioners (including handing out invitations to *Screw*'s 15th-anniversary party, to be held on the *Intrepid,* a WW II aircraft carrier mothballed on the Hudson River).

But the commissioners caught Al with his fly unzipped. They abruptly dismissed him without asking a single question.

"We flew five hours for this?" Goldstein's incredulous lawyer asked no one in particular.

"I'm fucking stunned," the usually inflappable entrepreneur said to a small group of reporters. Reverting to type, he surmised, "The commissioners must be tired from jerking off so much." But the targets of his bile were already out of the room.

Hollywood's chief spokesman, Jack Valenti, drove downtown to explain his industry's self-imposed rating system. The judges were flexible, he admitted—today's X is tomorrow's PG (Valenti mentioned *Midnight Cowboy*). But he defended its integrity—"The stongest and most powerful mogul in this town can't touch the chairman of that ratings board"—and its value—"the movie industry's attempt to be reasonable." Valenti said that just one percent of mainstream Hollywood films were slapped with an X, and 45 percent were rated R. He dumped on S&M flicks. "You have got to be terribly sick, you have to have something that is out of balance in the human condition to watch that without throwing up."

Hudson asked Valenti if he was "aware of the contents of some of the lyrics of rock music today." The chairman wondered if the witness had any thoughts about a "rating system for the record industry."

"I haven't given it that much thought," Valenti tiptoed. He suggested a sit-down meeting between PTA's, concerned parents and music executives.

Valenti was Ellen Levine's kind of witness. She tossed a few softball questions his way and thanked him for being "very patient," "very articulate." Most of the other commissioners were similarly deferential. Father Ritter was especially tough on Hollywood. He complained about all the sex in the movies today. But Valenti handled the padre deftly. Most of the complaints he gets nowadays do not concern erotica. "They deal with language," he said. "It really sends people up an emotional wall when they hear a word they find absolutely unacceptable." Father Ritter pursed his lips and nodded.

HERPES HIDEAWAY: BUNNY DEFECTORS

Los Angeles is a tough town in which to grab a headline. Short on worthy news, the hearings were buried. The *Los Angeles Times* had a short story deep in its second section on October 18 which criticized the unsubstantiated testimony of the anonymous witnesses.

Unlike Houston, public interest was nil in Los Angeles. No more than 30 spectators showed up at any one time.

The only excitement came when Mickey Garcia climbed onstage. A onetime *Playboy* centerfold (January 1973), Ms. Garcia had risen quickly in Hugh Hefner's organization to

Judge Edward Garcia: in vigorous 50s; calisthenics enthusiast; prominent Catholic layman with seven children; Reagan-appointed federal judge from Sacramento; under self-imposed gag order, he contributed almost nothing to the deliberations; when awake, he voted with hard-liners; told a reporter, "You know way more about this shit than I do."

become coordinator of Playmate Promotions, i.e., the Mother Superior to the bunnies. Flanked by her husband, a Chuck Norris-double in a short-sleeved flowered shirt, the aging beauty spoke of the unspeakable events that allegedly took place in Hefner's Los Angeles mansion: indiscriminate drug use, forced sex, her rape at the hands of an unidentified celebrity, a prostitution ring involving Playmates, and the bought silence of the LAPD.

Emotionally shaken, she told the hushed room that she had come forward to testify even though "threats" had been made against her family. The California journalists treated Mickey like a key Mafia informant. Cameras whirred and tape recorders turned as she stepped out into the bright sunshine in front of the municipal building. Although the commissioners had not one question for this bombshell witness, the media had plenty.

"Who made the threats to you?" several reporters shouted. Garcia would not elaborate.

"Why didn't you call the cops after your rape at the Playboy Mansion?" Garcia mumbled something about how Hef's chief of security was a former member of the LAPD's intelligence unit.

"Who told you to come forward now?" Garcia mentioned an attorney whom she refused to identify.

The skeptical press corps finally figured out Garcia's act when she revealed that she was peddling a manuscript dealing with her *Playboy* experience. No, she did not have a publisher as yet.

Playboy took the allegations in stride. Insiders said Hefner himself was "offended, but not perturbed." Burton Joseph, the corporation's special counsel, labeled Garcia's charges "patently absurd" and wondered if it were proper for the pornography commission to invite a disgruntled employee to dish up such slander.

In a letter to Sears the following month, Joseph quoted directly from the ex-Playmate's notes in her personnel file: "It might sound corny, but *Playboy* has been a wonderful influence on my life," she once wrote in happier days at the mansion. "I respect and admire Mr. Hefner and what he stands for . . . ."

Joseph concluded that "bearing false witness is as old as the recorded history of mankind and any further effort on my part to refute this testimony would only add a dignity that is undeserved."

The Garcia affair was the commission's second assault on Hef. In Chicago, Hudson wound up Brenda MacKillop, another former Bunny, who worked at the company's Chicago club from 1973 to 1976. The Arkady Shevchenko of porn established her bona fides quickly: "I frequented Hefner's mansion and I lived the Playboy philosophy." She went on to call Hef a pimp. "Many men came to the Playboy Club with the idea of purchasing sex. They offered me trips and money to go to bed with them. Although I never accepted, others may have. It is easy to see why these men would get the idea that pornography is associated with prostitution. Many centerfolds say they posed nude for the money."

But this Bunny eagerly hopped into bed without the promise of reward. "I found that premarital sex with single men led me to affairs with married men, then to using my body to get what I wanted . . . I got on casting couches in the attempt to become a movie star. Although I received small parts in *Godfather II* and *Funny Lady*, had sex with movie stars and producers, I felt worthless and empty." Then lightning from the heavens struck. She became a born-again Christian and embraced celibacy for three-and-a-half years, until her marriage. "There is no way I can describe the beauty, joy, fulfillment and peace of having sex within the bonds of my loving marriage," she concluded.

MacKillop's testimony was artfully scripted: She got away with calling Hef's mansion "Herpes Hideaway"; she included a reference to an aborted baby's "silent scream" (pornography leads, she noted, to many unwanted pregnancies); and she even managed to toss in a quote from *Dare to Discipline*, the bible of "tough love" written by Commissioner Dobson.

MacKillop is a familiar figure on the anti-porn circuit. "She pops up from time to time," remarked *Playboy* counsel Burton Joseph. "Her tenure as an employee, as far as we can tell, was unremarkable. We've got nothing on her."

IN DEFENSE OF *PLAYBOY* AND *PENTHOUSE*: BURTON JOSEPH AND ALAN DERSHOWITZ

By the time Meese unleashed his commission, America's two leading men's magazines, *Penthouse* and *Playboy*, were already enmeshed in warfare with the fundamentalists. The dogs of decency had targeted convenience stores for picketing and boycotts if they continued to sell a little T&A with their beer and cigarettes.

Jerry Falwell himself led a charge to the gates of the Southland Corporation, the parent company of the nationwide 7-Eleven chain, on Labor Day in 1985. Only 5000 true believers followed him. But some chain owners were concerned about the stream of rants against their outlets on the Christian Broadcasting Network. The magazines urged all distributors to hang tough against censorship. Bob Guccione and Hugh Hefner feared that the Meese commission would legitimize the campaigns against them. Smeared at almost every turn by Hudson, they nevertheless sent spokesmen to defend the right of adult Americans to read William F. Buckley, Jr., while eyeing a Pet of the Year.

Burton Joseph carried the *Playboy* standard in Chicago. A smartly dressed veteran of the obscenity wars (he fought for Henry Miller's *Tropic of Cancer* and for comedian Lenny Bruce), Joseph presented a high-minded First Amendment defense, shrewdly including a quote lifted from a text on obscenity by Commissioner Schauer. Joseph voiced a mistrust of any and all censorship. "Censors are insatiable," he said flatly.

Even so, the man who lawyers for *Playboy* did not want to be associated with *Jugs* and *Beaver*. His client published pictures for the elite. "The difference between *Playboy* and other so-called men's magazines is obvious," he said. "But when one is obsessed with 'pornography,' then quality, taste and content become irrelevant, and we, *Playboy,* are lumped with more explicit, violent, less informative, less enlightening and entertaining magazines."

Joseph finished with a rousing John Stuart Mill citation on freedom and settled back for questions. Commissioner Henry Hudson, no devotee of utilitarianism, went on the attack: "Your philosophy and viewpoint are remarkably similar to the ACLU. . . . Are you associated with that [organization]?"

Hudson already knew the answer. Joseph's résumé, provided with his written testimony, identified the attorney as a director of the ACLU in Illinois. But Hudson didn't want to waste a golden opportunity to link the pornographers and the civil libertarians together once again.

Hefner himself put down his Pepsi to dash off two editorials against sexual McCarthyism and the takeover of a federal commission by religious fanatics. "In America, they came first for your local convenience store. Who's next on their list?" asked the man who owned *Playboy*.

Penthouse, the largest-circulation men's magazine on the newsstands, upped the ante by hiring Harvard law professor and *Penthouse* columnist Alan Dershowitz to debate the panel in New York. One of the great polemical swordsmen of our day, Dershowitz had out-analogized William Buckley on "Firing Line" a few days earlier on the subject of AIDS. And now he seemed eager for fresh meat. Right from the start he went for the groin, challenging the legitimacy and objectivity of the panel. Pointing his finger at Father Bruce Ritter, the righteous Franciscan, he accused the moralists of trampling on sacred constitutional protections. "It is as American as apple pie to be sexually aroused and it is equally proper for a writer or photographer to design 'expression to be sexually arousing,' " he declared.

The fiery law professor put the commission on the griddle. He roasted its "self-selected, self-serving" witnesses and their testimony. "There is no basis for concluding that even a significant proportion of rapists or other sexual criminals have been exposed to pornography," he exclaimed.

Dershowitz treated the commission like a first-year law class. "Let's assume that every rapist in America in 1984 was exposed to *Playboy* and *Penthouse,*" he lectured. "We would still have to determine what proportion of their readers went out and committed rape. Even if we were to assume that each rape was committed by a different person, certainly not the case, approximately 99.97 percent of readers did not commit rapes.

"That," he said, "makes *Playboy* and *Penthouse* purer than Ivory Snow."

In preparing for his showdown, Dershowitz noted Father Ritter's remarks at a business session to the effect that if attitudes towards marriage are being affected by pornography, which says that extramarital and premarital sex is all right, then that represents a major attack on the family.

"Yes, yes, Father Ritter," Dershowitz boomed, "it is a direct attack on your beliefs, and I have the right to make that direct attack. Whether it be by getting a soapbox and standing on the corner and saying, 'I disagree with you, I think adultery is a good thing, and I think your view of sexuality is a bad thing.' I would have the right to say that, and I would have the right to advocate it through the use of pictures, words, devices or any other form of expression . . . .

"Let's debate it, let's argue about it . . . let's see who wins. You will probably win, but you have no right to shut down the marketplace and the stall from which dissenting ideas come."

In the question-and-answer period, chairman Hudson asked Dershowitz if he were familiar with a set of photos from the December 1984 *Penthouse* featuring bound Asian women. Dershowitz was fuzzy on the details.

"Maybe this will refresh your recollection," Hudson said dramatically as the room plunged into darkness. Then a slide from the pictorial flashed on a large screen at the front of the courtroom. The crowd was amazed by the sudden theatrics. Dershowitz responded quickly, urging that the record of the proceedings include the full text that accompanied the layout. The lights came back on; Hudson had no follow-up to his amateurish attempt to shake the witness.

Commissioner Dietz should not have asked why Dershowitz doubted the probity of the panelists. The law professor blasted the query out of the park. "I simply don't believe that there is a substantial possibility that the majority of this commission will come up with a recommendation that will

111

embarrass the attorney general, embarrass the President of the United States," Dershowitz cracked. "As you well know, if you happen to recommend any expansion of the gamut of erotic materials available to society, I guarantee it, I *guarantee* it . . . there would be no press conference with the Attorney General of the United States and the chairman of the commission. And the Attorney General of the United States getting up and saying: 'I've been wrong all my life, my president has been wrong all his life' . . . ."

Having lost the contest of wits, Dr. Dietz smiled and said, "I'm not going to ask you a question ever again." The audience laughed and applauded the professor's dash.

If Dershowitz was the climax, his *Penthouse* colleague Dottie Meyer was the resolution phase. A former Pet of the Year and now an executive with the magazine, Meyer sat at the witness table alongside the Harvard professor. When her turn came she spoke briefly about her career. "It hurts me when self-righteous, so-called do-gooders assume anyone who has been a centerfold is an empty-headed bubble-brained idiot being led down the garden path into a life of decadence with no moral future," said the 38-year-old wife of a Long Island cop. "I have definitely benefited from posing in *Penthouse* and would do it all over again."

Commissioner Dietz, fresh from his rout at the hands of Dershowitz, got rough with the tall and formidable enthusiast of erotica. Trying to undermine the truth of the text accompanying her nude layout, Dietz asked, "Is it true that you prefer men who dominate you in bed?"

"Yes," she replied.

"That you're preoccupied with sex?"

"On occasion."

"Do you have a collection of vibrators?"

"No."

Dr. Dietz, usually a kind man, came to regret this third degree.

BEHIND THE SCENES:
CENTERFOLD SESSION

Once more in Los Angeles, commissioners complained about time constraints. Progress was very slow. In a moment of rare candor, the chairman admitted that the quality of the panel's product was in jeopardy. "I am not sure we will be able to approach [this] with the exactitude that the commissioners think would be appropriate."

Over the next hour the commissioners talked cop shop. Tex Lezar had drawn up a huge list of law-enforcement proposals—i.e., amending standard police crime-scene reports to include space in which to record the presence of porn (tabled); state police should be encouraged to exchange information with federal law-enforcement officials (passed); and stiffer fines for those who aid and abet the interstate transportation of obscene materials. The current law on the books was 20 years old and set a maximum fine of $10,000. Cops testified that the figure of $100,000 would be a stronger deterrent. Hard-liner Dr. Dobson wondered if that was enough. Commissioner Ellen Levine delicately noted that she had "many questions on this one . . . ." The issue went unresolved, and the panel moved on to debate the wisdom of heavier minimum jail sentences for obscenity offenders. At this point the session reached a critical juncture. Father Bruce Ritter, a trained scholastic, was troubled. He wondered if the commission weren't going about its work all backward.

"We may be guilty of sort of begging the question [Does pornography cause harm?]" he said, as if his mind were open. "If we have not decided they exist, are we correct in establishing penalties for these harms that as yet do not exist?"

Chairman Hudson, who knew what Attorney General Meese expected, disagreed. In the clearest reflection of his own bias, he flatly stated that pornography was already outside the law. "I don't think in order to suggest law-enforc-ment initiatives we have to find that there is necessarily a harm, Father Ritter. *I believe that based upon the present fact that pornography is illegal,* and based upon what we have seen about the problem with enforcement control of pornography, it's in that vein that these recommendations are being made." (emphasis added)

But Father Ritter was worked up. Although he knew in his *medieval* heart that porn was the devil's work, he was smart enough to realize that good form was indispensable to the deliberations. "Suppose we found out there were no harms?" he mused. "Suppose this commission decided upon consideration of all the evidence that, in fact, the alleged harms were either nonexistent or relatively minor, and we are already on record as suggesting very large fines and jail sentences?"

Hudson's answer was lame: "Then I would think that each individual legislature could decide whether or not they felt there was no harm in their jurisdiction and adjust their laws accordingly."

Father Ritter kept the pressure up, urging the commission to face up to this key question or "we would rightly be accused of prejudging these matters."

Hudson's aide-de-porn Alan Sears said it all depended on how one interpreted the attorney general's charter. "You would look at the issue of harm as a question," he drawled. "You would look at the changes of law that might be done as a separate question. Now if the commission . . . writes all these recommendations about law enforcement. They are just recommendations on how to eliminate, close down or stop the flow of this material. [In] another part of your report you say the stuff is not harmful but in fact it's good for some folks. I think you have met your charter." (The government's interest in interdicting harmless material was not illuminated.)

Sears reminded them that the clock was running. "If we

defer until there is a final determination of harm to prepare work in all these areas . . . then I'm afraid we are not going to be able to do it physically.''

The scholastic was not placated. Hudson and Sears were turning the process upside-down. He hated pornography, but he had a logical mind, too. "Suppose this commission decided on a quarter-of-a-million-dollar fine and a five-year sentence would be necessary for adult pornography . . . and we voted and passed it unanimously, then three months later we decided, well, having reviewed all the evidence . . . we really don't think pornography is harmful.''

"At that point you can throw out the whole thing," Sears said.

Ritter was exasperated. "Alan, I understand your problem . . . but there is a logical imperative here . . . I, for one, think we would sabotage the credibility of this commission if we proceeded.''

Commissioner Dobson had no patience for the padre's pussyfooting. He said that the commission certainly had enough for "tentative conclusions." Despite Father Ritter's understandable uneasiness, the commission continued on its erratic erotic path.

Next up, a recommendation that police visit shops to tell proprietors what they may or may not sell. Hudson beamed enthusiastically. "It's a practice that we have in Arlington County. I make sure everyone is warned before they are prosecuted.''

Levine shuddered. "I can see that as a tool that could be taken in a very negative way by some people who seem to think they keep the public's morals in their hands," she said. "I think a lot of merchants would be scared to death to have a police officer walk in off the street to educate them.''

Hudson got testy. "What you are saying is the merchant

makes his own decision. If they are wrong, they get arrested."

"I am, in fact, more comfortable with that," said Levine, "than having the police have the ability to go around and suggest that selling this book is not a good idea because that's been taken off the library shelves in the town next door and it may go to court. I think it can lead to too-vigorous enforcement."

"I don't think many police officers are going around having library books taken off the shelves," Hudson retorted. "We are talking about more graphic photographs and books."

But Levine's chilling vision of gumshoe thought-police was effective: Her colleagues voted to request that police merely provide "upon request" obscenity law information to interested parties.

One of the mandates of the commission was to determine the "changing nature" of pornography in the years since the 1970 commission studied the issue. The vice cops' slide shows were full of the most extreme example of bizarre sexual practices and child pornography. In order to get a less jaundiced view of the proceedings, Levine had asked the staff to do its own investigation.

On the second day in Los Angeles, Sears unveiled a slide presentation put together by staff social scientist Edna Einsiedel. The show turned out to be an historical review of nudes, mostly centerfolds, from *Playboy, Penthouse* and *Hustler* since 1957. (The slides came courtesy of Dr. Judith Reisman, who was studying men's-magazine cartoons in another wing of the Justice Department.) When the lights dimmed, Einsiedel began, "I am not going to give you any commentary on this." She kept her word—merely calling off the years when each blonde, brunette or redhead disrobed for the citizenry.

"1957"; "1958"; "1959"; "1960"; "1961," Einsiedel droned as a few commissioners solemnly took notes.

"What year is this, Edna?" asked Diane Cusack when a bovine blonde flashed up.

"1978," said Edna as Cusack recorded the data on a yellow legal pad.

When the lights came back on, Sears grinned. "I hope we have met your requirements. If there is anything else you need, please let me know. Thank you, Edna."

Even Hudson seemed shocked by the pathetic level of staff support on this crucial matter. "Before we open this up for discussion, I want to make one comment," he said sternly. ". . . accepting the charge of the commission doesn't mean you are to abandon all common sense or your experience in life."

That said, he called on a shocked Ellen Levine. She pointed out that centerfolds "are not necessarily indicative of the distinctions between these three books." Dr. Einsiedel made excuses: "We only had these magazines for two days."

Diane Tilton thought it might have been more helpful if the staff had presented captions with the photos.

Unhappy with the all-American slide show, Dr. Dobson wondered if the staff were doing more to find examples of "perversions." Dr. Dietz suggested that a similar extravaganza could be mounted starring the covers of detective magazines. (He offered to lend them 20 such pictures he had in a personal collection.)

And what about the forgotten consumers of porn? Although traffic in explicit pictures was a multibillion-dollar business, the commission was unable to nail down a single contented customer. Sears informed the panel that he had been diligently laboring to find some "beneficiaries of pornography. We are working very hard." He mentioned that Chairman Hudson was quoted in the *Washington Post* earlier in the week on that point.

"We asked the reporter during that interview, if he knew of any, to send them to us."

117

TABLOID

The following is a description of a newspaperlike publication entitled *All Pleazure*. Page 4 contains three photographs. One photograph is a close-up of a female's labia being spread by fingers. Another photograph depicts a nude Caucasian female lying on her back with her legs spread. Her left hand is on her right breast. Her right hand is on her pubic area; lying beside her is a stuffed animal.

The last photo is a nude Caucasian female lying on her side. She has her right hand on her right buttock and her left hand is spreading her labia from under her body. Her face is turned toward the camera.

Pages 5 and 6 is all text. It is titled "OVERSEXED JUNGLE BUNNY." The text is about a female named Margaret Manners. It first explains how hair grows on most female vaginal and anal areas and how Margaret Manners is lucky because she doesn't have much hair on those areas. It tells how she manicures her own finger-and toenails and becomes very upset when a nail breaks. She also fantasizes about having sex with a black male.

Page 10 contains a large photo and text to another story titled, "FUCK ME, TUFF." The photo shows a partially clothed Caucasian female lying on her back with her knees in the air. Her hands are across the backs of her thighs with her fingers spreading her labia. She is wearing light-colored socks.

(Excerpted from the Final Report of the Attorney General's Commission on Pornography—Government Printing Office, 1986)

"Have we received any, Mr. Sears?" asked Hudson.

"To date, no comment," Sears shrugged. "We will keep up our search."

Father Ritter suggested calling Dr. Ruth Westheimer. "I know she has recommended that married couples seek out programs from their local video stores to bring some spice to a fading marriage."

Dr. Dobson said maybe the Church could help. "I believe that the Lutheran Social Service located, I believe, in Minneapolis, at one time used pornographic materials extensively in desensitizing young people referred by the court for various offenses."

Hudson said he would look into it.

6

DEFINING THE UNDEFINABLE

C hairman Hudson took flak from inside and outside for flying the commission blindly through three hearings without a definition of pornography. Reporters wanted to know if he was merely interested in bizarre sexual depictions, like pregnant-lesbian photo books. Or was pornography smiling naked girls skipping on a beach?

The 1970 commissioners did not even use the term "pornography." They said the word had "no legal significance and . . . it most often denotes subjective disapproval of certain materials, rather than their content or effect."

But this caveat did not stop the current chairman.

Dr. Park Dietz: the chairman's favorite shrink; expert on autoerotic hanging, rubber fetishes and detective magazines; plays drums to relax; brightest member of panel but sometimes space cadet on sex; taught at Harvard Medical School, currently professor at University of Virginia; testified against John Hinckley; FBI consultant; more worried about violence than Deep Throat; *late 30s; masturbation to centerfolds okay; won 1986 Krafft-Ebing Award from Academy of Forensic Sciences.*

Hudson got the long-delayed discussion rolling at the second business meeting in Los Angeles. The prosecutor distributed a working definition he had drafted. "Don't feel wedded to it," he said.

Pornography, according to Henry Hudson, was:

"1. [T]he graphic sexually explicit portrayal of women, men or children presented as sexual objects who enjoy pain or humiliation, or

"2. women, men or children are presented as sexual objects for the mere purpose of pleasure;

"3. women, men or children are presented as the objects of physical sexual abuse or

"4. women, men or children are presented being penetrated by objects or animals."

Women Against Pornography would have tingled. Hudson's second clause was lifted from WAP texts. WAP polemicist Catharine MacKinnon had obviously wooed the impressionable Hudson in Chicago. This remarkable document offered an invaluable insight into the prosecutorial mind. Its head-scratching specificity (the "being penetrated" in number 4); its moral undertone (number 2's "mere"); and its reactionary impulses (the porn label goes back on *Ulysses*) were almost Victorian.

Not surprisingly, Ellen Levine pounced first. Twirling the salt-and-pepper strands of her long hair, she went straight for number two. "Sexual pleasure is often a purpose of *normal* relations," she delicately pointed out. "I don't understand it in the definition of pornography." And neither did the grim-faced Hudson, who refused to argue the point.

As an increasingly awkward silence filled the room, Hudson called upon Dr. Dietz, who had been working out a formulation of his own. The apple-cheeked professor from the University of Virginia, dressed in khaki pants, a blue blazer and topsiders, eagerly strode to the front of the room and began to write on a large sheet of paper.

"Pornography is any presentation of felonious or violent behavior which is sexually arousing," he read aloud when he was finished scribbling. His colleagues let that sink in. Levine made a pained face and shook her head from side to side. Then pointed questions were raised.

For example, how could one determine what was "sexually arousing"? Dr. Dietz, soon to win the 1986 Krafft-Ebing Award, suggested that "might be a reasonable person's response to stimuli." Perhaps, he added with a Frankensteinian touch, medical "laboratories" could certify what is or is not sexually exciting. He meant hooking machines—penile plethymographs—up to erections to measure blood flow. If more than 5 percent of the guys got it up, the picture was pornographic.

Someone asked about the term "felonious." The accommodating Dr. Dietz said that he was open to changing it to "unlawful." "In some states fornication could be a misdemeanor, I guess," he reasoned.

As commissioners pondered further, Dr. Dietz returned to his seat and leaned back in his chair. Father Ritter spoke next, wondering whether he could put the following remarks "off the record." This caused the few reporters in attendance to lean forward. He gently chided Dietz's Clockwork Orange scenario and said the professor had a "blurred criterion" of sexual arousal.

Levine piped up that Dr. Dietz's arousal tests might be "expensive" and slumped low in her seat. But the psychiatrist emphasized that his definition concerned material in which an "eroticized object is bad." He gave an example: "A boy who masturbates while looking at the covers of detective magazines three times a week for two years has a high probability of finding women that are tied up to be arousing. . . ."

Deanne Tilton was fuzzy on the connection between unlawful activity and pornography. "Would you be talking about someone being sexy in the process of embezzling?" she asked.

Dr. Dietz countered. "I know of no embezzlophiliacs that have ever been reported."

Dr. Dobson went on record as saying he would prefer a "simpler definition." Hudson urged the panel to "get back on track."

Dr. Dietz, who wandered into the corridor for a smoke, stuck his head back in the room to announce that his definition dealt only with the issue of "learned association." "It doesn't go far enough to handle all the harmful effects of pornography."

This remark aroused Dr. Dobson. "What was it—*Asian Sluts*—that we saw yesterday? Anal sex or young girls over the age of maturity having sex with older men." He wanted something to cover all that.

Levine asked whether the definitions being bandied about would affect "art photography" and mentioned Helmut Newton.

The group returned to Hudson's definition. Tilton had a question about his fourth clause—people being penetrated by animals.

124

"Isn't it usually the other way around?" the well-exercised blonde asked with a wince. "The animals being penetrated?"

"Depends on whether it's a man or a woman animal," shot back Levine.

The intrepid executive director tried to clarify the situation. "We went to Times Square—one of the largest stores in the nation," he said. "We counted one entire wall that was covered with animal films—45 different animals being portrayed. Everything I could imagine was pictured, and I would say it was equal who was penetrating who."

In addition, Sears discovered a fascinating new genre. "For the first time in my experience, I saw sadomasochistic bestiality films . . . where young women were bound, tied up and animals were being lowered onto the woman." Sears was impressed—he would mention this exotica several times over the course of the next few months.

His eye on the clock, the chairman asked the commissioners to read the transcript of this debate before the next meeting in Miami, where deliberations would resume.

In the Sunshine State a month later, Hudson tried again. Still smarting from a definitional Bay of Pigs in Los Angeles, the tenacious prosecutor tossed out what he termed "a very succinct yet very workable" effort: "Pornography is any representation designed to be sexually arousing and portrays pain, humiliation, and unlawful sexual conduct, as a dominant theme."

"Father," he confessed to the priest, "I got the idea from reading some of your materials."

"Why'd you use the term 'unlawful'?" immediately asked Judge Garcia.

"To delineate the sexual conduct, Judge, to that which is socially unacceptable. To perhaps eliminate some nudity."

"Okay," said the jurist.

"Would bestiality be excluded from this definition?"

inquired Father Ritter.

"It would be sexually unlawful conduct, would it not?" answered Hudson.

"Is private sexual contact with an animal unlawful?" asked the friar.

"It is in Virginia," nodded Henry Hudson.

"It is in California," chimed in Judge Garcia.

"It is everywhere," announced Dr. Dietz.

But Father Ritter was bothered by an apparent loophole. "Group sex would not be considered unlawful. Let me theorize, Mr. Chairman. Five men and five women having sex together is not unlawful."

"I suppose you're right," Hudson shook his head, staring down at his definition.

"That gets us back to fornication and what its status is," said Dr. Dietz. "Also, sodomy ought to be introduced into that."

Tex Lezar sighed. "I don't understand the purpose of defining pornography."

Father Ritter did. "If this commission were asked what was the subject matter of its survey, what would you tell them?"

"Well, you wouldn't tell them one word," answered Judge Garcia.

"The problem we face, Tex, is no one on the commission can really say what we are talking about," said the friar.

Hudson offered to trade "unlawful" for "explicit" in his definition.

Father Ritter was delighted.

Lezar was working overtime now. "We want a definition that will allow us to include everything that other people are saying is pornography. It's not a value judgment. This would cover everything that people have come before the commission and have said, 'This is pornography.' Dr. Dietz politely corrected him. "No, this doesn't cover everything."

126

"What else is there?" asked Tex.

They danced around with child porn a little bit before Tex moved in for the kill. "Any representation is pornographic if it is designed to be sexually arousing and portrays pain, humiliation or sexual conduct or organs as the dominant theme."

But the ever-unpredictable Dr. Dietz threw a forensic monkey wrench on the table. "The only other thing that leaps to mind would be portrayals of corpses, in which there would no longer be pain." He also posed the possibility of having sex with "anesthetized persons."

"Could we just add that as a footnote, Doctor?" pleaded an exasperated chairman.

"Well," answered Dr. Dietz, "I would hate to divert the entire industry to necrophilic pornography."

Lezar agreed.

"Is it legal to have sex with a corpse if you are married to it?" asked Mrs. Tilton.

"One could be doing other things than sexual things with a corpse legally," said Dr. Dietz.

"Could you do things with a corpse legally?" inquired Tilton.

"It's beyond my ken," Hudson exclaimed.

"Me, too," said Cusack. "They lost me on that."

Tilton thought corpses were getting an undeserved knock. "What's the difference between a corpse and a beast? I don't like adding 'corpse,' I'm sorry, Park."

Hudson put the definition to a vote, without "corpse." Dr. Dietz did not protest. Cusack soothed him: "Your words will live forever in the transcript, Park."

All the commissioners in attendance—Hudson, Cusack, Lezar, Tilton, Judge Garcia, Father Ritter and Dr. Dietz—voted to adopt the following working definition: "A representation is pornographic if it is designed to be sexually arousing and portrays children, pain, humiliation, sexual abuse, conduct or organs as a dominant theme."

One of the commissioners conceded that mainstream erotica like *The Joy of Sex,* Christian love manuals and Nabokov's *Lolita* would now be considered pornographic under this broad formulation.

But in the end, the Meese commission, like its predecessor, surrendered on the definition of pornography.

The final report noted that marking the boundaries of "pornography" is essentially a "futile" task. So what did they mean when they referred to pornographic materials? Merely that the materials were "predominantly sexually explicit and intended primarily for the purpose of sexual arousal."

DR. DIETZ'S PORNOGRAPHIC LADDER

At an earlier business meeting, the commissioners wanted pornography—whatever that was—to be broken down into digestible components. Dr. Dietz accepted the assignment of creating a scale of harmfulness. In Los Angeles, he handed his fellow commissioners the fruits of his labors:

The following scheme seeks to provide a means of classifying materials with erotic, sexual, or obscene content other than those involving children. It is a "scale" at least in the sense that I intend that any given material be assigned to the highest-numbered class applicable. Whether this is a scale of "harmfulness," with high-numbered classes considered to be more harmful than lower numbered classes, is a separate issue. If all else were equal, I would think that this scale corresponds well to our best current information on potentially harmful effects, but I think there are factors other than those used in the classification scheme that are related to harmfulness, such as the number of persons exposed, the age at exposure, and the moral context of exposure.

One advantage of developing a classification system or scale along these or other lines is that it would be possible for various users of such a system or scale to make their own choices about the types of materials they wish to produce, publish, display, sell, purchase, and so on. The classes of materials acceptable in school books or for purchase by children ought to differ from the classes acceptable for purchase by adults. In making these or other distinctions, it would be valuable to decision makers to have a functional classification system or scale. The classes defined here are merely a first draft set forth for discussion by the Commission.

The sources of examples given for each class are by no means exhaustive.

I recognize that there are those who would consider all displays of the naked body as degrading and others who would view as degrading any display of a person who is being treated as an object (i.e., "objectification"). The sense in which the term "degradation" is used here, however, is narrower and is limited to instances in which a person is portrayed as less than human, in humiliating circumstances, as defiled, or with the exposure of tissues ordinarily concealed by the labia majora or the buttocks.

Class 0: One or more adults displayed in full or partial nudity without behavior, pose, garments, props, or context suggestive of provocativeness, sexual behavior, domination, submission, degradation or violence. Many examples are found among classic paintings and sculptures; photographic figure studies; medical illustrations; and photographs published in *National Geographic*.

Class 1: One adult displaying behavior, pose, garments, props, or context suggestive of sexual behavior, but without stimulation of the genitals or penile erection, regardless of nudity, without suggestions of domination, submission, degradation or violence. Many examples are found among the centerfolds of *Playboy, Penthouse,* and other magazines; lingerie advertisements and window displays; mailorder catalogs; televised situation comedies and soap operas; and mainstream films.

Class 2: Two adults displaying behavior, pose, garments, props, or context suggestive of sexual behavior, but without stimulation of the genitals or penile erection, regardless of nudity, without suggestions of domination, submission, degradation, or violence. Many examples are found in network television broadcasts and mainstream films. Examples are also found in fashionable advertisements.

Class 3: One adult displaying behavior, pose, garments, props, or context suggestive of sexual behavior, with stimulation of the genitals or penile erection, regardless of nudity, without suggestions of domination, submission, degradation, or violence. Many examples are found in magazines such as *Hustler, Chic, Club International,* and in the magazines sold in "Adult" bookstores; some examples are found in *Penthouse.*

Class 4: Two adults displaying behavior, pose, garments, props, or context suggestive of sexual behavior, with stimulation of the genitals or penile erection, regardless of nudity, without suggestions of domination, submission, degradation, or violence. Examples are not plentiful, but may be found among sex education books and films.

Class 5: One adult displaying behavior, pose, garments, props, or context suggestive of sexual behavior, with any suggestion of domination, submission, degradation, or violence but without stimulation of the genitals or penile erection, regardless of nudity. Many examples are found in music videos; television and film portrayals of abduction, sexual assault, and other crimes; the covers of detective magazines; and magazines of the bondage and domination or sadomasochistic variety. Occasional examples are found in fashionable advertisements.

Class 6: Two adults displaying behavior, pose, garments, props, or context suggestive of sexual behavior, with any suggestion of domination, submission, degradation, or violence but without stimulation of the genitals or penile erection, regardless of nudity. Many examples are found in music videos; television and portrayals of abduction, sexual assault, and other crimes; the covers of detective magazines; magazines of the bondage and domination or sadomasochistic variety; and "Adult films." Occasional examples are found in fashionable advertisements.

Class 7: One adult displaying behavior, pose, garments, props, or context suggestive of sexual behavior, with stimulation of the genitals or penile erection, and with any suggestion of domination, submission, degradation, or violence, and regardless of nudity. Many examples are found among high-circulation magazines with sexual content; magazines and films sold in "Adult" bookstores; and films, pamphlets, illustrated books, and catalogs directed toward sexual masochists. Some examples are found in magazines of the bondage and domination or sadomasochistic variety; occasional examples are found in mainstream films.

Class 8: Two adults displaying behavior, pose, garments, props, or context suggestive of sexual behavior, with stimulation of the genitals or penile erection, and with any suggestion of domination, submission, degradation, or violence, regardless of nudity. Many examples are found among films and magazines sold in "Adult" bookstores and in *Hustler* and certain other widely circulated magazines with sexual content.

Class 9: One or more adults displaying behavior, pose, garments, props, or context that is unquestionably sexual coupled with explicit domination, submission, or degradation, regardless of nudity or stimulation of the genitals or penile erection. Many examples are found among the films and magazines sold in "Adult" bookstores; *Hustler* and certain other widely circulated magazines with sexual content; television and film portrayals of abduction, sexual assault, and other crimes; and magazines of the bondage and domination or sadomasochistic variety.

Class 10: One or more adults displaying behavior, pose, garments, props, or context that is unquestionably sexual coupled with explicit violence, regardless of nudity or stimulation of the genitals or penile erection. Many examples are found among R-rated films; "Adult" bookstores; *Hustler* and certain other widely circulated magazines with sexual content; television and film portrayals of abduction, sexual assault, and other crimes; and magazines of the bondage and domination or sadomasochistic variety.

The commissioners ultimately found the 10 classes unwieldly; Dr. Dietz whittled them down further. He unveiled his new classes in February in Scottsdale.

7

EXPLOITING
THE CHILDREN

The commission arrived in Miami on the eve of Hurricane Kate in mid-November. Sandbags were tightly packed against the seaside doors of the Doral Hotel, a garish Miami Beach resort where panelists dormed. Hudson and his team braved gale-force winds to drive home the horror of child pornography. They invited several Florida cops to describe their best kiddie-porn busts. Nevertheless, the police admitted that tough laws had already forced the hideous product off the open market; even under-the-counter purchases were rare. So rare that FBI Director William Webster told the commission that his bureau did not require any new laws.

133

Even a few commissioners thought the matter was a dead horse. Father Ritter pleaded that Hudson kick his "overriding preoccupation" with the topic. "I'm not sure that it should be a major concern of this commission," he had remarked in Los Angeles. "It is already outside the pale, constitutionally, and if we keep bringing it back into the hearings over and over again, it takes us away from the more difficult matters," the priest implored.

THE KIDDIE-PORN CONNECTION

But Hudson needed to exploit the kiddie porn. He used it to smear the whole erotic industry.

Showcasing the children's issue in Florida was a shrewd move. Republican Senator Paula Hawkins is a national figure in the battle against child molestation. The cosponsor of the 1984 Child Protection Act commanded media attention when she went public with tales of her own abuse as a girl. And Anita Bryant's antigay rights campaign succeeded in the state a few years back, in good measure because of its Save the Children theme.

At his Miami press conference, the chairman made a point of noting that the René Guyon Society and the North American Man-Boy Love Association declined to send representatives to testify.

Ken Lanning was brought back again to turn stomachs with grisly slides from crime scenes. He linked adult erotica to child molestation by noting that such material is used to lower the inhibitions of kids by pedophiles. "What you find out is all the adult magazines that [a pedophile] had, every one of them contained at least one story about children or sexual abuse of children," he continued.

Cops, clinicians and recovering molesters jammed the witness slots in this city of vice. Commissioners heard more than they needed to know about the aberrations in this category. For instance, a detective from San Bernadino, Sergeant R.P. "Toby" Tyler, testified that "panties" can be child erotica. "In one bizarre case I heard of, I didn't work it, toenail clippings [were erotic to one man]."

Some of the previous testimony had wildly inflated the problem. Sears' senator, Mitch McConnell of Kentucky, testified that kiddie porn represented 10 to 15 percent of the putative $4.5 billion porn empire. (He lowballed NBC's white paper "The Silent Shame," which bumped the statistic up to $3 billion per annum, a sum equal to the entire gross receipts of Hollywood movies in 1984.)

Cornered outside the Great Hall following his Washington testimony, Agent Lanning winced when asked for his reaction to these estimates. "You know how it is when there's not much time and people have to dramatize their point," he shrugged. "Nobody really knows the size of it."

In fact, a U.S. postal inspector commented that no one is becoming "a millionaire" on child pornography. And Lanning himself has previously averred that kiddie porn is really a cottage industry in which private practitioners trade photos of young children on the black market like baseball cards.

The hysteria over kiddie porn has frightened nudists all over the country. The panel was even talking about mandatory jail sentences for mere possession of kiddie porn. Producing innocent snapshots of kids at nude volleyball games is a federal crime. Nudist hell loomed. The head of the American Sunbathing Association came to say, "Think of us."

"We are a family-oriented organization, and we have been since our inception in 1931," the fully clothed Richard Lane said. "We would like to portray . . . what we believe in and what we are and who we are: namely, family. If we are going to leave members of our families out, then we are not truly portraying ourselves . . . ."

135

The commissioners thanked him for his concern and then forgot the nudists.

THE WITNESS FROM "CAPTAIN KANGAROO"

The only hard news out of Miami was the sneak preview of Dr. Judith Reisman's $734,000 study of cartoons in *Playboy, Penthouse* and *Hustler*. Her survey, funded by a noncompetitive Justice Department grant, was controversial from the start.

Congressmen denounced the exorbitant price tag and questioned the value of this unusual undertaking. They looked askance at Dr. Reisman's amazing résumé, which identified her as a former songwriter for "Captain Kangaroo" and disclosed a surprising lack of scholarly credentials. (No books, no scientific studies, no university teaching.)

But Dr. Reisman had bona fides of a different sort. She was a familiar face on the antipornography bandwagon: In a book titled *Take Back the Night,* she compared Hugh Hefner, Bob Guccione and Larry Flynt to Hitler, Mussolini and Tojo. In 1983, on CNN's "Crossfire" program (cohosted by future Reagan adviser Pat Buchanan), she accused the late Alfred Kinsey of permitting pedophiles to abuse children as part of his sex research. (The Kinsey Institute denounced the charges and demanded proof. Dr. Reisman promised to lay out her case in a "nearly completed" book—a genre in which she seems to specialize. But three years later the book is still to be published.)

This showmanship caught the eye of Alfred Regnery, a Reaganaut hack who then headed the Justice Department's Office of Juvenile Justice and Delinquency Prevention. He doled out almost double the entire budget of the porn commission—in discretionary funds—to zap the Big Three of men's sophisticates. But first Dr. Reisman had to find academic cover. No university affiliation, no grant. However, the connection was easily arranged. After learning that she had her hands on a mother lode, American University in Washington made her a full research professor in its school of education. Coincidentally or not, Attorney General Ed Meese's wife serves on the university's board of trustees.

Consequently, Dr. Reisman and her staff of coders launched the federal government's most frontal assault on skin magazines. The angle of attack was below the waist. Unable to combat the adult erotica in *Playboy, Penthouse* and *Hustler,* she attempted to drag in the kids by putting a magnifying glass to all the cartoons ever published in these mainstream monthlies. So her crew clipped away for several months in 1985. As expected, they were not amused by what they found—taking at face value what most readers would regard as satire or sexual burlesque.

The $734,000 presentation to the commission was hurried and, at times, incomprehensible. With lights dimmed, Dr. Reisman—a short, chunky, middle-aged woman in a white suit—narrated her slide show with the aid of expensive computer graphics. Her statistics seemed astonishing at first glance: "The coders identified 2016 child cartoons and 3988 child visuals, of which 681 were pseudo-children, in all issues [of *Playboy, Penthouse* and *Hustler*]," she claimed. *Playboy* accounted for 3045 cartoons and visuals, *Penthouse* for 1180 and *Hustler* for 1179 for a total of 6004 child-linked images. The total count of 6004 images means children or surrogate children were involved pictorially an average of 8.2 times for the *Playboy* issue, 6.4 times for a *Penthouse* issue and 14.17 times per *Hustler* issue. The 2016 child cartoons comprised 12.14 percent of all cartoons published in the magazines."

Among other alleged horrors, Reisman discovered "exaggerated sexual parts" on some of the cartoon children. This was mostly ample cleavage on teenage characters whom Dr. Reisman identified, contrary to the impressions of the audience, as pre-teen adolescents.

She unearthed hidden messages in some "fairy tale" cartoons. One pathetic example involved the evolution of the Dorothy character from *The Wizard of Oz*. In a November 1968 *Playboy*, Dr. Reisman saw Dorothy as a "flat-chested little youngster in a small black-and-white implied sex scene with the scarecrow." Actually, the cartoon featured a leering man of straw telling our heroine, "You know what I really want."

She then displayed a *Playboy* cartoon published a decade later in which a just-ravaged Dorothy turns over the Tinman, Lion and Scarecrow to a cop. "That's them, Officer," read the caption. Dr. Reisman fretted about the implications of Dorothy "gang-raped as a child-woman . . . exploited by surrogate protectors with no help given by other authority adults." And so on.

The songwriter had cast her net wide. She found evil in Gahan Wilson's cartoons and Helmut Newton's photos. "Shaved genitalia," she intoned solemnly, "has emerged as a troublesome new phenomenon." One pictorial starred a young woman who was clearly in her late teens. Yet Dr. Reisman noted that the model was diagnosed as a six- or seven-year-old by a group of Georgetown pediatricians.

What was Dr. Reisman getting at? What did all this cartoon guilt-by-association mean? Regrettably, she offered no evaluation of her own, hiding behind the facade of objective research. Instead, she quoted two "child-development specialists" who speculated that "[r]epeated exposure to scenes with adolescent or young girls could stimulate *hidden* sexual feelings toward young girls, which the man had been keeping at bay [emphasis added] . . . . To a person who has difficulty separating fantasy from reality, the magazines give tremendously confusing records."

Maybe so. But *Field & Stream* is probably just as confusing to such psychologically impaired souls. Despite her inflammatory past, Dr. Reisman concluded with a calm constitutional call for a "moratorium on child or pseudo-child depictions until verifiable answers are obtained."

Only the skeptical Dr. Judith Becker questioned the weird methodology. After fending off Dr. Becker's concerns, Dr. Reisman was dismissed by the chairman. The next and last witness in Miami was a Baltimore detective who walked the pedophile beat.

The commission eventually decided to ignore the inventor of the "pseudo-child" and left out all reference to the controversial project in the final report. It was one of the panel's few shrewd judgments. This unexpected repudiation made Dr. Reisman an even sadder figure. But she pledged to continue her work at her own recently established institute. At the last commission session in May, she was spotted handing out her new business cards.

BEHIND THE SCENES: NUKING SEX ED

The inane dialogue at the business meetings indicated the need for universal sex education in the United States. Unfortunately, the commissioners ran away from this controversial issue. Although the 1970 panel called for a massive sex-ed campaign, Meese's group shamefully kept their silence. Nevertheless, Father Ritter, God bless him, asked his colleagues to back a national curriculum in Miami. "I can hardly think of anything more important to our country," he emphasized.

Dr. Dobson, a moralist of a fundamentalist kind, blinked incredulously at the Franciscan's proposal. "For us to endorse sex education . . . and not guidelines . . . could open the door to things I would be very much opposed to," he said.

Levine leaned forward in her seat and endorsed Ritter's suggestion. Ever the dunce, Hudson immediately went for a compromise. He suggested that "[t]he commission would recommend that those jurisdictions that elect to integrate

Deanne Tilton: most congenial; 40-ish; soft-spoken; sounds like Beaver Cleaver's mom; on second marriage, to child psychologist; president of the California Consortium of Child Abuse Councils; child pornography is principal interest; weirdest moment—when she asked Colleen Dewhurst at a public hearing if Actors' Equity had been infiltrated by organized crime.

sex education into their school curriculum should include, as part of that program, appropriate instruction in the potential harm that pornography may have on adolescents and young people.'' (This came from a man who dared to tell reporters that the commission had not yet decided whether pornography was harmful.)

Tex Lezar rubbed the sides of his black cowboy boots and wondered why the ''negatives'' of sex should not be emphasized to kids.

Tilton then delivered a touching speech killing Lezar's dirty mind with kindness. She lamented the tragic fallout from the notorious McMartin preschool case in Los Angeles. ''They fired male workers and then they instructed their workers to stop holding kids . . . there are certain needs kids have . . . [t]hey have to be touched . . . a curriculum [shouldn't be negative] it [should] be talking to kids about the healthy kinds of outlets . . . .''

Father Ritter plowed ahead, stressing that sex education must be taught ''within moral and ethical values: The problem is that we live in a very pluralistic society, we must accept some core curriculum. It is not enough to say that sex

140

PAPERBACK BOOKS

Abused Vietnamese
  Virgins
A Girl and Her Dog
Bondage Brat
Bound, Whipped and
  Raped Schoolgirls
Chain Whipped Bride
Cock Starved Nympho
Convict Lesbian
Dog Loving Daughter
Dripping Dykes
Eager Naked Daughter
Frank's Oversexed Aunt
Fuck-Crazy Wives
G.I. Blow
Going Down on Her
  Dad
Greta's Dungeon Ordeal
Her Mean Stepmother
Horny Balling Babysitter
Horny Holy Roller
  Family
Hot Chains, Cold Wife
Hot Cock Nazi Master
Incest Mommy
I Want All-Night Abuse
Japanese Sadist
  Dungeon
Mom's Golden Shower
  Nights
Naked Teen on a Leash

Nazi Dungeon Slave
New Kid in Prison
Over Daddy's Knee
Overheated Mother
P.O.W. Sex Slave
Raped by Arab
  Terrorists
Rent a Nude Model
Sex Swamp Camp
Slant-Eyed Savages
Soviet Sex Slaves
Suck Eager Daughter
Take It, Wimp
Teen Rape Orgy
Tied Up Tits
Tongue Fucked Asshole
Ummm! Mom's a Hot
  One
Up the Ying Yang
Used by the Gestapo
Vicky's Cock Fucking
  Throat
Wet Teen Lezzie
Young Legs Wide Open

(Excerpted from the Final
Report of the Attorney
General's Commission
on Pornography—Gov-
ernment Printing Office,
1986)

141

education must be provided within the context of family . . . . [Otherwise] we are doing our kids an enormous
disservice and we are opening them up to [learning about
sex] from hard-core pornography.''

Dr. Dobson, who stared intently at Father Ritter,
wouldn't budge: ''I feel there's too much too soon. I think
the wrong kind of sex education increases promiscuity,'' he
harrumphed. The evangelist eventually prevailed; his para-
noia perverted any possibility of recommending a more sensible way of teaching children about the facts of life. This
was the commission's greatest failure of nerve.

8

THE MOB, THE MILITANT AND THE MINISTERS

Henry Hudson had just declared a lunch recess on the opening day of the New York hearings in January when the commotion began.

Dorchen Leidholdt, the Squeaky Fromme of Women Against Pornography, rushed the microphone at the witness table and nervously began reading out 12 nonnegotiable demands. Surprised by this ambush, the panelists froze in their chairs. "We demand that the commission acknowledge that the eight-billion-dollar-a-year pornography industry is built on sexual enslavement and exploitation of *wom-*

143

en," said Leidholdt. Realizing that the commissioners were listening to her, she relaxed and spoke more slowly. "We demand that the commission acknowledge that pornography targets *all women* for rape, battery, sexual harassment, prostitution, incest and murder."

Flanked by a dozen anti-porn lieutenants including the forlorn founder of Men Against Pornography, Leidholdt kept on for four tense minutes. Chairman Hudson could have shut the demonstration down at any point, but instead he chose to permit the takeover and even asked for a written version of her statement.

This last courtesy offended some in the gallery. "This is a farce," yelled Lindsay Flora, a vice president of the Adult Film Association. "The commission is staging this," screamed Leanne Katz of the National Coalition Against Censorship. "Why wasn't the microphone turned off?" another woman grumbled loudly. But for naught. A majority of the panel and its staff were blood brothers with the anti-porn extremists and liked to extend all privileges to them.

"IF ONLY HOOVER WERE ALIVE"

New York's intelligentsia were ready for Henry Hudson's road show. Literary luminaries like Gay Talese and Kurt Vonnegut issued rebukes. Writers' groups, gay activists and the usual Jeffersonians convened their own panels on Meese's ominous mandate and urged retaliation.

When the commissioners appeared at the International Court of Trade near New York's City Hall early on January 24, they got a rough greeting. A small crowd of female protesters called No More Nice Girls dressed up as constables, wore signs saying "Sex Police" and chanted, "Stop Meese, not sex." Yet the panel plowed forward with its hearing on pornography and "organized crime." The topic brought on more detectives. Consequently some of the opponents of the smut-busters were locked out once again. For example, the American Booksellers Association, whose members can be arrested for selling sexually explicit materials, was denied a slot, while the vice police and D.A.'s from Los Angeles, Chicago and North Carolina—who had *already testified*—repeated their routines.

Hudson ordered out-of-town talent because local cops stayed away. The NYPD practically boycotted the event, sending over a single detective. Jerry Piazza, a sergeant from Midtown South, noted that obscenity busts are not a high priority among New York's finest. He said that his unit, which covers the Times Square flesh parlors, received only two public complaints in the last two years. Gotham's media-conscious U.S. attorney Rudolph Giuliani, an organized-crime expert himself, nixed an invitation to testify. The star witnesses for the prosecution were second bananas—a pair of retired FBI agents from another era.

"The problem is, the average prosecutor is about the age of Alan Sears up there," growled jowly William Kelly. "He is like thirty years old, he is three years out of law school. He is scared to death of the defense attorneys, some of whom are in here in the courtroom, he is a product of the new generation and he is afraid of getting beaten, because sometimes he gets beaten. A lot of the United States attorneys have told me, 'What are you getting so stirred up about dirty pictures for? Kelly, didn't you used to go to stag parties when you were in college?' And the answer to that is, no, I didn't. So that makes me weird, right?"

Kelly asserted wistfully that things would be different "if J. Edgar Hoover was still alive." Those were the Golden Years. "I was a high-paid agent. I had a car. I had backup," he recalled. His former colleague Homer Young shot the breeze about Bugsy Siegal, Meyer Lansky and the Gam-Bee-Nos. "Since 1955, I have felt that this is more or less a mission in which I have been involved, and I thank the Good Lord each day that I can continue my fight," he said. "Without His help I too may have fallen or become addicted [to pornography]."

The duo was questioned respectfully by commissioners, who typically failed to notice the bias in their backgrounds. Young, for example, was a close associate of the late Reverend Morton Hill, the Jesuit who dissented from the report of the 1970 presidential commission.

Both ex-G-men made the astonishing claim that vigorous prosecution by the United States attorneys could shut down America's porn business in 18 months. At various points in their testimonies, they labeled the erotic materials, "filth," "degradation of our humanity," "sickness," "a disease" and "garbage."

Young disclosed the unknown connection between pornography and Pearl Harbor while reminiscing about the early days of his career. Back in 1940, on his first night on duty in the L.A. office, he was assigned to a top-secret sex case that threatened national security. "Commander Itaru Tachibana of the Imperial Japanese Navy, with five of his staff members, used what we call stag-type films to lure American-born Japanese men in the fishing fleets to meetings . . . and thereby knew the soundings of our harbors, the comings and goings of our ships," he said. "I point this out to show the lure of the films."

Tojo's spies used films made in Spain, Italy, France, Hong Kong and Manila. "Practically all the films degraded religion of any type," Young continued. "Some depicted priests and nuns involved in intercourse in wheelbarrows in the fields."

Young finished up with a quote from Norman Vincent Peale. "Today we are so concerned with the cleanliness of our streams, rivers and lakes. What is wrong with a clean mind and a clean body?"

Hoover's Sunshine Boys were followed by the tape-recorded testimony of another old-timer—Aladena ("Jimmy the Weasel") Frattiano—a mob turncoat who has been

146

singing for years. The obliging ex-mobster—now a member of the Federal Witness Protection Program—pleased his handlers by confiding that, yes, the porn industry was rife with unsavory characters.

Ed Chapman, a commission staffer on leave from the Arlington, Virginia, police department, then played an interview that he conducted with an adult-bookstore owner in Chicago. The streetwise entrepreneur admitted that paying protection was a cost of doing business but defended the practice with wise-guy logic:

"You've got the FBI, the cops, to protect copyright on pocketbooks . . . right. Well, they have an enforcement arm to protect them, right, it's the same thing. . . . Somebody . . . asked me, 'Do you pay extortion?' What's extortion?

"I feel the federal government extorts me every time that I pay taxes and they piss the money away . . . overseas, right. Okay, I pay extortion to the mob, and they piss my money away, sending their kids to Harvard Law School and making him a member of the Justice Department."

The Godfather connection was tangential to the panel's real mission—which was to wipe out dirty pictures and movies "consistent with constitutional guarantees"—Mafia or no Mafia. ACLU attorney Jeremiah Gutman made the obvious point in his submission: "We recognize that it has been suggested that organized crime has moved in to capitalize upon the public's taste for what some call pornography. That may indeed be true, just as organized crime has apparently moved into the building trades, transportation, some unions, legal casino gambling and, as I recall from my youth, the sale of avocados in New York City.

"The solution to these problems is to enforce the law against the criminals, not eliminate the lawful activities. Constitutionally protected activities infected by organized crime require protection, not suppression. One does not kill the patient to cure the disease. One excises the infected areas or eliminates the invading organisms."

THE NEW LINDA LOVELACE

The morning session moved quickly into the excitement stage when Linda Marciano damned her former profession. Better known by her nom de porn—Linda Lovelace—the astonishing fellatrix of *Deep Throat,* now the 37-year-old mother of two, claimed once again that she was forced on threat of death to make that film. After telling her revisionary story in *Ordeal* (1980) and in *Linda Lovelace Out of Bondage,* published in 1986 (with an introduction by Gloria Steinem), she emerged as the most famous "victim" of pornography. In her colloquy Mrs. Marciano endorsed early sex education. "The biggest mistake my parents made was that they protected me too much," she said. "Growing up, I didn't know what a prostitute was."

She broke down for a moment when Dr. Dobson wondered why she didn't inform her parents while the ordeal was going on. Marciano said that she often asked herself why her father—a police officer—didn't rescue her just as the George C. Scott character saved his daughter in *Hard Core.*

Dr. Dietz, the panel's Krafft-Ebing, relished the occasion to question a friendly witness with possible insider knowledge about snuff films. Marciano did not express personal knowledge but asserted that the "wife of a friend of my husband [said she saw one]."

"And you believe that?" asked Dr. Dietz.

"Yes," said Linda.

MAU-MAUING MEN: DWORKIN AGAINST ERECTIONS

The enduring mystery of snuff films, the UFO of anti-porn votaries, came up the next day when the long-suffering

Andrea Dworkin took the stand.

The Rubenesque zealot testified that she too had never caught one but has heard about their current availability in the Las Vegas area for $2500-$3000 per print. Private screenings, she alleged, cost $250 a ticket. "We have information from prostitutes from all parts of the country that they are being forced to watch snuff films before then being forced to engage in heavily sadomasochistic acts."

In her view, all pornography is snuff. The 38-year-old absolutist is a La Rouchite of feminist politics. Once an abused and battered wife, she seems to have transformed personal struggles into public issues. Through her writings, speeches and anti-porn civil-rights ordinance, she has commanded national attention. Despite a snarling and insulting polemical style, she can also tug at the heartstrings. Dworkin undraped that side of herself in New York.

"In the country where I live as a citizen," she began, "there is a pornography of the humiliation of women, where every single way of humiliating a human being is taken to be a form of sexual pleasure for the viewer and the victim; where the women are covered in filth, including feces, including mud, including paint, including blood, including semen; where women are tortured for the sexual pleasure of those who watch and those who do the torture.

"Women are murdered for the sexual pleasure of murdering women. And this material exists because it's fun, because it's entertainment, because it's a form of pleasure. And there are those who say it is a form of freedom."

Dworkin raked the lawyers who defend porn entrepreneurs and called the ACLU a front for pimps.

She made Dr. Dietz's day when she unveiled the new paraphilia of "skull-fucking." "Apparently brought back from Vietnam . . . these are films in which a woman is killed and the orifices in her head are penetrated with a man's penis—her eyes, her mouth and so on," cried Dworkin. "This information comes from women who have seen the films and escaped."

Some panelists were knocked out by the zealot's rhetoric (Dr. Dietz's eyes teared at one point in her performance) and the majority would eventually vote to quote her at length in the final report.

But they stayed away from her most quotable remarks about sex between men and women, from *In Our Blood* (1976):

> I think men will have to give up their precious erections and begin to make love as women do together. I am saying that men will have to renounce their phallocentric personalities, and the privileges and powers given to them at birth as a consequence of their anatomy, that they will have to excise everything in them that they now value as distinctively "male." No reform, or matching of orgasms, will accomplish this.

> Rape remains our primary model for heterosexual relating.

> Men agree, by law, custom, and habit, that women are sluts and liars.

Her extreme views are reviled by many feminists. "Dworkin has gone so far she's come full circle, preaching the opposite of feminism," said Marcia Pally of the Feminist Anti-Censorship Taskforce. "She's not simply misguided, she's dangerous. By telling women their problems begin with porn, she distracts them from real solutions to sexism and rape. Instead of encouraging women to go out and get what they like sexually, she teaches women to be afraid of sex. In the end, Dworkin tells women that sex is sexist."

150

RELIGION TO SEX: GO TO HELL

Sex and religion do not go together well. Over the centuries Judaism and Christianity have been especially hard on sinners of the flesh. Although the Testaments are short on specifics, lesser holy writs covered the erogenous zone with moral microscopy. Theologians have gnashed their teeth over matters as exotic as the enjoyment of wet dreams and the presence of domestic animals in the marital chamber.

Strictly speaking, as religion tends to do, all sex outside marriage (and not a little within) is absolutely forbidden. This ban includes almost universal acts like masturbation, premarital intercourse and fantasies, as well as perennial practices like extramarital encounters and homosexuality. Monogamous Catholics and Orthodox Jews are not off the hook in bed unless ejaculation occurs inside the vagina while husband and wife imagine only each other. The Church permits nonorgasmic oral and anal explorations, but fundamentalists frown on gourmet tours. *Intended For Pleasure* (1977), a best-selling biblical love manual by Dr. Ed and Gaye Wheat, noted that the Eternal Anatomist would not have designed equipment specifically for intercourse if He wanted his children to climax otherwise. The Wheats object to cunnilingus and fellatio on practical grounds too. "Oral-genital sex definitely limits the amount of loving verbal communication that husband and wife can have as they make love," they wrote with straight faces. (Apparently the deaf and dumb are exempted from the latter observation.)

Since church and temple have always preached against temptations of the venereal type, the religious witnesses who crowded the New York hearings said nothing unexpected about pornography. In a single day, the commissioners heard an anti-masturbation bishop, a Mormon official claiming that "erotic stories and pictures are worse than filthy or polluted food," a lady missionary in praise of a

151

novice nun who lay in a casket for three days dressed in a bridal gown, a priest from Father Flanagan's Boys' Town who believes that a photo of a naked woman "destroys the will to live," a self-styled pro-sex but anti-porn Presbyterian pastor from Cincinnati who boasted of having a ball with his wife of 29 years, and a gentleman from the American Jewish Committee who submitted a statement noting that Jewish law considers nakedness itself "dehumanizing" and thus Jews may not even pray in the nude. Absent from this ecumenical liturgy was a representative from the Southern Baptist tradition, who might have mentioned an aversion to standing intercourse because it leads to dancing.

Most Reverend Edward Egan, auxiliary bishop of the Archdiocese of New York and the highest-ranking prelate to address the commission, soft-pedaled his denomination's credo of repression and omitted any reference to the divine. Realizing that modern Catholics turn a deaf ear to saintly sexology, the bishop cast his brief sermon in secular terms. "Purely as a human being," he told the commissioners, "I am convinced, as are most Americans, that sex is not a plaything" and "has its true meaning only as an expression of love between two persons who have committed their lives to each other." (With this loose language he inadvertently blessed homosexual marriage and marriage between divorced people, which are expressly anathematized by his church.)

If pornography were absolved of fostering rape and molestation, the bishop would still deplore its commerce. Afraid to repeat the Catholic knock on "impure thoughts," a mortal sin in every catechism, he cited the pollution of men's and women's minds. "The essential question is not simply what pornography does to a person's immediate behavior, but what it does to his or her thinking as well." Not a gifted critic of human sexuality, the celibate clergyman went no farther into the dynamics of arousal. But he felt sufficiently sure of himself to recommend more legal and citizen action.

In keeping with the worldly tone of his remarks, Bishop Egan closed with an embrace of the 1985 *Newsweek*/Gallup poll that seemed to support his hidden heavenly agenda. He observed that "three out of every four Americans believe that sexually explicit material degrades women and leads at least some people to sexual violence; and two out of every three believe that such material forces the breakdown of public morals. Clearly then, what I have expressed in this testimony represents the thinking of mainstream America."

The bishop had greviously misspoken. Actually, the *Newsweek*/Gallup poll should encourage sexual moralists of all faiths to seek vocational retraining. Despite the statistics on the degradation of women and moral decay, less than half of all Americans polled want stricter controls on sexually explicit materials.

Although the bishop discreetly stayed away from his church's prohibition of masturbation (no exceptions for testing sperm or artificial insemination, either), he handed over for the record a copy of the Pastoral Statement Against Pornography by the Catholic Bishops of New York State, who, seven centuries after Aquinas called masturbation a vice against nature, complain about "so-called health network commentators who repeatedly advise autoeroticism as a sexual panacea" on cable TV.

In fact, masturbation is the common and frequent experience of men and women today. To declare that it is unnatural is to repeat the condemnation of Galileo in another branch of science. Yet the bishops of New York dare; they just do not dare to speak very loudly. If moralists are wrong about masturbation, should their wisdom be trusted on pornography?

Ironically, the most popular and prolific pornographic novelist writing in English today is Catholic priest Andrew Greeley. His steamy fiction—seven books since 1981—fea-

153

tures a peculiarly violent approach to sex. It seems that
Father Greeley's lovers cannot lust without tearing off
clothes or drawing blood. Take Patrick Cardinal Donohue,
a hero of his first blockbuster, *The Cardinal Sins*, who
comes on to his old girlfriend the hard way:

> "There's something I have to do first," he said, con-
> scious of the smoothness of her shoulders and back, of
> the scent that drifted from her, of her breasts inviting
> his touch.
> At the doorway of the apartment now, she turned to
> him, uneasy at the tone of his voice.
> "What do you mean, Pat? Why do you look so fun-
> ny? Oh . . . please, don't."
> He muffled her startled scream with his mouth,
> pressed her body against his. He pulled her down on
> the sofa and ripped her dress, stripping her to the
> waist. He wanted to stop. Principle began to reassert
> itself. His fingers slipped away from her breasts. He
> breathed deeply. Oh, my God, she'll never forgive
> me. I must apologize and run. Never see her again.
> Find a monastery. He was no longer touching flesh,
> only black lace, much less dangerous.

Then there was the coke-snorting Father Hugh Donlon in
Ascent to Hell. When he was high, he got down:

> After Hugh's family and friends had gone, one of the
> younger traders offered Hugh a sniff of coke.
> He then left for the apartment and his rendezvous
> with Helen in a glorious daze. Her cry of pain shocked
> him out of his daze. He pulled away from her, his
> potency gone, his whole body quaking as though he
> had been seized by a sudden high fever.
> "I'm sorry, Helen, my God I'm sorry . . . the
> damn cocaine . . ." he moaned, horrified at the

rivulet of blood running down her breast. "I didn't mean to hurt you."

Helen put her arm around his waist and caressed him maternally. "You're a violent man, Hugh," she said sadly. "A woman who loves you knows she runs the risk . . ."

"Forgive me," he pleaded.

She laughed cheerfully. "Of course, I forgive you."

Even snuff scenes are not against Father Greeley's conscience. For example, the vicious sexual murder of the lovely Lisa Malone in his forthcoming Father Blackie Ryan mystery book, *Happy Are the Clean of Heart*:

I sat down on the sofa, beside which Lisa was lying, passive, beautiful, powerless. Slowly, gently, tenderly, I removed her terry-cloth robe, loving preparation by a pagan pirate for the ravishing of a frightened Christian matron.

Such a lovely body, slim, lithe, yet intensely erotic. Marvelous breasts, full yet neatly sculpted. Perhaps eventually the knife would be used. All in good time.

I lit a cigarette, puffed on it leisurely and then delicately pressed the glowing tip to the smooth skin on Lisa's belly, savoring the sweet smell of burning human flesh.

Lisa tried to scream. All that emerged from her lips was a soft whimper.

Her eyes dulled with pain and then looked at me with a mute plea for mercy, a plea that faded into resignation. Almost as though she had expected her death sentence and was resigned to it. A single tear appeared in each eye . . . .

Drink in one hand, I began to fondle Lisa with the

other, caressing and hurting at the same time. "Do I see a touch of fear in those lovely, if glazed, blue eyes of yours?" I kissed her lightly on the lips. "Well, there's nothing to be afraid about, Lisa dear, not for a while, anyway. Let me go through the agenda and tell you exactly what I'm going to do to you."

I twisted one of her beautiful breasts viciously. Lisa's attempt to shriek with pain was only a faint whimper.

"And let me tell you the ending first. After everything else is over, and after I've had all the fun I possibly can with you"—I held up the cosh—"I'm going to smash your brains out!"

How does Father Greeley get away with it? On literary grounds, he cannot escape punishment. But on moral grounds, the porno-priest takes refuge in the idea that God loves both passionate sinners and passionate books about marital intercourse, rape, seduction, adultery, prostitution, jealousy, incest and murder. The Bible told him so.

"Life might be a wedding feast," he explained in the afterword to *The Cardinal Sins*. "We've been given an invitation to a great party and we're crazy not to go." Unfortunately, the commission did not invite this mainstream porno-priest/novelist to share his views of sin and salvation. What is degrading to Bishop Egan is practically salvific to Father Greeley.

BEHIND THE SCENES: SEX-TAX REFORM

The New York work sessions belonged to the prosecutors. Hudson and Sears pushed the panel into endorsing an arsenal of anti-porn weapons. For example: using pandering statutes against producers of XXX-rated films, per the LAPD; creating a federal task force to battle obscenity; utilizing forfeiture procedures against stores selling the wrong

156

magazines (a representative of the Southland Corporation—the parent company of 7-Eleven—shook his head from side to side in the gallery). It was all too much for Ellen Levine; she tossed barbs the chairman's way whenever she found an opportunity.

On the question of cable television, Hudson wanted support for a Senate bill pushed by Senator Jesse Helms (R-North Carolina) that would restrict or prohibit the airing of "indecent" material. Levine wondered how many cable systems actually presented X-rated materials. The staff had no idea. Father Ritter seemed to feel the problem was widespread. But Levine wanted to hear facts and figures. "Let's find out," she said flatly. (Barry Lynn of the American Civil Liberties Union reported that only one cable system, in Bethlehem, Pennsylvania, slips in X-rated fare with a regular cable package.)

Sexual activity in adult bookstores also bugged a few panelists. Chairman Hudson took a hard line, suggesting those stores that permit live sex be shut down. "I think there is a health aspect to consider," he said. Levine surged, arguing that closing the stores would force anonymous sex fans into other places. "In New York that means public bathrooms . . . . If you close bookstores, this doesn't go away. So who are we protecting?"

Dr. Dobson had a problem with the nontaxed income derived from the bookstores. "Why can't they [the IRS] install equipment and see how much money is coming through the booths? They could hire a staff to monitor this . . . . They make millions in nontaxed profits."

Dr. Dobson, who takes in a bundle on his syndicated radio show and assorted Judeo-Christian capitalist ventures, knew from the IRS. In an overt display of special pleading, he wished evil on the profiteers of peep. "The IRS monitors me and profits quite well . . . . They monitored me for an entire year. Why not them?"

Father Ritter said that a tax on each peep-show machine

FILMS

Anal Annie Just Can't Say No

Bizarre Marriage Counselor

Bizarre Wrestling Women

Black Bun Busters

Black Lesbian Orgy

Butter Me Up

College Girls in Bondage

Couple on a Leash

Cram Course

Creme de Banana

Cumming of Age

Deliveries in the Rear

Der Lang Finger

Der Perverse Onkel

Dog Fuckers

The Extra Testicle

Everything But the Kitchen Sink

Finger Lickin' Good

Gwen's Tit Torment

Gym Coach Bondage

Hard to Swallow

Hill Street Blacks

Hong Kong Dong

Horror in the Wax Museum

Huge Bras

Kinkorama

Lesbian Foot Lovers

Lust at First Bite

Maid to be Spanked

Mondo Fetish

Never a Tender Moment

New Cummers

Night of Loving Dangerously

Nine Lives of a Wet Pussycat

Oriental Sexpress

Ozark Virgin

Passionate Pissing

Rambone the Destroyer

Rear Ended

Romancing the Bone

Rubber Party

Rump Humpers

Snake Fuckers

Space Virgins

Sperma

Sticky Fingers

Street Heat Orgy

(Excerpted from the Final Report of the Attorney General's Commission on Pornography—Government Printing Office, 1986)

158

was a good idea and urged "a special assessment tax like alcohol or tobacco." But Tex Lezar, suddenly roused from his constitutional slumber, was unhappy with the analogy. "Since this is *speech* . . . . It's like determining what newspaper to tax."

Dr. Dietz proposed that the tax revenues from erotic establishments be earmarked for pornography "victims' services." Dr. Dobson, who advises the president on tax matters, objected. "Giving humanitarian aid would hurt the deficit." His parsimony carried the day. Hudson pimped the victims' bodies at his hearings and then tossed them away.

9

GETTING DOWN
IN SCOTTSDALE

After six public hearings and several group meetings
scattered over eight months, the panel retreated to
Scottsdale, Arizona, for four days of uninterrupted
debate in late February. The main issue was harm: Did pornography cause it or not? Until now no government commission had been able to prove any connection. Without an
unambiguous declaration of harmful effects, the final report
would be merely another whitewash and a Bitburg-sized
disaster for Ed Meese. If the panel's token liberals were
going to mount a serious challenge, Scottsdale was the
place. Ellen Levine, the titular head of the left wing, knew
Arizona was not going to be a vacation. Only she—and

maybe Dr. Becker—stood in harm's way.

Levine often appeared exasperated by the proceedings. Smart, sophisticated and well upholstered in colorful ensembles and sweeping hairdos, she resisted the Revenge of the Herbs, in her fashion.

In her heart Levine knew that the process was insane and that some of her colleagues were certifiable on the subject, yet she continued to play along. As a vice president of CBS Magazines, which owns *Woman's Day,* and a member of the board of the New Jersey Bell Telephone Company, she enjoyed the inside game.

Some observers familiar with the commission felt that she was being used and that her polite demurrers had little effect. They were disappointed that she had not risen up and denounced the deviant sexual politics of all the attorney general's men.

Meanwhile, Barry Lynn of the ACLU was hard at work. In February, he released a 34-page syllabus of errors that demolished the bona fides of the enterprise in midstream. He ridiculed the commission's procedures as "so intellectually indefensible that they will taint the integrity and credibility of any recommendations." Lynn predicted that the Arizona sessions would be more of the same.

THE REVOLT OF THE WOMEN

The pivotal meeting of the commission began on Wednesday morning, February 27, in the windowless basement of Scottsdale's white adobe city hall. All the members were present except for Vice Chairman Tex Lezar, who was otherwise occupied at a trial in Texas.

The first item on the agenda was the so-called Koop report, a slippery inside move indicating both the right-wing tilt and the methodological madness of the panel. Way back at the first public hearing, Chairman Hudson beseeched

Dr. Judith Becker: *most uncomfortable commissioner; Catholic college grad; single; resented attempts to bend scientific data; Columbia University psychologist specializing in sex aggression; early 40s; scandalized by some staff maneuvers; wrote dissent with Levine for final report.*

Surgeon General Everett Koop, himself an ardent foe of pornography, for some help in reviewing the scientific literature. Although Dr. Koop promised cooperation, nothing ever happened. Instead, the commission relied on the limited offices of Dr. Edna Einsiedel, the staff social scientist, to do all the hard researching and analysis. Some of the professors who testified at the Houston hearings provided further data of the laboratory kind. Yet no consensus had emerged. The scientific case against porn, as previous commissions in England, Canada and the U.S. had discovered, did not stand up to scrutiny.

Phyllis Schlafly, the scourge of tennis-shoe Republicans, got wind of this discouraging development and wrote Ed Meese a letter of complaint. Schlafly pressed the attorney general to follow up the Dr. Koop option, with the expectation that he would turn up some smoking data and save the commission from the same mistake that the 1970 body made. Schlafly's wish came true. Eight months after Hudson struck his failed bargain with Koop, Meese decided to fork over an additional $50,000 to pay the bill for a "meta-analysis" of the scientific data. Another $50,000 would come from Dr. Koop's department.

Hudson warmed to the idea of accommodating a friendly administration witness, even if it delayed the final report, but he was not going to postpone Scottsdale's overdue plebiscite on harm. "There may be no substantial departure from our findings," Hudson said of the surgeon general's study. "If there is, I think we have a duty to reconcile it and incorporate it into our findings."

Dr. Park Dietz, who had no tolerance for violent porn, spoke against the fishing expedition. But the evangelical Dr. James Dobson, who boasts about not sleeping around, was insatiable. Expecting damaging evidence, he wanted everything Dr. Koop could lay his hands on. "The issue of causal relationships and psychological harm is the foundation of everything else that we're doing," said Dr. Dobson.

At this point, the *Cosmo* girl inside Ellen Levine quietly erupted. "I find this very difficult," she said. "Meta-analysis and statistical extrapolation that would go to the core of whether or not something was a harm seems to me something we should have had before we started to talk—not at the end. It doesn't affect just the social sciences, but anything we do. To say that we're waiting for this [Koop] report and we're going to look at it five minutes before we go to press doesn't work for me. We would want to be able to verify the response itself."

Hudson, a palooka when put on the spot, had no comment. Since Alan Sears was the lone contact with the Surgeon General, Levine suggested tabling the discussion until Sears himself showed his face later in the morning. (In the end, the fabled Koop connection fizzled into a two-day gathering of scientists in late June of 1986. According to the Surgeon General's maverick mandate, which ignored the specific requests of the commission, the experts were charged with discussing only one question—the effect of adult pornography on children. Since there was no data on

164

the subject, the experts made no recommendations except to call for more research.)

Now aroused for combat, Levine waited for the right moment to strike harder. But first she listed to Dr. Dietz's taxonomy of pornography. Before harm could be assessed, the genre needed to be classified into various types. Dr. Dietz had devised an unwieldly scale of 10 different species of porn that he whittled down to four. Nudity was assumed in all categories, but not genital display, which Dr. Dietz called "irrelevant." Keeping covered below the waist did not save materials from pornographic labeling.

Herewith Dr. Dietz's scale:

Class I—Sexual activity, actual or simulated, with violence, regardless of what else is present (i.e., slasher films, rape scenes)

Class II—Sexual activity, actual or simulated, degradation, humiliation or domination, but no violence, regardless of genital display (i.e., scatology, fisting)

Class III—Sexual activity, actual or simulated, without domination, humiliation or violence, regardless of genitals (i.e., Hollywood films, prime-time TV, men's magazines like *Penthouse* and *Playboy*)

Class IV—Pure nudity, without sexual activity, violence or degradation (i.e., works of art, Calvin Klein ads, men's magazines)

Dr. Dobson objected to this elaborate porn grid because it neglected any reference to perversion, "a component that is present in most pornography today."

Levine pounced on the commissioner who sees Satan's mouth on the other side of the glory hole. "It's not necessarily present in most pornography," she said. "It varies between five and fifteen percent, depending on how you define it."

Having settled on the procrustean classes, the panel moved next to judge their supposed harms. The aberrant method of analysis proposed by the chairman assured a hostile verdict. Unlike the 1970 presidential commission, which based its conclusion on the evidence of social science, the Meese 11 were not satisfied with mere facts. Realizing that facts alone would probably exonerate pornography, Hudson cleverly constructed a three-tiered approach to evaluating harm.

First, the panel would consider social-science data—what the professors and researchers had discovered about the effects of porn. The second tier involved the "totality of evidence"—the accumulated testimony of all the witnesses at the hearings and good common sense. And third, "moral and ethical considerations"—God's take on centerfolds. Whatever Hudson lost on the first tier he could swiftly regain on the second, because the witness list was stacked with conscious and dedicated antieroticists. The moral and ethical tier merely added a heavenly whack. It would be easier for Al Goldstein to pass through the eye of a needle than for porn to escape this triple-threat booby trap.

It was the task of Dr. Einsiedel to brief the panelists on the research. Her part-time position was not exalted. The hiring of five gun-toting cops to just a single university scholar revealed the chairman's gumshoe approach to the problem. Who was this shy Filipino-American, and why was she selected above all the social-scientist professors in the country for this crucial post?

Dr. Einsiedel had two special qualifications. Her Ph.D. is in communications, where the anti-porn action is today. The title of her thesis was "Reporter Source Orientation, Source Attraction, Topic Importance, and Reporter Information-Seeking Behavior."

Secondly, Dr. Einsiedel's mentor was the longtime anti-porn professor, the Marquis de Zillman. He was her doctoral adviser at Indiana University in the 1970s, and the two even coauthored an article on pornography and women.

Was her close association with the Marquis' school of thought a conflict of interest? Of course, but Sears probably would not have hired a more objective person in this sensitive slot.

Dr. Einsiedel's sympathy never seemed in doubt. Although she did not jigger the evidence, she hardly made the best case for the other side. Her benign neglect extended to opposition witnesses. Deborah Weinstein, executive director of the Society for the Scientific Study of Sex, wrote Dr. Einsiedel a letter with a blank-check offer to supply experts from its membership of 1000 sexologists. Weinstein waited in vain.

If the communications scholar could be said to have a handicap apart from her general unfamiliarity with sex research, it was her foreign residence. During the heyday of the investigation, Dr. Einsiedel lived in Canada because she got a job at the University of Calgary after joining the commission. As the year went on, she became little more than a paper-pusher and go-between for the panelists. She felt frozen out by Hudson and Sears and was eventually forbidden to talk to the press. At Scottsdale she should have dominated the discussion of the social-science data. She was the expert. But she was not a tough woman, and she just faded away in the heat.

This morning she explained the alleged harms of Class-I violent porn to the group. According to laboratory tests, young college fellows purposely overdosed on sex and slasher movies like *Swept Away* and *Hallowe'en* pressed shock buttons too long, expressed untoward sympathy for rapists in mock trials and tended to blame the victims. "So, on the basis of exposure to sexually violent materials in the laboratory," Einsiedel said, "the evidence shows that these harms have been demonstrated in these areas."

Hudson called for a vote on the social-science findings in Class I: Did violent pornography cause harm? This was a decisive moment. Once harm gained an official foothold, Hudson would never let go. The chairman went around the table. Diane Cusack, Scottsdale councilwoman, yes. Dr.

Dobson, yes. Dr. Dietz, yes. Judge Garcia, yes. But Levine said no. She was not impressed by the narrow scope of the experiments and felt that Hudson was pushing the commission beyond the claims of the scientists themselves. Her polite rejection of Hudson's harm-at-any-cost agenda started a chain reaction that risked sabotaging the main purpose of the commission.

Dr. Judith Becker, the psychologist from Columbia University, voted next. She was Levine's closest pal on the panel and seemed skeptical about turning the screw on popular forms of erotica. "I have some difficulty with the word 'harm,' " she said. "I'd call it harm if people then went out and raped or engaged in violent behavior against someone. What the laboratory experiments demonstrate is a negative impact of exposure to sexually violent material. That's all I'm willing to say."

Deanne Tilton, the faint-spoken California child-abuse expert who usually went along with the majority, joined Levine and Becker in protesting the verbal overkill.

Father Bruce Ritter, the fighting Franciscan, preferred the mortal sin of harm to the misdemeanor of negative effect. But Professor Fred Schauer endorsed negativity.

The revolt of the three women was fouling the works. If Hudson could not squeeze "harm" out of this class, the whole ball game might be lost. Given the shift of terminology suggested by Dr. Becker, the chairman decided to go around the table again. Astonishingly, the lesser evil won (5-4-1), because Dr. Dietz suddenly threw in with Schauer and the liberal triumvirate of females. The pro-harm bloc could have tied the vote if the inscrutable Judge Garcia, who had sworn himself to silence, had not flaked out when his turn came to choose, saying, "I don't care."

The commission immediately recessed for lunch. Levine stood up, glanced at the small gallery of observers and strutted out of the room, looking satisfied at last.

168

The afternoon session had to cheer the chairman. Freed from the straitjacket of social science, the panelists could vote their passions on the next two tiers.

Sears, reflecting the Justice Department line, acted as a cheerleader for harms. Stepping out of his auxiliary role, he implored the commissioners not to drag their feet in this critical area:

"I think there are probably only three of us at this table who have had real-world experience in the courtroom with the way . . . people use these reports . . . I think we all know the games that are played in legislative bodies and the games that were played with the 1970 report.

"I think if the commission believes there are twenty-eight harms from the violent stuff, you ought to say so.

"Well, if we want to emphasize the worst ones, that there are only three, there are only four, you will hear shouted from the rafters in trial after trial and legislative proceeding after legislative proceeding, 'This right-wing, extremist commission could only find three or four harms of violent material.'

"I just throw that out for your consideration."

However, the chairman listed just five types of specific harms for discussion: acceptance of rape myths, degradation of women, modeling or copycat effect, and wrongs to society and family.

The tallies were unanimous except on the "institution of the family."

Father Ritter argued that depictions of sexual violence were worse than child porn and poisoned the possibility of stable family life. Levine disagreed once more, puncturing the romantic idea of the golden age of families immune from violent stimuli. "Pornography is a symptom, not a cause," she said. The five-member Levine coalition forced a tie.

Unanimity returned in the evening deliberations when the panel got to play God (Old Testament version) in the third tier, that is, moral and ethical considerations. They all supported Dr. Dietz's proclamation: "Sexually violent materials are immoral and unethical, and the willing production, distribution and consumption of them are an offense against humanity." (ACLU lawyer Barry Lynn amused some of the spectators by cracking that the press should headline this news: FED PANEL SAYS R-RATED FILM FANS AKIN TO NAZI EXECUTIONERS.)

Amazingly, the panel voted that consumption of sexually violent materials is an offense against humanity, but they deadlocked on whether they actually hurt the institution of the family! This dissonance was a symptom of the commission's cognitive erotomania.

The relatively rare pornography of Class II was next.

"Among the things that some might consider being within this category would be those depictions that show ejaculation in the face of a woman, a camera focused on the labia, the use of excrement or urine," Dr. Dietz explained. He expanded the orbit to include a woman submitting to a man "acting like a dog."

Research on the material in this class was not extensive. The best the commission could do on the social-science tier was to vote the following: "Social-science research is limited in quantity and very few sources. Most that exist show negative effects of very few kinds."

As for the second tier, the panel agreed that the totality of evidence indicated several so-called harms apropos men, women, family and society.

Sears told of a bookstore tour on which he uncovered some Class II horrors—*The Master's Revenge,* the "Slave Horror" series, "the Nazi genre," "Soviet domination of women," and "racist materials"—one strain was particularly unflattering toward southern Europeans, Czechoslo-

170

THE SCOTTSDALE VOTES
ON THE HARMS OF PORNOGRAPHY

CLASS I: Sexually violent materials

Tier 1. Social Science Evidence
finding: negative effects demonstrated by testing (10-0)

Tier 2. Totality of Evidence
finding: harms in most sub-tiers
a. acceptance of rape myths (10-0)
b. degradation of status of women (10-0)
c. modeling of copycat effect (10-0)
d. institution of family (5-5)
e. societal harm (10-0)

Tier 3. Moral, Ethical and Cultural Evidence
finding: sexually violent materials are immoral and unethical and the willing production, distribution and consumption of them are an offense against humanity. (10-0)

CLASS II: Sexual activity without violence but with degradation, submission, domination or humiliation.

Tier 1. Social Science Evidence
finding: harm in all sub-tiers
a. acceptance of rape myths (10-0)
b. violence against women (10-0)
c. feminine degradation (10-0)
d. masculine degradation (7-3)
e. family (10-0)

f. modeling or copycat effect (10-0)
g. societal harm (10-0)

Tier 3. Moral, Ethical and Cultural Evidence
finding: sexually explicit degrading materials are un-ethical and immoral and on both grounds are an offense to human dignity. (10-0)

CLASS III: Sexual activity without violence, degradation, dominance, humiliation or submission.

Tier 1. Social Science Evidence
finding: predominantly no negative effects (10-0)

Tier 2. Totality of Evidence
finding: no harm in sub-tiers
a. does not foster rape myth (10-0)
b. no feminine degradation (6-3-1)
c. positive and negative effects on family (5-4-1)

CLASS IV: Non-provocative nudity

Tier 1. Social Science Evidence
finding: no harm (10-0)

Tier 2. Totality of Evidence
finding: no harm (10-0)

vakians and Poles.

Dr. Dietz wanted to include in this class the cover of the Rolling Stones album *Black and Blue,* which featured a bruised woman tied to a chair.

"Most people buying that record would not think it's pornography. I think they are wrong," said Dr. Dietz. "I think part of our job is to be educative about this." The rest of the panel let that sink in without comment.

Sears thought this was an appropriate time to speak up for a special group of people. "I am particularly concerned about prostitutes," he admitted. The bleeding heart argued that porno-magazine readers often ordered hookers to act out scenes of degradation. Sears zapped magazines sympathetic to the life. "I think it's a harm to advocate decriminalization of pandering."

Professor Schauer was dim on Sears' analysis. "I am very uncomfortable with characterizing as a harm [of pornography] an argument that the *law* ought to be different," he said.

The chairman had jotted down a few words to summarize his Jeffersonian theory on the point. "We will add there is an indefinable connection between pornography and prostitution and that to the extent that such a connection exists, pornography has a degrading effect on women in the prostitution industry," he said, reading his notes.

Ms. Tilton was befuddled: "I am not sure where we got the information that pornography contributes to prostitution."

"Do you want the witness list?" growled the chivalrous Sears. "How do you have pornography without someone engaging in an act of sex for consideration?"

Hudson closed the matter: "We'll put what I said into the narrative."

Dr. Dietz, a detail man, convinced the commission to endorse the notion that materials in this class also degraded "biological males, including homosexuals, heterosexuals

173

portrayed in infantile and scatological settings, and partial transsexuals.''

Consensus was achieved on the divine tier, too, but rather than call Class II ''an offense against humanity,'' they knocked down the charge to ''an offense to human dignity.''

Having done most of the Right Thing about violent and degrading pornography, the commission moved on to more accessible turn-ons Thursday morning. Dr. Dietz labeled this third universe of sex fantasia ''depictions of sexual activity without violence, dominance or humiliation.'' In other words, the broad mainstream of soft-core men's magazines, sex-education texts and videos, Hollywood movies, and, at the extreme end of the class, hard-core without any rough stuff.

''Is this erotica?'' Father Ritter wondered.

''No, that's Group Four,'' said the chairman.

Although conceding taxonomic fuzziness, the commission plunged into the social-science findings. Had the experts determined that mainstream entertainments like *Hot and Saucy Pizza Girls* and centerfold sensuality caused crime?

The evidence, as usual, was sketchy. Edna Einsiedel said that the experiments she reviewed didn't isolate Class III porn. One Canadian paper which used very tame erotica reported no negative effects.

''I thought that a large number of studies showed . . . positive effects,'' Dr. Dietz piped up. Chairman Hudson make the mistake of asking Dr. Becker for clarification. ''I don't believe that there has been demonstrated a negative impact of exposure to sexually explicit material for adults [viewing] this category of materials,'' she said in a steady, soft voice.

A few investigators reported that nondegrading porn ''has been helpful to some'' and ''often serves an educational purpose,'' she added. Dr. Becker mentioned having personally conducted a survey of sex offenders which exonerated this material.

Father Ritter grasped for some shred of evil. Didn't this class help in the "maintenance" of perversions? he inquired.

Sears joined the assault on Class III. Eschewing social science altogether, he went for the anecdote. The adult bookstores he personally cruised sold many pictures of anal intercourse and oral sex in which the man assumed the "dominant" posture. Was this material harmless? Sears did not seem to think so.

"It's a matter of preference," answered Dr. Becker, who was annoyed by his unsophisticated approach to sex. "There are some people who would argue that the missionary position puts a woman in a submissive position." Sears twitched in his seat.

Dr. Dietz asserted that this "whole issue hangs on what one wants to include as domination and submission."

Dr. Becker had something in writing. She read a letter from Professor Edward Donnerstein reporting four unpublished studies of his that found no negative effects from exposure to X-rated "nonviolent materials."

Dr. Dobson wanted to know if Category III interfered with the "relationship between a husband and wife" or affected the "tendency toward promiscuity of teenagers."

Out of nowhere Father Ritter decided to roast same-sex erotica. "So much of the available pornography is homosexual pornography," he whined.

"Is this commission obliged to say that . . . heterosexual activity is no more normative for the good of society than homosexual activity?" he asked.

Sears thought that the commission could squeeze in another deviation. Its charter, he reminded everyone, ordered an examination of pornography and antisocial *behavior*.

Chairman Hudson put the matter to a vote. Did the panel

175

have the mandate to determine "what certain types of sexual behavior [are] normal, abnormal"? Gay activists had warned that homophobia was on the Meese agenda. And here it was.

But Hudson, who constantly fretted over a looming deadline, did not want the panel sidetracked by faggotry. The forlorn friar rallied only the freethinking Professor Schauer to his side and lost an 8-2 vote. Incredibly, Dr. Dobson chose not to gay-bait.

The commissioner from Vatican City was a sore loser. He broke in every few moments to sermonize about the panel's duty to take up proper and improper sexual behavior.

When the vote on the social-science data was finally called, they found unanimously that the available research indicated "predominantly no negative effects" among users of Class III porn.

This was an important ballot. The beheading of violent and degrading erotica in the previous classes was not surprising. But this category, Father Ritter astutely noted, was the panel's "biggest challenge." Anti-porn zealots—counting on the Meese 11 to nuke *Playboy, Penthouse* and the like—could not have been pleased by this unanimous vote.

Next up was the freewheeling "totality of evidence" tier. First concern: "Did the material foster the pernicious myth that women enjoy rape?"

Speaking for the prosecution, Sears recalled testimony that this porn depicted "women as whores by nature."

The executive director also remembered that some witnesses claimed the material at hand propagated the notion that "women love to expose themselves, love to perform acts that some people believe to be degrading." Specifically, he noted "anal intercourse . . . even in a nonviolent, nondominant, non-humiliating setting."

Dr. Dietz cried foul. "I think that a case can be made for this class of material increasing tolerance toward rape myth, but that case is no stronger for this than it is for use of the word prostitution in newspaper columns, or television portrayals of women in subordinate positions and employment hierarchies.''

Dr. Dietz carried the day. The panel voted 10-0 to forget the rape myth. Sears was having a tough morning.

Hudson then asked whether the panel felt that Class III perpetuated "feminine degradation." Dr. Dobson hardly thought at all before exclaiming: "I think there is overwhelming evidence as to the harm . . . . We have heard about it for ten months."

But Professor Schauer was not so sure. Spinning his own wheels, he said that he agreed with Andrea Dworkin's definition of degradation and so placed most of mainstream erotica in Class II. To him, Class III included only consensual, non-degrading sex. He could not remember a witness who claimed this stuff dumped on women.

Dr. Dietz tried to clarify the situation:

"A very standard theme in movies of this class that are of the X-rated variety is, a man comes to a home; he is the electrician or the plumber or the newspaper salesman or whoever. He comes to the house. The housewife seduces him. He has sex with her, and there are many sexual scenes.

"That could be argued from either side as being degrading to women, because the woman is portrayed as sexually available to any man who comes knocking; or it could be argued that the only reason that one sees that as degrading is the stereotype—the acceptance of the stereotype that men should; or it's accepted for the men to pursue sexual intercourse with any attractive women, but it's not acceptable for women to do that; and I think that's where some of the witnesses we have heard have argued that this is not degrading to women."

Dr. Schauer countered.

"If we go a little bit closer to the center and imagine,

once again, . . . a motion picture showing with unquestioned explicitness a man and a woman engaged in what is unquestionably consensual sexual intercourse. It is the view of virtually all and maybe all of the people who have presented to us the concept of feminine degradation, that that material is not itself degrading and would not be likely to have a causal relationship to feminine degradation; is that a fair statement?"

The commission agreed—no female degradation—by a 6-3-1 vote. Father Ritter said, "I don't know."

The commission soon came to the sensitive question of "effects upon the family." Father Ritter argued that promiscuity-promoting books and pictures negated the "concepts of permanence, stability, love and affection" and threatened marriages.

Dr. Dietz lit another cigarette and explained the case for "mixed effects." On the upside, porn of this class showed new positions and techniques for family members in need of more fulfilling sex lives. For moms and dads with desire problems, X-rated books and videos could be aphrodisiacs.

On the downside, such material stimulated dangerous sexual appetites; some fellows may see a deep-throat scene and demand that same treatment at home.

Mrs. Cusack expressed sympathy for wives who feel "inadequate" next to the beautiful babes in their husbands' dirty magazines.

Hudson moved the question quickly. Commissioners could vote that the material was "predominantly harmful" or "predominantly not harmful" or that it had "mixed consequences" for the family.

Cusack, sitting on Hudson's left, led off and chose "mixed."

Dr. Dobson, worried about kids who get hooked on men's magazines and then switch to harder stuff, said, "Predominantly harmful."

Judge Garcia, once more off reservation, okayed "mixed effects." For him, it was a clear matter of vocabulary. He heard some good, he heard some bad, so it had to be mixed.

Likewise Dr. Dietz.

Ellen Levine complained that the material was poorly defined and opted out with a, "No answer."

Dr. Becker went with a firm "predominantly not harmful."

Ms. Tilton—sometimes taken for Linda Evans, according to her husband—furrowed her brow and seconded Levine's "No answer."

Father Ritter predictably annointed "predominantly harmful."

No surprise, Professor Schauer selected "mixed effects."

Chairman Hudson found Class III "predominantly harmful" to the family.

When the dust cleared, "mixed effects" had four votes; "predominantly harmful" got three; "predominantly not harmful" had one vote; and there were two abstentions.

What on earth? The Meese commission—conceived by prosecutors and ordained by legions of decency—had just voted that much pornography did not degrade women, did not promote rape and could actually help families. The panel retired for the day with the cloud of failure looming over Scottsdale.

THE AGONIZING AFTERNOON OF DIANE CUSACK

Diane Cusack, the Margaret Dumont of the panel, had a miserable afternoon. While her colleagues took siestas or swims, she agonized over her "mixed" vote. Although a conservative Catholic who obviously despised pornography, Cusack had joined the liberals in winking at coffee-

Diane Cusack: *conservative Catholic politician from Scottsdale, Arizona; Rosary College; certificate from Harvard Business School; married, three grown children; longtime community hyper-activist; as town planner, used zoning laws to harass adult theaters; lost council seat as panel met; foe of sex education; took "commonsense" approach to complex issues; consistently voted the vice squad's agenda.*

table erotica. Why had this mother of two turned her back on Jim Dobson, Father Bruce and Henry Hudson? She blew the family vote and she felt awful. When the commission reconvened for the evening session, she asked the chairman for the microphone.

"Henry," she said in a strong voice, "I want to reconsider [sic] my vote to 'predominantly harmful.' "

She had three reasons. First, she explained, the pornography in question did not "strengthen" the family. Second, she feared bestowing legitimacy on anything which could be legally obscene in some communities. And third, Cusack speculated about the effect of this material "upon one's spouse." She admitted that the last point was born out of "my own historical experience," but she provided no details.

Dr. Dobson asked whether this material would include depictions of "five women" engaging in sexual activities, including "cunnilingus" and "fellatio." Told that it did, Dobson blinked: "So this commission is going on record saying that legally obscene material is not harmful to the family?"

180

Chairman Hudson said no—that with Mrs. Cusack's switch, the panel had voted to find "predominantly harmful" effects.

Ellen Levine recoiled and made her move. "I want to change my abstaining vote to "mixed effects," she said forcefully. The panel was now deadlocked 4-4-1 with one abstention.

Father Ritter broke the silence with another sermon against casual sex: "Sex-educational materials can be helpful but [don't belong] in the same category as group sex. I can hardly imagine that this kind of depiction is healthy; it attacks the very institution of marriage."

After the priest was spent, Tilton decided to shift out of neutrality. Her sisters needed her. She requested that her abstention be changed to "mixed effects." "I just don't think we know enough . . . I don't want to take the chance of diluting our credibility," she said softly. Now the vote was 5-4-1 for "mixed effects."

This maneuvering, which exposed the raw politics of the panel, led to a fierce three-hour debate.

Father Ritter wanted "sex education" materials in this category segregated from rougher items.

Levine asked where the priest drew the line on what was educational and what was a sin. The editor pointed out that *The Joy of Sex* and hard-core films could be educational to married couples. The medievalist rubbed his chin.

Dr. Dietz tried to ride to the rescue. He rose from his chair with a Magic Marker in hand and strode to the front of the room. The boyish criminologist listed sexual activities contained in the category that seemed at odds in some minds with therapeutic and educational aims. On a large sheet of white paper, he wrote:

More than one man
More than one woman
Prostitution

Promiscuity
Adultery
Fornication
Oral-Genital
Anal-Oral
and maybe masturbation.

He sat down while the commissioners bit pencil tips and stared at his work. They were more confused than ever. As debate raged anew, Dr. Becker seemed a million miles away. She passed the time leafing through a marked copy of *Vogue*. At one point she came to a sizzling spread for Calvin Klein's Obsession perfume, featuring an erect female nipple. She brought the scratch-'n'-sniff strip next to her nose, inhaled and then offered a hit to Ms. Tilton, who breathed deeply and smiled. They neglected to offer Father Ritter a whiff.

At his end of the table, Dr. Dobson did not like the smell of things. Apparently he needed consolation from another world. During a break he huddled in prayer with Michael McManus, a sympathetic religious journalist, who put his arm around his besieged brother. They bowed their heads and closed their eyes long enough to call down a storm of locusts and frogs upon Levine, Becker and Tilton.

Back at the debate, it appeared that consensus was beyond reach. Still, Father Ritter urged a last-ditch united stand. "If this commission is split . . . in this category, we'll be laughed out of existence." But even the indefatigable chairman was worn down and floated the notion of a "hung jury" on the family issue.

A reflective Levine said that the panel's task was impossible. "If the commission had three years . . . to investigate this particular category broken out in 322 puzzle pieces of possibilities, you might be able to get your arms around it and separate out this material.

"We have not been given the time, we have not been

given the money; and the format of the way the information has been funneled into the committee does not give us tools to make a determination of this."

Hudson plowed forward. He proposed separating out materials used in therapeutic settings. Dr. Dietz did not think that that would solve the dilemma. "Is it a therapeutic use," he asked Hudson, "for a couple to jointly select a video tape to watch at home together Friday night which they think will enhance their evening's entertainment? Is it a therapeutic use for a man to select one that he thinks will teach his wife how to do a better job at oral-genital sex? Who is to say what is legitimate therapeutic use?"

Hudson blanched and Father Ritter seemed stunned. "You look perplexed, Father," the chairman said, throwing the priest the ball.

"I certainly am," said Father Ritter. But he was not giving up the struggle. "Let me in a very gingerly way propose the possibility of another basis for division that may fly."

The weary commissioners nodded their okay.

The Franciscan asked the federal panel to endorse the proposition that "a loving, committed, faithful relationship" between a man and woman is the relationship on which are based sound families, healthy children and a sound society. Other expressions of human sexuality "that do not totally support that relationship," he suggested cheerily, should be looked upon with less favor.

"Say that again," an incredulous Levine insisted.

Ritter did, and Levine, his New York neighbor, was outraged. "Aren't you saying, by leaving out other people, that they don't have value?"

"No," said the priest.

"That they have a lower value?" the editor followed up.

"A lesser value," corrected the friar, who always thought in holy hierarchies. "I was simply saying that if this commission affirms the value of the heterosexual, monogamous, faithful, loving commitment as the ideal, then we can safely say anything which does not support and maintain that ideal is of lesser value within a social context.''

"We are talking about images of these portrayals," Levine shot back. "We are not necessarily talking about duplication of this behavior.''

"Can you separate?" asked Father Ritter. "Pornography is the image.''

"You would have to assume, then, that everybody who saw it went out and did it," said Levine.

Father Ritter gently corrected: "We are simply saying that the behavior portrayed by pornography fits somewhere in a hierarchy of value. I think we have to say it. I don't think we can say by our silence that group sex and incest are in the same category as a loving monogamous relationship. We can't say that.''

Dr. Dietz dissented. "I think we are beyond our mandate when we say whether the encouragement of things like oral-genital sex is a good thing or bad thing. I *don't* think we are beyond our mandate to say that depictions of oral-genital sex probably encourage oral-genital sex. I think many readers will have no trouble determining whether for them that is a good or a bad thing.''

Such laissez-faire morality horrified Dr. Dobson. "So you would like to see a virtually value-free final report?" he sneered.

Dr. Dietz defended his position. "I think we have made value statements," he insisted, "but so far we have confined them to things that I think are universal human rights.''

Father Ritter reminded the panel that "we are not talking about oral-genital sex within *a marriage*." That, he noted, was outside the "province" of the commission.

Consensus began to slip away, and the night got longer and longer. Ellen Levine did nothing to lift spirits when she posed the impossible question for this jury of prudes:

"What if we had this wonderfully happily married couple. They rent a videotape that is not normal heterosexual—it has some sadomasochistic tinge to it—but that particular element contributes to their fantasy enjoyment. They are not going to go out and mimic the behavior. It is not going to break up their family . . . . Now, where does that leave us?"

She went on in this difficult mode: "Let's say adultery. They have a fantasy about adultery and in some ways it's better to go rent a videotape because it satiates them and they do not go out [and commit it]."

Avoiding Levine's practical concern because his church forbids such illicit fantasies, Father Ritter brought up real nasty examples. "May I ask about a videotape of group sex or a videotape of incest?"

"What about it? What about it?" asked Levine, all worked up now. "What if they rent it, look at it and it is an idea that does not harm the family . . . . We cannot assume that just because you see this, you therefore do it. That would be assuming that people don't make any distinctions and can't control themselves." Which is precisely the church's assumption.

Dr. Dobson said that if you made the material available to that couple, you release it into the "bloodstream of the society" and "you don't know where it's used."

Father Ritter sighed deeply. "Our problem is we are really approaching this material with fundamentally different value systems." One rooted in the ninth century and one modern.

Chairman Hudson threw up the white flag and proposed that 11 separate statements be prepared on Class III porn and the family. The exhausted group accepted the assignment.

Thus, after condemning the most egregious and extreme forms of pornography (S&M, chain-saw sex), the Meese commission failed to nuke corner-store erotica—where most of the action is. Hudson's fail-safe, three-tiered approach to porn fell apart in the crunch. The women's revolt stripped the smooth-running gears of the majority. Scottsdale spelled stalemate in the erogenous zone.

THE $100,000 GIFT

Scottsdale happens to be the national headquarters of the Citizens for Decency Through Law (CDL), the legal arm of the anti-porn far Right. Founded by Charles Keating, the embittered dissenter of the 1970 presidential panel, the CDL provides counsel and strategy for obscenity prosecutors nationwide.

The CDL's squeamish counsel, Bruce Taylor, slipped into the city hall basement one afternoon during the Scottsdale meeting and passed a 15-minute recess in whispers with commission attorney David Cayer. Taylor was somehow sanguine about the panel's progress: "Let's wait and see."

Taylor, a nice but finicky kind of guy, is still in the diaper stage of sexual analysis. "Dirty pictures are bad, everyone knows that to be true," he testified at the New York hearings. "Kids know you aren't supposed to look at pictures of naked women. Certainly teenagers know you're not supposed to have pictures of people doing it. Adults know you don't show it to kids. It's not the kind of thing that you would discuss with each other."

But those fellows who peek end up in a pool of sadomasochistic voyeurism. Here is Taylor's Vaselined description of porn's slippery slope.

"Once a man becomes desensitized to seeing pictures of naked women, he wants them to do something. If you see breasts, then you want to see the spread shot. If you have seen the spread shot, you ask, 'Have you got anything with people in it? I want to see her doing it with somebody and

186

then doing it with two or three guys, then maybe roughing it up a little bit.' " And soon after that, a Tommy Lasorda-look-alike tying up an entire reunion of naked Doublemint twins . . .

Zealous in pursuit of its goals, the CDL paid public tribute to a sitting commissioner last November, a week before the panel's hearing in Miami. The occasion was a $1000-a-plate ball to raise money to fight child pornography. Offering the benediction was commission chaplain—Father Bruce Ritter. CDL honored the priest with its first annual Charles Keating Award and a $100,000 check for his Covenant House activities.

Although Father Ritter accepted his "gift" in plain sight, nobody noticed this conflict of interest. But imagine the uproar if Morton Thiokol, Inc. had donated six figures to Challenger investigator Dr. Richard Feynman's Cal Tech department while the presidential panel was investigating the shuttle tragedy. Dr. Feynman would have been disgraced and thrown off the case.

Father Ritter's impropriety was especially hypocritical considering that some unfriendly witnesses before the commission were grilled on their financial ties.

When *Penthouse* pointed out this vivid conflict of interest last April, Father Ritter cried "smear" in a casuistic letter to the attorney general. Yes, his House got the CDL money. And yes, his House took $1.25 million from Ed Meese's department in the past three years. But all the funds went to his kids. So the priest denied "even the slightest appearance of 'conflict of interest.' "

Hometown commissioner Diane Cusack of Scottsdale also attended the gala event. Mrs. Cusack said in an interview that she did not pay for a ticket and was not a friend of Charles Keating. "I've met him only once." The matronly councilwoman must have made an impression. The head of the CDL and his business associates contributed $11,250 to the reelection of Mrs. Cusack and her two running mates in early 1986. (The slate of the incumbents was defeated in March.)

Asked whether it was a conflict of interest for a sitting pornography commissioner to accept money from a leading anti-pornography lobbyist, Mrs. Cusack said that such a conclusion was "totally unfounded."

"He [Keating] may have known the other two members of the slate," she squirmed. Did he? "I do not know," she said, adding, "It was really an insignificant amount compared to other money he gave [to other local candidates]." Keating and his aides invested $78,000 in council candidates in Chandler, Phoenix, Tempe and Scottsdale in the spring balloting.

Apparently such largesse can produce results. After Keating bankrolled the campaign of Maricopa County District Attorney Tom Collins a few years back, the prosecutor soon moved to indict video-store merchants in the Phoenix area for selling X-rated tapes. The only case that went to trial, however, failed to result in a conviction.

Mrs. Cusack refused to say whether she agreed with Keating's organization's views on pornography. "I can't answer that," she said. "I don't recall exactly what the [CDL] witness said." When she voted on the issues, however, her affinity with the earlier pornography commissioner was quite apparent.

NUDITY BEATS THE RAP

Back in the bunker in city hall, it was time for softball. If Class IV nudity were all the porn there was, then there would not be a Meese commission in the first place.

Class IV pornography, as outlined by Dr. Dietz on Friday morning, meant nudity without force, sexual activity, violence or degradation. Vulgar photos of genitals fell into Class II degradation, and in-and-out shots were covered in Class III explicitness. The comparatively innocent range of

188

this group encompassed Joan Collins in *Playboy,* Greta Garbo topless in *People,* The White Rock Girl and Manet's *Déjeuner sur l'Herbe.* Surely the panel would gallop through this material without embarrassing itself. But noooooooo.

Father Ritter, a prisoner of a Catholic sexual morality that divides the naked body into *partes honestas* and *partes inhonestas,* worried about close-ups of the genitals in Michelangelo's *David.* Dr. Dietz cited nudes of obese and deformed persons as a potential trouble spot.

Dr. Dobson said: "There's a tremendous difference between a nude woman with a bandolier with one foot on a chair shot from below compared to a Michelangelo nude. Can't we have a category for artistic nudes?"

"Who is to judge?" asked Levine.

"Who is to judge anything?" replied Dobson.

"That's the trouble here," Levine snickered.

On and on they went, but in the end, despite Father Ritter's giant leap into anthropology and cross-cultural nudity taboos, Class IV was officially exculpated on all three tiers by a landslide.

The accumulated dottiness of the Scottsdale summit, culminating in Friday afternoon's Buñuelian symposium on provocative-versus-unprovocative nudity, pushed Dr. Becker over the edge. Like Levine and Tilton, she had kept her distance from the bashers on the panel. Although she pondered resignation in the fall, the psychologist specializing in sex aggression and sex victims stuck around without stirring up a large fuss. But no longer. In apparent solidarity with Levine, she was ready to burn some bridges. Asking for the floor, she launched into a tirade against the intellectual treasons of the string-'em-up caucus of Hudson-Ritter-Dobson-Cusack.

"One of the mandates was to determine the relationship between pornography and antisocial behavior and the commission of sexual crimes. I'd like to comment that I don't

189

think there is in the social-science data any conclusive causal relationship between this type of material and the commission of sexual crimes. I think the data show that in certain experiments attitudes change, and I think one makes a quantum leap from attitudinal changes to committing sexual crimes.

"My request is that when we write our essay, we state why we have come to the conclusion that we have. My opinions are based on ten years of experience in work with sex offenders and a knowledge of the literature on violence and antisocial behavior. But I think that some people have come to their opinions because of divine revelation, because of common sense, because they know in their heart of hearts that pornography is wrong, because you've heard compelling evidence from criminal-justice people and from victims.

"I don't believe in what I call the Simple Simon theory of antisocial personality. That is, people will see something and go do it. I think human behavior is much more complicated than that."

How did Hudson greet this grapefruit in the kisser? In over his head when ideas are in dispute, the chairman said, "It is your belief that . . . we have inadequately addressed the connection between certain forms of pornography and their behavioral effects?"

"I do," replied Dr. Becker. "I don't think the evidence is in yet, because some of the studies have not been done or can't be done to show that pornography causes people to commit sexual crimes . . . . What we're saying is going to determine public policy. People should know why these individuals have come to the conclusions they have."

After lunch, Hudson tried to blunt Dr. Becker's nut-crunching attack by calling on Dr. Dietz, whose credentials in psychiatry and publications equal or surpass Dr. Becker's.

Anticipating the question, Dr. Dietz was ready with a

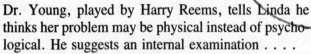

<u>DEEP THROAT</u>

Dr. Young, played by Harry Reems, tells Linda he thinks her problem may be physical instead of psychological. He suggests an internal examination . . . .

He then spreads her labia . . .

"Miss Lovelace, you don't have one," Reems exclaims.

"You clutz, I'm a woman, I'm not supposed to have one."

"I didn't mean one of those. You don't have a clitoris," he says. He tells her to look for herself. She does.

"No wonder you hear no bells, you have no tingler."

Linda starts to cry and says, "That's not funny."

He asks her, "When you have sexual intercourse, what excites you the most?"

"Giving head," she replies.

"What do you feel?" he asks.

"I get excited."

"Where?" he asks.

"You'll laugh," she says.

He says he won't.

She points to her throat and says, "Here." He laughs. He then examines her mouth and discovers her clitoris in her throat. She cries some more.

He says, "Having your clitoris in your throat is better than having no clitoris at all."

(Excerpted from the Final Report of the Attorney General's Commission on Pornography—Government Printing Office, 1986)

chart indicating an indirect connection between the beaver and the bludgeon. After all, he explained, social science cannot even prove a causal link between "proper guidance at home and healthy children." Dr. Dietz was convinced that pornography is somewhere in the overall picture of sex crimes. "A factor that counts for some nontrivial share is called one of the causes," he put it.

At this remark, Levine jumped in, subverting his argument by inquiring, "So is alcohol more or less a contributing factor to sex crimes [than pornography]?"

Apparently squelched, Dr. Dietz responded honestly, "My estimate is that it's more."

The panel's schedule shattered under the weight of the agenda. By the end of its workweek, the commission still had to discuss organized crime, finally define pornography, and attend to other key matters. An additional four days of work sessions were scheduled for the end of April in Washington. But, incredibly, Hudson and Sears were still insisting that they could meet the June 20 deadline for the final report. They explained that they had no choice—the allocation was almost spent and the staff would soon be history.

Levine was astounded. She saw no way the panel could wrap so quickly. Along with Professor Schauer, she pleaded with Hudson to get more money from Meese. Henry promised to do what he could.

But the chairman was not going to make waves. An admiring president had just nominated him to be the next U.S. attorney from the eastern district of Virginia.

10

COMMISSION CORRESPON- DENCE

S everal of America's most accomplished writers expressed serious reservations about the censorious impulses of the Attorney General's Commission on Pornography. At a briefing in New York convened by the National Coalition Against Censorship in January of 1986, Kurt Vonnegut noted ironically that: "It is not enough that sex crimes of every sort are already against the law and are punished with admirable severity. It is up to our leaders, and particularly to our attorney general, to persuade a large part of our citizenry that even the most awful sex crimes are

193

perfectly legal, and even celebrated in some godless quarters, because of the permissiveness of our Constitution. Only then will an aroused and thoroughly misinformed citizenry rise up in righteous wrath to smash the First Amendment—and many other only slightly less offensive parts of the Bill of Rights."

Some of Vonnegut's literary colleagues wrote Henry Hudson directly to express their concerns.

February 16, 1986

Chairman
Attorney General's Commission on Pornography
Washington, D.C.

Dear Sir:

Since around 1960, when Vladimir Nabokov's *Lolita,* Henry Miller's *Tropic of Cancer,* and D.H. Lawrence's *Lady Chatterly's Lover* were published in this country and made available in bookstores, American writers have been free to attempt sexual realism—to describe sexual events and transactions between people in as much detail as seems appropriate, in the language that people actually use. Please do not take this freedom from us, or from artists of any kind, or from those therapists and scientists who wish to address in printed form the subject of sexuality.

Any legislation or ruling which abridges this freedom of expression is regressive, and will not succeed in stamping out pornography, which will flourish underground, but in making the publishers, writers, and editors of this country timid and self-censoring in an area where the dominant standard for twenty-five years has been honesty and vividness and understanding in portraying this important side of human activity.

I think that the relative sexual openness of recent times,

194

including the public sale of magazines and books which many consider reprehensible, has made my fellow-Americans more tolerant and genial, less condemnatory and ignorant than they were before, in these long-shrouded areas of human intimacy. It would be great step backwards to rescind this openness, and to strengthen the dark forces of censorship. Already these forces, in the shape of school librarians, local vigilantes, and groups informally pressuring bookstores and newsstands, are too powerful. They would make our society less adult and less free. As a person and as a professional writer, I deplore any abridgment of our First Amendment rights as presently interpreted.

Yours sincerely,
John Updike, author

February 25, 1986

Chairman,
Attorney General's Commission on Pornography

Dear Sir:
It is a frightening time to be a novelist, and to be an American citizen devoted to the freedom to write—and the freedom to read—throughout the world. As an active member of the Executive Board of P.E.N., I'm very aware of writers who've been imprisoned for what they write, and writers who are tortured for what they write; and I am very aware of the censorship that is standard in the Soviet Union, and in other countries not committed to democracy. I am also aware of an increase in censorship within my own country; but this is not a letter where I will indulge in any political name-calling—I will not suggest, either, that the enthusiasm for censorship among my fellow Americans is solely to be blamed on an increasingly right-wing agenda,

influenced by an increasingly self-righteous Moral Majority (so-called). I have seen a rise in censorship of a left-wing inspiration, too—to ban Mark Twain and Faulkner, for example for alleged "racism"; to ban Bernard Malamud for alleged "anti-Semitism." I find this form of censorship as wrong-headed and as anti-American as the censorship of Kurt Vonnegut or John Updike—or John Irving—because we are "obscene."

I'm translated into more than fifteen languages; I'm both critically acclaimed, as they say, and critically trounced in all those languages, too. And that's as it should be. It's hard to delineate my so-called *themes*; I've often said that a novel is a search for a victim, or victims—that a novelist's moral and social responsibility is to show who the victims of stories are. In my books, they tend to be women and children; it's difficult to show victims without being explicit. It takes an appalling lack of education to miss hearing the sympathy in the voice that describes those victims—but, of course, critics do this "missing" all the time. And some of them get it right, too. The point is: readers can hear the sympathy or fail to hear it for themselves—in this country, anyway. There's rape in my novels; children are hurt, even killed. My last novel was about an obstetrician at an orphanage hospital in Maine, in the first half of this century—when abortion was illegal. The hero of the book is an abortionist. You can imagine how many people there are who'd like to censor the sympathy taken toward such a "hero." But not in America; they can't censor me here.

Not yet.

Here's what Charlotte Bronte wrote in her Introduction to *Jane Eyre* in 1847: "Conventionality is not morality. Self-righteousness is not religion. To attack the first is not to assail the last." She said this because the English critics of her day suggested censoring *her*.

Recently I read that Attorney General Meese was critical of the present Supreme Court. Among the things that the

196

Attorney General sought were ways to protect our constitution, and our laws, from what he called an ideological predilection. I am one hundred percent in favor of protecting us from that, too. And if you legislate against pornography in the United States, *who* is going to tell us what pornography *is*? Someone free of the taint of any ideological predilection, I suppose?

This is the United States, not the Soviet Union; and this is not the United States of Cotton Mather, either. I don't trust a single one of my fellow Americans to tell me what pornography is.

Should the Commission wish to speak with me, in person, on this matter, I would be happy to make myself available.

Respectfully,
John Irving

November 7, 1985

Dear _____ :

A half-dozen times a year since 1976 and the publication of *Saving the Queen* I receive reproachful letters bearing on the sexual promiscuity of Blackford Oakes. I have answered these; but after a year or two it occurred to me that always the same basic questions were being posed, and correspondingly answered. I decided for that reason to write out my answers to the generic questions raised. I cannot claim for them that they will persuade my critics, only that they are sincerely set down in an effort to clarify. And I add, with regret, that I cannot undertake to say more than is here set down.

Why do you introduce sex in your novels?

Because sex is in our time treated as a public and publicized feature of modern life. A generation or two back it was otherwise. Not so any more. A novel that shrinks from treating concerns almost universally treated in modern fiction tends to lose credibility.

But even if that is so, why do you sometimes deal erotically with sex?

Most sexual encounters are (and indeed should be by their nature) erotic. A writer's challenge is to attempt to communicate feelings that inhere in sexual attraction and sexual behavior. It is as much the writer's responsibility to communicate the feel of lust in sexual union as the feel of fright in combat.

Aren't you actually engaged in trying to please the publisher and make money?

If you don't please the publisher, you don't get published. I have written twenty-three books, only seven of them novels. In the other fourteen, sex does not figure. The two books I have written which have sold most copies are non-fiction. Anyone who buys a Blackford Oakes novel when primarily in search of sex will feel sorely cheated.

But aren't you on record as opposing pornography?

Yes, and I reiterate my opposition to pornography. But I distinguish between pornography and eroticism. The latter is natural, the former unnatural. Sexual attraction is described with a candid knowledge of the factor of lubricity. Sexual union as described pornographically is a corruption of eroticism. There are great erotic poets, no great pornographic poets.

Don't you acknowledge that illicit sex is just that— illicit?

I do. And so label it in situations where it becomes relevant to recite my credenda. I do not do so in books in which it would be intrusive to do so. That rule applies to my treatment of other sins, including gluttony, pride, sacrilege, sloth, anger, and despair.

How do you reconcile Blackford Oakes' explicit commitment to Christianity and his sexual behavior?

Blackford Oakes behaves before his marriage much as

most members of his class and generation behave before their marriage. How such behavior is finally incorporated in the Christian life is as puzzling to moralists now as it has been through recorded history including biblical history, where illicit sexual activity is probably the most commonplace sin. Oakes is a paragon in many respects: looks, education, intelligence, patriotism. His sins are of the flesh, no less sinful for that reason, but no more surprising than the dismaying fact that we are all sinners. And I am trying to write about real people.

Yours faithfully,
Wm. F. Buckley Jr.

February 26, 1986

Chairman
Attorney General's Commission on Pornography

Dear Sir:
On the matter of restricting language in books, on grounds that it serves the cause of anti-pornography, may I please differ? What such legislation would do is restrict a writer's ability to reflect the truth of his time; for language is one of the major instruments that defines time.

Mark Twain's nineteenth century novel, "Huckleberry Finn", is an indisputable masterpiece of that century and this, yet the book is under fire for its recurring use of the word "nigger". Had Twain used more polite language in the telling of Huck's and Jim's odyssey, the novel today would very probably belong to the Nice Nelly literature of that age: which is to say, it would be in the discard pile as false history. The word "nigger," as it was and is used in the English vulgate, has no equal in being expressive, terrible, and historically significant, and Twain, in using it, was railing against its significance as the supreme epithet of

199

slavery.

Closer to our own day, Ernest Hemingway, in the 1920s and 1930s, because of the laws and mores of that period, was unable to use the language of his choice in his novels. Through the use of dashes, or circumvention, he occasionally suggested such words, but that suggestion was a compromise with fidelity to the truth of his time and himself. We know from Hemingway's letters, recently published, what a vulgar and bawdy man he was, his obscenities capable of surprising even the most sophisticated modern reader. But that never entered into his published fiction. It fell to the writers of World War Two—Norman Mailer, James Jones and others—to truly convey the way it was, in speech, for men at war. Hemingway is a great and innovative stylist, a wonderful storyteller, but his language is the vulgate whitewashed, and therefore only half true. One cannot say this of the greatest of writers, Shakespeare, whose unbridled poetry enshrines both the glory and the grossness of the Elizabethan world.

American writers should be free to emulate the bard in whatever large or small way their talents allow. They should have no legalistic fetters that confine the imagination as it seeks to define the raw and radiant truths of the age. If lawmakers feel so strongly about the language, let them use it themselves; let them write their own books and compete in the marketplace for the attention of the public mind. In resorting to censorship they not only imprison writers, they imprison readers as well, denying them the right to know. Censorship is pernicious, it is un-American, and it is stupid.

Sincerely,
William Kennedy

Stacking witness lists and controlling the agenda were not enough for Meese's minor-league Torquemadas. Hudson and Sears also wrote letters on Department of Justice stationery to chill suspected purveyors.

Back at the Los Angeles hearings, the book-burning Reverend Donald Wildmon, executive director of the National Federation for Decency, had his shot at porn. Unlike other religious witnesses, Reverend Wildmon did not quote Scripture, give a sermon or wail against filth and degeneracy. Instead, the calculating Reverend went after mainstream erotica's choke points—the retailers.

"The general public usually associates pornography with sleazy porno bookstores and theaters," Wildmon testified. "However, many of the major players in the game of pornography are well-known household names. Few people realize that 7-Eleven convenience stores are the leading retailers of porn magazines in America. Indeed, 7-Eleven is perhaps the most important key to successful marketing of pornography in the family marketplace. In my opinion, should 7-Eleven discontinue the sale of porn magazines, both *Playboy* and *Penthouse* would be seriously crippled financially. The profits made by 7-Eleven on pornography run into the millions of dollars. Irwin Billman, then executive vice president of *Penthouse* magazine, testified that Southland Corporation, that is, 7-Eleven, was the single most important outlet for the sales of *Penthouse* magazine.

"7-Eleven convenience stores boasted to *Dallas Times Herald* columnist John Bloom in 1980 that they sell 20 percent of all *Playboy* magazines sold in America; and according to *Everybody's Business—An Almanac,* published by Harper & Row, 7-Eleven sells more *Playboy* magazines through its stores than any other retailer in America.

"Pornographic magazines rely heavily for their circulation on single-issue or over-the-counter sales in addition to subscriptions. Therefore their display at newsstands and in stores is vital to their existence. In fact, the subscription market of *Penthouse* magazine amounts to only 5 percent of total sales. Only 202,877 subscribed to *Penthouse* magazine during the last half of 1984, but 3,568,517 were purchased monthly over the counter.

"In addition to 7-Eleven, there are other well-known retailers who market pornography. They include the Rite-Aid Corporation, Dart Drug Corporation, People's Drugs, Lil' Champ Food Stores, Sunshine Jr. Stores, Revco Drugs, Dairy Mart Convenience Stores that recently bought Lawson Convenience Stores, National Convenience Stores, Circle K Corporation, Thrifty Corporation and K-Mart Corporation through their subsidiary Walden Books."

Reverend Wildmon methodically listed other leading American conglomerates with alleged porn connections: CBS owned an interest in a company that distributed the Playboy Channel; Time Inc. had a cable outlet which aired "Hollywood Hot Tubs"; Ramada Inns were showing adult films to guests; and RCA and Coca-Cola were in the porn business in Australia.

Commissioners had no questions for the witness, and Hudson thanked him: "We appreciate the statistics you have compiled and presented to us."

Reverend Wildmon's testimony was just the latest salvo in the fanatic's decade-long harassment of the entertainment industry. His newsletter blasts the networks for T&A sitcoms, and a recent number even went after NBC's hit "Golden Girls," calling it a "geriatric-sex series."

Reverend Wildmon's charges surfaced in a staff-prepared section for the commission's final report on "retailers, soft-core pornography."

When Ellen Levine saw it at a business meeting in New York, she balked. "I would open up discussion on whether or not we should, in the final document, be naming these

202

kinds of names and targeting these kinds of people."

Professor Schauer suggested sending a letter to the companies fingered by Reverend Wildmon. "I am very reluctant to name the names of specific individuals or specific corporations in our final report unless they have been given an opportunity to respond," he said.

Hudson thought that was a great idea. "I think the record we have heard this far is ample to support the naming of corporations that sell these types of products . . . . I want to make sure their information is accurate."

Sears began to draft a letter immediately. He told commissioners that he "would note that a lack of reply would indicate they did not differ."

Professor Schauer did not like that approach. "I hope we did not presume to find something true by lack of response."

Sears would not budge. "Lack of response might mean they didn't have a problem about it; it may be they want to ignore the commission," he reasoned.

Dr. Becker thought Sears should include "who the person was who gave the testimony."

Sears said that might be difficult—he claimed that more than one individual made some of the allegations. "We will try to attempt at least to identify one person that made the statement," he sighed.

Dr. Dobson told Sears not to knock himself out. "It's already in the record if they want to get it out," he grumbled.

After some more haggling over wording, Hudson agreed to write a letter for Sears to send to the named companies.

Dated February 11, 1986, this message from the attorney general's men went forth:

"Authorized Representative:
"The Attorney General's Commission on Pornography

has held six hearings across the United States during the past seven months on issues relating to pornography. During the hearing in Los Angeles, in October 1985, the Commission received testimony alleging that your company is involved in the sale or distribution of pornography. The Commission has determined that it would be appropriate to allow the company to respond to the allegations prior to drafting its final report section on identified distributors.

"You will find a copy of the relevant testimony enclosed herewith. Please review the allegations and advise the Commission on or before March 3, 1986, if you disagree with the statements enclosed. Failure to respond will necessarily be accepted as an indication of no objection.

"Thank you for your assistance."

The letter was signed by Sears. He attached Reverend Wildmon's testimony—but not his name.

Most of the accused simply denied Wildmon's charges. But the Southland Corporation, the parent company of the 7-Eleven chain, apparently took the threat seriously. On April 10, Jere W. Thompson, Southland's president, announced that *Penthouse, Playboy* and *Forum* would be permanently pulled after the May issues.

Thompson said that the Meese commission was responsible: "After reviewing the testimony and evidence presented [to the commission], we have made the decision to remove the magazines from our 4500 company-operated stores." Southland also mentioned that customer surveys reflected a possible connection between adult magazines and crime, violence and child abuse. The move was a reversal of the company's hang-tough policy against the fundamentalists. Apparently the Justice Department pressure was just too much.

Down at NFD headquarters in Tupelo, Mississippi, Reverend Wildmon's gang went crazy with joy. Up north, *Penthouse* and *Playboy* went to court.

Penthouse publisher Bob Guccione, flanked by attorneys

Alan Dershowitz and Arnold Forster, called a press conference at the magazine's headquarters in New York to decry "intellectual terrorism."

"Every court which has considered the issue has decided that *Penthouse, Playboy* and *Forum* magazines are not obscene and are protected by the First Amendment," Guccione told the press.

"Yet, the Justice Department—the prosecuting arm of the United States government—has threatened to include stores which sell these magazines on an attorney general's list as 'identified distributors' of pornography."

The publisher said the whole affair smacked of blacklisting and McCarthyism. *Penthouse* filed suit in New York. *Playboy* and the American Booksellers Association sued in Washington.

They wanted to stop publication of any government list of identified pornography distributors. Further, they asked that a second letter be sent to the corporations stating that the commission did not consider their publications obscene or unlawful.

The commission was criticized on editorial pages across the country for its star-chamber procedure. At their final conclave in D.C., several shell-shocked commissioners including Levine and Professor Schauer led a successful effort to delete any reference to specific companies in the final report.

Hudson and Sears hardly fought—their letter had already borne fruit. Ultimately, the Meese commission failed to specifically condemn as pornographic or obscene any mainstream men's magazines. *Penthouse* and *Playboy* were not included in a list of more than 4500 pornographic materials included in the final report. A clear majority of the commissioners polled by the authors at the final meeting in Washington felt that men's sophisticates could not be linked to sex crimes.

Executive Director   *Washington, D.C. 20530*

FEB 11 1986

Authorized Representative:

　　　　The Attorney General's Commission on Pornography has
held six hearings across the Unites States during the past seven
months on issues related to pornography. During the hearing in
Los Angeles, in October 1985, the Commission received testimony
alleging that your company is involved in the sale or
distribution of pornography. The Commission has determined that
it would be appropriate to allow your company an opportunity to
respond to the allegations prior to drafting its final report
section on identified distributors.

　　　　You will find a copy of the relevant testimony enclosed
herewith. Please review the allegations and advise the
Commission on or before March 3, 1986, if you disagree with the
statements enclosed. Failure to respond will necessarily be
accepted as an indication of no objection.

　　　　Please call Ms. Genny McSweeney, Attorney, at (202)
724-7837 if you have any questions.

　　　　Thank you for your assistance.

                              Truly yours,

                              Ian E. Sears
                              Executive Director

enc: Self-Addressed
      Postage Paid Mailing Label

Even some of the most censorious panelists noted that these magazines did not particularly trouble them. For instance, Dr. Dobson went on radio to clear the air: "You see, at issue here is not the publication of *Hustler* magazine," he said on KNX in Hollywood. "Most of the popular men's magazines include subject matter that is protected by the First Amendment and would continue to do so."

Even chairman Hudson said that *Penthouse* and *Playboy* "do not violate the community standards" in his pristine jurisdiction, according to the unpublished transcript of his interview with Philip Shenon of the *New York Times*.

And Dr. Dietz said it was not at all immoral for someone to gape at centerfolds.

They felt the real issue was hard-core. But fundamentalists like Reverend Wildmon would use the commission's final report as ammunition against any sexually explicit material in the culture.

INCOMING MAIL: THE SCHAUER LETTER

Several commissioners were distressed by the draft of their findings as drawn up by executive director Alan Sears and his staff of young Republicans. After distributing it to panelists in Scottsdale, Sears tried to keep the poorly written and researched document behind closed doors. The American Civil Liberties Union sued in federal court in March. "I know that many members of this commission would like to cover up pornography, but that is no reason for the commission to operate behind a brown-paper wrapper," cracked Barry Lynn. The Justice Department relented without a fight. Lynn ridiculed the now-public 1200-page text for its "factual errors, preposterous legal theories, undocumented allegations and unwarranted hysterics about the effects of sexually explicit material on viewers and readers."

In this dispiriting atmosphere, Commissioner Fred Schauer made his move. The University of Michigan law professor had a different agenda from that of the constables who had run the operation from the beginning. The blue knights were only hoping for additional weapons with which to sanitize American sexual fantasies, but Professor Schauer wanted a statement he could sleep with *and* respect afterward. He had graduated from Dartmouth College (1967) and Harvard Law School (1972), studied at Cambridge University and written three books on constitutional law. A man who takes himself and his work very seriously, Professor Schauer had a huge professional stake in the commission's final product.

Hudson and Sears risked ruining his good name in law-school common rooms. The staff draft was just impossible: a monument of little minds. Something had to be done fast, so the professor took the disastrous work-in-progress into his own hands. He wrote a frank eight-page letter of complaint to his fellow commissioners on March 7, a few days after Scottsdale.

He was especially irritated by the chapter on pornography victims, a 200-page martyrology with lurid but unsubstantiated accounts of sexual abuse, beatings and mental trauma, all laid at the altar of porn:

"Much of this material is powerful, credible and important. Some of it is less credible, and some of it is of little use to us. If we are indicating that we believe or endorse all of this, I can not conceive of going along. If we are merely reporting what was told to us, I wonder how we can justify reprinting 199 pages of victim testimony while not reprinting a single page of testimony about the dangers of overregulation or the alleged benefits of some of this material. If this section is included as is, we will have confirmed all the worst fears about the information on which we relied, and all of the worst fears about our biases."

As for legal and constitutional considerations, the scholarly Schauer said: "I still find this portion so one-sided and oversimplified that I can not imagine signing anything that looks remotely like this.''

The professor was also angry about the comments on organized crime, because Sears relied on the testimony of an FBI agent of dubious character. This G-man, Professor Schauer discovered, had been busted for shoplifting. The trial judge remarked that the defendant ''has a great propensity to lie.''

Schauer likewise deplored the staff's proclivity for accentuating the bizarre. He hated the chapter on ''Types and Forms of Pornography'': ''I have a hunch that one publication was included because it was astoundingly gross, bizarre and disgusting. But that does not make it legally obscene, and it does not make us any less of a laughing stock for including it. This whole section, in my view, needs a lot of rebuilding from the ground up.''

What was to be done? The professor promised to pleasure himself with his own document: ''Obviously it is for each of us to decide what we will or can sign, but as I review all of the above I am extremely pessimistic about the possibility that the existing drafts can be converted into a version that I could accept within the time constraints that we have. I may be wrong about this, but I have reluctantly concluded that I must commence drafting a document that will satisfy me, and my notions of minimally acceptable quality. I am convinced that all eleven of us have engaged in an extremely fair, thorough and open-minded inquiry. Obviously, we have differences in point of view, experiences, areas of expertise, and the like, but I remain extremely pleased with the course of our hearings and deliberations. As a result, I feel it is crucially important to produce a document that will reflect this open-mindedness and thoroughness. This draft just is not it, and does not look to me as if it is close to becoming it. I am proud of what we have done, and I do not want the result to be a document of which we would be ashamed.

''In thinking about how to proceed now that I have

decided that I must at least have the contingency plan of a complete report that I have written, I am faced with two alternatives. One is to produce a document that reflects how Fred Schauer now feels about all of this, and what Fred Schauer thinks should be done with pornography. The other is to produce a document that Fred Schauer thinks reflects the collective judgment, where it exists, of all of us. This will obviously require some subjugation of issues where I am in the minority. But I want at least to try to produce something that others, and perhaps even all others, might find a persuasive exposition of views congenial to them, and accurately reflective of areas of agreement and disagreement. Maybe I am whistling in the wind, and no one will be interested in putting their name to what I have written. In that case, I will rewrite it for myself, putting my own views back in a more prominent place even when I am in the minority. But I have decided to try to produce something that all of us might be more comfortable with, and I have today started on a process that I am confident will take almost all of my time for the next six weeks, but which I think will result in a complete report before we meet in Washington. I will of course send out pieces of what I am doing to each of you as I proceed.

"This decision to strike out on what may be my own has not been an easy one. I came to Scottsdale a bit uneasy about what we had so far, and I left Scottsdale happy about what we had accomplished there, but even more uneasy about how much was left to do. I have agonized almost continually since I returned home . . . . Please be assured that this is no search for individual glory. I can think of nothing that would make me happier than if a majority of the Commission would be comfortable enough with what I write, subject of course to the give and take of compromise that we have so successfully engaged in so far, that this would no longer be my report but ours. In that case if there is any glory attached to the report it will go not to me but to

> The general public usually associates pornography with sleazy porno bookstores and theaters. However, many of the major players in the game of pornography are well-known household names. Few people realize that 7-Eleven convenience stores are the leading retailers of porn magazines in America.
>
> Indeed, 7-Eleven is perhaps the most important key to successful marketing of pornography in the family marketplace.

Henry, and he is the one who deserves it.

"In closing this most difficult of letters to write (and I know the task before me may be even more difficult), let me remind you of Alan's memorable words in Houston: 'My reputation is on the line.' In terms of the final report, it is *my* reputation that is now on the line. I am willing to compromise on difficult questions for policy, and I am willing to compromise on matters of wording, style, and the form of the report and our recommendations. But I will not compromise my commitment to quality. I hope you won't either, and I urge all of you to bear in mind that your reputations are on the line too."

11

THE FINAL CONCLAVE

After ten months on the rack, the sex tribunal was nearing self-destruction when it convened for the final four-day conclave on April 29. Although the last draft of its report was due at the Government Printing Office in less than three weeks, the commission had still not resolved the central dilemma of its enterprise: What kinds of pornography, if any, are really harmful? With typical methodological madness, the panelists had already endorsed tough new laws to harass the adult-entertainment industry. They had even urged the formation of citizen sex-spy networks to monitor newsstands and other purveyors of allegedly obscene materials.

213

But they had failed to condemn the mainstream of erotica. This had Dr. Dobson hopping mad. In a long letter to his fellow panelists, the evangelist wailed about the "river of smut" cascading across America: "Does it not insult every self-respecting female in the world to see a woman sip semen from a champagne glass after men have filled it with ejaculate? Is it degrading to women to depict prostitution as a noble and respectable profession? Is it degrading to women to show their genitalia shaved and spread to the eye of the camera? Is it degrading to women to publish magazines entitled *Oriental Snatch, Blond Fuckers, Cum Hungry Girls, Chocolate Pussy, Super Bitch, Cum Sucking Vipers, Hot Fucking She Male* and *Pussy Pumping Ass Fuckers?*

"Is it degrading to women to cast them in the role of insatiable nymphomaniacs who throw off their clothes and spread their legs at the slightest provocation? Not degrading to women? Have we gone completely mad?! Such pornographic depictions are an affront to an entire gender, and I would take that case to any jury in the land. Remember that *men* are the purchasers of pornography. Many witnesses testified that women are typically repulsed by visual depictions of this type herein described. Category III is provided primarily for the lustful pleasure of men and boys, who use it as a masturbatory aid. And it is my belief that, though evidence is not easily obtained, that violence against women is a by-product of all obscene material, including that represented in this third classification. Pornography is the theory; rape is the practice.

"In conclusion, I plead with my fellow commissioners to reexamine the issues discussed at Scottsdale. We still have time to bring our decisions in harmony with the evidence, with the time-honored values of society and with the collective heart of the American people.

"Columnist George Will wrote in *Statecraft as Soulcraft*, 'Even more injurious than the flood of obscenity that has been let loose have been the arguments for letting it loose.'

Those disturbing arguments have again been placed before us, and history will judge what we do with them.''

Pressured by several commissioners, including Dr. Dobson, Chairman Henry Hudson had reluctantly requested more time in which to do a decent job. But the attorney general was in a rush. According to Washington speculation, Ed Meese wanted his anti-porn report out in time for the fall elections. He approved only a 15-day extension.

Professor Schauer's extra-credit effort was revealed in the *New York Times* in mid-April, catching Sears and Hudson by surprise. The smartest-kid-in-the-class flew to the capital to confront Meese's vice squad.

"We were just talking about you, Fred,'' said Ellen Levine when Professor Schauer entered the eighth-floor conference room a few minutes after nine on that fateful morning in April.

Smiling nervously, as is his custom, the bearded scholar with black, curly hair reached into a canvas bag. ''Let me distribute these,'' he said, taking out photocopies of his homework.

The commission recessed to ponder the Schauer report. Reporters, cable-TV lobbyists, ACLU lawyers, anticensorship feminists and a young blonde from Phyllis Schlafly's Eagle Forum perused it as well.

THE SCHAUER REPORT

Entombed in turgid and Talmudic prose, the professor's opus shared most of the assumptions of the staff draft. He lamented under-enforcement, wanted more money for police to fight porn with and backed tougher penalties for obscenity-law violators.

Unlike Hudson and Sears, he did not seek new and constitutionally questionable laws against obscene or indecent materials; he felt there were adequate measures on the books already. Despite the staff's obsession with kiddie porn, he dismissed this small pocket of erotica as merely a "cottage industry" (but he condemned the possession as well as the production and distribution of the genre). Finally, the professor called the task of defining pornography "essentially futile" and downplayed the relevance of the term.

Where he did use the word "pornographic" in his report, Professor Schauer said it meant only that the material "is predominantly sexually explicit and intended primarily for the purpose of sexual arousal." On the key issue of "harms," Professor Schauer condemned a wide range of materials. Citing a handful of controversial studies, the professor was persuaded that sexually violent materials caused sex crimes. So, too, depictions which "degraded" its subjects—usually women. These categories would include materials in the mainstream of American entertainment— i.e., R-rated slasher films, men's magazines.

But the professor's mountainous accusation brought forth a mouse. He merely recommended stepped-up prosecution of *already* legally obscene materials in the violent-and-degrading category. As for the less arousing mainstream, Schauer said the panel was split as to harms—so prosecution should be determined by community standards. The Law was advised to go after Class I and Class II before Class III. Thus the Schauer report was a Magna Carta for censors.

When the commission reconvened, Commissioner Dobson expressed problems with Schauer's failure to go all the way in beefing up the constabulary. "All of our work is up for grabs now," said the angriest commissioner, pounding the table. "What happened to the critique of lax government action?" Chairman Hudson tried to calm Dobson down. The two reports could be integrated. But Dobson, still seething, could not see how. "It's like putting oil and water together. They don't mix."

The spanker in Dr. Dobson wanted the report to leave

welts, moaning that Professor Schauer lacked "punch." "We need to react dramatically to the offense of pornography," he said. "This is all technicalities."

"Punch is not my game," replied the professor, who preferred the slow water torture of his convoluted condemnation. "If it is the wish of the commission to write something more dramatic . . . get another boy."

After debating the final format, the panel voted to use the Schauer report as a framework and to include, where possible, sections of the staff document. Then they started on the tedious but important last-minute debate over details.

Where were Ellen Levine and Dr. Judith Becker, the most skeptical panelists in the midst of the Golden Schauer Report? They blocked their colleagues from going to town on harms in Scottsdale and practically brought the inquisition to a standstill. Yet they disappointed many liberal observers by keeping their peace when the commission hastily reviewed the professor's "Harms" chapter in Washington.

Levine was exhausted from months of trench warfare. "I'm tired of being in the minority," she said during a break in the deliberations. Obviously her heart was not with the majority. She showed a few onlookers a letter from a happily married young mother of two who reads *Woman's Day* and occasionally turns on to hard-core videocassettes with her husband. The correspondent wanted Levine to understand that her private delights were not degrading.

Even so, Levine surrendered. She was not going to make a stink at this last supper. "I believe it's much better to work behind the scenes," she said.

"But you just voted to approve Schauer's version of harms," a bearded reporter pointed out. "How are you going to fix that behind the scenes?"

"I don't know," she said. "Fred's going to China in three days."

Dr. Becker was weary as well. She accused some of her

colleagues of voting their personal and religious prejudices in Scottsdale and loudly protested the "Simple Simon" view that porn causes crime. However, Professor Schauer's more complicated version of the same theory did not equally get her goat in Washington. "They don't listen to me, I can't persuade them," she complained. "It's not my style to stomp my feet."

Instead, Dr. Becker decided to join Levine in a strong personal statement for the final report that would outline their differences with the majority.

Some of Professor Schauer's proposals inspired close votes. Dr. Dobson protested the recommendation that cops give priority to collaring violent and degrading filth. The professor was soft on Class III, but Dr. Dobson demanded a crackdown on all three types simultaneously.

The latter did not want to send a signal to police and prosecutors that explicit oral sex—even if mutual and loving—was no big deal. Hudson agreed: "This could be read as justification for ignoring Class III materials."

"Obscene is obscene is obscene," insisted Dr. Dobson.

Judge Garcia did not understand the fuss. He said that D.A.'s almost always brought obscenity cases on the basis of "what we can win."

Professor Schauer was thinking more broadly. "Shouldn't factors other than 'what we can win' be involved in society's general determination of what it wants to get rid of and what it doesn't?" he asked.

Finally the commission voted 6-5 that cops go after Class I and II first. Dr. Dobson and Hudson sighed.

Next they turned to specific media of erotica. First up—literature, a subject barely touched all year long. Professor Schauer pleaded in his report to exonerate the Printed Word. Ellen Levine, roused by her pals in publishing, supported him.

Sears dug in. He had come back alive from a five-city

tour of adult bookstores with bags full of hard-core titles featuring bestiality, bondage and brutal "backdoor" sex. Dr. Dobson deplored exonerating books like *After-School Rapist*.

When the vote was called, only five commissioners (Dobson, Garcia, Cusack, Lezar and Hudson) favored screwing books. Librarians across the country could now tell local pests to buzz off.

As industry lobbyists looked on, the panel debated a staff recommendation that "indecent" material be banned from cable-TV transmission. The proposal would have covered many R-rated films with sexually explicit themes. The measure, identical to a bill introduced in the Senate by Jesse Helms, went down in a 6-5 vote as the cops fumed.

The swing vote on both important ballots was cast by the commission's official exorcist, who was suddenly possessed by reality. Since the freedom of dirty words was locked into the constitution, Father Ritter proudly washed his hands of prosecuting books that degrade love, sex, marriage and family.

Magnanimous in victory, this theocrat in Franciscan tunic tossed the civil libertarians a bone. "Fear of censorship was a constant theme of many witnesses who appeared before this commission," he explained in his personal statement published in the final report. "I do not think we are entitled to judge that concern lightly, or to consider that those who express such anxiety are motivated by self-interest. First Amendment values are crucial to American life and the virtual sanctity and integrity of the printed word central to the absolute freedom of political debate and dissent."

His cable cave-in would have brought a smile to the cheeks of Cardinal Wolsey, the accommodating cleric who smoothed things over for Henry VIII. Apart from his temporary fit of constitutionality over concupiscence, Father Ritter rendered homage to the religious interest in keeping cable filthy: "There is still another compelling reason why many thoughtful people in this country would actively oppose any attempt to apply the same standards of broadcasting television to cable," he explained. "Indeed, almost all of the principal religious denominations and religious broadcasters unanimously fought such an equation of broadcast and cable television on the grounds that it might seriously impede their own religious freedom to control their programming as they saw fit and might compel them to grant equal time to atheist or agnostic or anti-religious presentations."

When the censors come for religious cable, Pastor Ritter wanted somebody left to help stop them.

THE STAFF REPORT
THAT WOULD NOT DIE

All infighting dissipated, however, when the commission turned to the staff's pet projects. With relatively little rancor, it voted to drown the mellower parts of the professor's report under a law-and-order tidal wave. The panel endorsed:

—Using pandering statutes against the makers of adult fare—that is, charging film producers with procuring another person for the purpose of prostitution;

—Treating any second conviction of selling pornography as a felony, with a mandatory one-year prison term;

—Adopting forfeiture laws to seize the assets of any business engaged in the sale of proscribed materials (this would permit the seizing of an entire convenience store if it sold the wrong magazine);

—The appointment of a "high-level" Justice Department task force on obscenity cases;

—The establishment of a data base on the pornography industry for use by law-enforcement personnel;

—Considering the employment of models under the age

of 21 in sexually explicit poses as *child* pornography;

—Using state racketeering laws and federal racketeering statutes to obtain seizure of sexual materials;

—Increased federal, state and local prosecution of obscenity statutes;

—Making it an unfair labor practice to have actors and actresses under 21 engage in sexual activity;

—An FCC crackdown against "obscene" dial-a-porn services.

The panel also wanted the community to enlist in the frontline Battle Against Smut. Going beyond Professor Schauer's restrained approach, it explained how citizens could form "effective community-action groups" to keep tabs on pornography in their towns.

Under the flimsy guise of "educating" the public, the commission approved a how-to-protest manual which mentioned boycotts of porn retailers and the support of corporations which use their powers "responsibly" (i.e., don't do business with peddlers of offensive materials).

The queer matter of vibrators haunted the commission until the very end. For months Sears had asked his colleagues to label sex aids obscene. Most of these, he said, were marketed by two companies controlled by organized crime. He was referring to the nipple clamps, dildos, bondage masks and cock-rings sold in the back rooms of peep shows. A Georgia law branding such items as obscene per se had survived State Supreme Court review. But some commissioners counseled caution on rubber goods.

Dr. Dietz was concerned that condoms might fall in this category. "And it might include the surgical implants available for erections in men who are impotent, and as-yet-uncreated medical devices," he stated in New York. "On the point of obscenity, while I certainly agree that there are dildos and artificial vaginas that may be obscene in their own right, it seems to me that the ordinary vibrator is no more obscene than the Washington Monument."

Ellen Levine spoke in defense of the vibrator whenever she could. She made a last-ditch plea to Sears in Washington: "I can't think of any harms . . . . You can go to the best drugstores on Madison Avenue and find quality vibrators made by reputable companies."

Sears refused to withdraw. He told Levine that the Food and Drug Administration was investigating two cases of injury to individuals using these products.

But even Hudson allowed American women good vibrations: "I'm willing to take out 'vibrator' if that would give you some comfort, Miss Levine." This indelicate phrasing caused Levine to break up. The chairman did not crack a smile.

Some years hence, the Meese commission may be called the Dworkin commission after Andrea Dworkin, the long-suffering soul of Women Against Pornography. By a quirk of sexual politics, the Moral Majority of the Meese panel enshrined the man-hating feminism of Dworkin in their report. Not only did Professor Schauer hijack her absolutism on porn's degradation of women, which puts *I Spit on Your Grave* on the same moral plane as some Maidenform bra ads, but the commission backed the concept of her civil-rights ordinance, which would allow women to sue anybody in the pornography industry for violating their erotic space. Although the Supreme Court ruled that the ordinance passed in Indianapolis was unconstitutional, the Meese court liked the idea anyway.

It seemed that Dworkin's emotional testimony at the New York hearings impressed several members of the panel.

Dr. Dobson even wanted the government to quote the woman at length in the final report. Sears telephoned Dworkin at the last minute about using parts of her testimony to introduce the "Victims" chapter. She consented.

Although Dr. Dietz edited the martyrology down to 68 pages, it now had an extra kick. The mother superior of the pornoplegics would preface their arranged and orchestrated confessions.

THE AFTERMATH

The Administration's hit on the 1970 commission was complete. The cops got almost everything they desired. Andrea Dworkin was hugged by Ronald Reagan; and the legions of decency were warmed by an industrial-strength dose of morality in government.

Henry Hudson tipped his fedora and settled into his new, higher-paying job. Professor Schauer went to China. Dr. Dobson called his commission service "one of the most unpleasant things I've ever done in my life." This First-Class Christian complained about the 12-hour days, the 30-minute lunch breaks and a "very meager meal served because of budgetary constraints." He also whined about the lack of compensation. "I haven't even received a refund for my expenses for some of the trips. At one point they were $1500 behind on paying me and not in a terrible hurry. Let me tell you about it, it was all give."

And Ellen Levine and Dr. Becker shuttled home to New York.

Once there, the women retreated to Dr. Becker's office to hammer out a 20-page dissent blasting the operation from top to bottom.

As they worked, Barry Lynn of the ACLU told the *New York Times* "for this commission, intuition has taken the place of science."

Times science correspondent Daniel Goleman, a Ph.D. in psychology, was smart enough to call up the social scientists whose research was quoted in the final report. Two of them were astounded by the perversion of their scholarship. "These conclusions sound bizarre," said Dr. Donnerstein. "I dispute their conclusions because they are not in accord with my understanding of the scientific data," said Professor Murray Straus, the head of the University of New Hampshire's Family Research Lab.

All the press to the left of *Human Events* was bad. For example, the editors of the *New York Times* told the commission to put their pistols down: "Opinion about sexually arousing material is hopelessly divided. There's no faulting the commission for failing to resolve age-old doubts and deeply personal conflicts. But the report, widely circulated without formal publication, must be faulted for relying on questionable evidence and recklessly encouraging censorship . . . .

"There is a pornographic problem in the United States. Offensively explicit sex and violence are dispensed with too little regard for the rights and sensibilities of those who want themselves or their children shielded from such material. But the consumers of it also have rights. The Meese commission's connection of pornography and crime outruns its own evidence and its cure of censorship is worse than the disease."

The *Washington Post*'s William Raspberry praised the dissenting Levine and Becker for their "intellectual integrity and guts." He admired their refusal to be "buffaloed into unsupported conclusions." Another *Post* columnist, Richard Cohen, ridiculed the commission's discovery of a causal link between porn and violence as "more a wish than a scientific finding."

"Certainly if violence is our concern, there ought to be a presidential commission to study Sylvester Stallone," he argued. Dr. Dietz would certainly agree.

Mike Royko, the blue-collar columnist for the *Chicago Tribune,* hit the panel over the head with a brick.

"When I was a young crime reporter, I hung around police stations and watched the dregs drift by.

"They included every sort of sexual adventurer: rapists, peepers, flashers, child molesters, zoo invaders and guys who wore pink negligees.

"Some were harmless, others were deadly. But one thing that I never saw was a dirty book sticking out of any of their pockets.

"Nor did any of them confess to having dashed from a porno movie to satisfy their lusts . . . .

"But for the sake of argument, let's concede that pornography does inspire a certain amount of violence.

"If that's the case, we should be consistent in outlawing things that cause violence.

"Consider that in recent years, there have been more than 220 bombings of abortion clinics . . . .

"And what motivates the bombers? Those who have been arrested have expressed deep religious convictions. They say their beliefs justified setting off bombs.

"Then there have been the extremist groups that shoot rural sheriffs, talk-show hosts and lawyers they suspect of being liberal. They, too, spout religious devotion.

"So maybe we should begin considering the outlawing of religion because it is the root cause of so much violence.

"But you, as a religious person, answer that religion isn't the cause; that people who set off bombs or shoot talk-show hosts have a few screws loose and will always find a reason to be violent.

"I agree. Just as I agree with those who say that the guy who crawls through a window and rapes and murders a woman or child didn't get turned on by some six-dollar paperback he bought in Times Square.

"Maybe he did it because his brain cells aren't arranged right, or he was dropped on his head as a kid, or he is simply evil. And there have been people like that long before the first book was printed."

Even George Will, a Chestertonian between the sheets, zinged Reverend Jerry Falwell during a colloquy about the commission on ABC's *This Week with David Brinkley*. "Mr. Falwell, in response to David's question about what pornography is, you took a complicated term—pornogra-

225

phy—and substituted another difficult one; that is, you said it is the literature of the depiction of deviance," he said.

"Now, this is a country in which seventy-five million people rented adult tapes last year to show in their own living rooms. Pornography is a multibillion-dollar industry. Given this, the fact that Americans are voting with their dollars—in a way that conservatives say a market is a form of democratic voting—why isn't it fair to say that pornography now is accepted as part of the recreation of this nation as demonstrated by market spending?"

Shaken by Will's intelligent perspective, the Reverend fumbled.

Following up, Will noted, "The president's son is a contributing editor of *Playboy*. William Buckley writes for *Playboy* and *Penthouse*. Are you quite sure you're representing community values and if so, what community?"

The usually glib Reverend had no comeback.

Alan Sears put the finishing touches on the final document and hit the road to stump for the report. The executive director jetted to Maine at the invitation of the Christian Civic League, which was pushing a proposal to make it a crime to sell or promote obscene material. He stopped just short of officially endorsing the measure, citing restriction on government employees, but he gave it his blessing anyway. "I looked it over and it appears to me . . . to parallel one of the recommendations of the commission."

Maine voters defeated the measure in a referendum by a 3-to-1 margin (48,976-16,101). Barry Lynn of the ACLU crowed: "Citizens don't like government to tell them what they cannot see and read." The Meese commission report had failed to rouse the citizenry in its first exhibition contest.

The commission had yet a final misadventure in store. The staff added a little something to the chapter on the "Production and Distribution of Pornography." Sears inserted a list of 2345 separate magazine titles, 725 books

226

MAGAZINES

Asian Suck Mistress
Asshole Buddies
Big Busted Ball Buster
Big Tit Dildo Bondage
Big Titted Lezzies
Black Beaver Fever
Black Bush Fuckers
Black Jumbo Jugs
Bondage Latex Catalog
Butt Fuckin' with Soul
Celebrity Fuckers
Chocolate Pussy
Climax Corner
Cock Stuffed Sluts
Cum Coated Lips
Cum Soaked Threeway
Dracula Fucks
Eat Out My Hole
Enema Thrills
Europe on 5 Fucks a
    Day
Fat Fucks
Fuck This Job and Suck
    It
Girls Who Love Uncut
    Dicks
Head Waiter
Here's the Beef
I Love to Fuck Cowboys
If It Moves Fuck It
Leather Pussies

Menage-A-Twat
Milky Mamas
Mulatto Splits and Tits
Naughty Daughter in
    Heat
New Cummers
Oriental Orgasms
Peach Fuzz Pussies
Poolside Pricks
Pregnant Dildo Bondage
Quadrafuck
Ream-O-Rama
Romancing the Bone
Rumpbusters
Savage Sucker
Shave Me and Fuck Me
Swallow Party
Teeny Tits
Ten Inch Tools
This Butt's for You
Tit Fuckers
Wham Bam Window
    Washers
Young and Shaved

(Excerpted from the Final
Report of the Attorney
General's Commission
on Pornography—Gov-
ernment Printing Office,
1986)

and 2370 film titles found by commission investigators in 16 pornographic bookstores in six cities.

He also tossed in 31 pages detailing the book *Tying Up Rebecca* and scene-by-scene descriptions plus dialogue from the triple bill of *The Devil in Miss Jones, Debbie Does Dallas* and *Biker Slave Girls.*

Barry Lynn of the ACLU termed the addenda a "national bibliography of pornography complete with graphic descriptions of every conceivable—and some inconceivable—sexual practices."

This was a first in United States history—government-produced smut. Only in America could a conservative administration pay to publish:

"Let your big sister show you how it's done. Suck that pussy. Bury your tongue way in it. Yeah all of it in and out. Do it, Brad, suck that pussy, suck that cunt. Come on, make me cum right in your face. Do it, Brad."

The Meese commission was cartoon fodder for a week. "Although I personally find much of the material in this volume highly offensive," Lynn quipped, "I would nevertheless defend absolutely the federal government's right to print it."

As a final humiliation, U.S. District Judge John Garrett Penn, in response to *Playboy*'s lawsuit, ordered the commission to retract Alan Sears's threatening letter to bookstores and drug and convenience store chains. As if to escape his unsavory association with the panel, Sears quit Justice for the Interior Department.

The F Troopers of the Erogenous Zone limped offstage with arrows in their derrieres.

12

THE
MISSING LINK:
PORNOGRAPHY AND CRIME

Harm was not everything to the Meese commission; it was the only thing. If the new evidence did not show credible links between explicit pictures and passionate crimes, all its labors would be wasted. The panel was convened for one purpose: to reverse history by overturning the not-guilty verdict of 1970. To fulfill this imperative they had to construct a case for evil consequences. Although the president denounced pornography in his State of the Union address in February of 1986, the Justice Department's jury was officially still out. At the business meeting in Scottsdale in March, the question of harm had led to bitter stalemate.

There were two vexing concerns in the desert. First, scientific research seemed to take pornography off the hook—just as it did in the 1970 presidential report. Even violent and hard-core kinds—from *Tool Box Murders* to *Deep Throat*—were cleared of *causing* bad behavior. The studies merely indicated that some college boys overdosed on porn pressed a shock buzzer longer than the controls did. And sometimes a rise in sympathy for extramarital sex followed a festival of racy films. Since laboratory reactions prove nothing about real-world actions and since sex offenders themselves did not seem to depend on porn to inflame their loins, the panel concluded that social science, taken alone, did not come close to implicating any genre of arousing materials in any kind of sexual aggression. This was a dangerous finding, and it threatened the success of the entire mission.

THE SCOTTSDALE CONUNDRUM

Second, the ten commissioners who attended the Scottsdale session (Tex Lezar was away at trial) went into meltdown when the discussion turned to mainstream erotica (e.g. *Debbie Does Dallas*, men's magazines, Hollywood movies and scenes from soap operas and miniseries). Six of the panelists (Levine, Becker, Tilton, Dietz, Garcia and Schauer) dared to vote that this class of porn actually had positive effects on the family. But the debate was extremely divisive. Citing the perils of promiscuity, Father Ritter would not settle for less than a smut-free City of God from Maine to California. He granted no absolution for soft-core sins. Dr. Dobson was so distraught by the laxity of the majority on Class III that he publicly prayed to the Almighty Commissioner during a coffee break. Meanwhile, the gang of three liberal women—Levine, Becker and Tilton—sneered

230

at the notion that even erotica had to be predominantly harmful. Dr. Becker, who blew up after a barrage of holy admonitions from Father Ritter, gave the mainstream a "predominantly not harmful" blessing. Being very honest, but not very enthusiastic, Professor Schauer, Dr. Dietz and Judge Garcia had to admit that this nonviolent and non-degrading class had some exciting benefits.

Since the pro-harms faction—the prosecutor, the priest, the spanker and the city councilwoman—felt their opposition keenly, Chairman Hudson called for 11 individual statements, suspending the most popular forms of sexual entertainment in limbo just out of Ed Meese's reach. This compromise tabled the issue until Washington.

Despite the staff's attempt at a frame-up, pornography was coming out of Scottsdale unexpectedly clean. The commission was running away from the president and the attorney general and the gathering momentum on the religious Right.

The prospect of repeating the findings of the 1970 report must have revolted Professor Schauer. In his own carelessly worded chapter on harms, he ignored the limitations of the social-science research and the positive side of porn that he himself affirmed in Scottsdale.

According to the Meese report as drafted by Professor Schauer, science has finally implicated porn in crimes of passion and mainstream (i.e., degrading) erotica was almost as awful. How did this transubstantiation occur? By sweeping aside reasonable doubt and applying the "common sense" solution.

THE INCREDIBLE HARMS CHAPTER

The chapter on harms is the foundation of the anti-porn verdict. The entire Meese report stands or falls on its rigor. But even the author of this crucial section has apologized for its intellectual shortcomings, especially the lowered standard

Professor Frederick Schauer: Andrea Dworkin's dream date; nonstop talker; in love with own thoughts; admitted Pac-Man addict; lectured by Harvard law professor Alan Dershowitz on Constitution at New York hearings; sour apple with press; twice-married; wrote the heart of the final report; fled to China after last business meeting.

of proof. Eschewing traditional formulas like "clear and convincing evidence" and "rational basis," Professor Schauer noted that the commission rested its conclusions more on gut instinct than good reason. "We have felt it best to rely on the language that people ordinarily use, words like 'convinced,' 'satisfied,' and 'concluded,' " he admitted.

Much of the testimony had structural faults, too. The professor did not trust either the porn addicts or the offenders. Nor did he believe that the "victims" were the tip of a vast iceberg. "We do not deceive ourselves into thinking that the sample before us is an accurate statistical reflection of the state of the world," he wrote. The same was true of clinicians who described the unhappiness of their porno-patients.

Correlational evidence was also risky business. The professor put it simply: "We recognize, therefore, that a positive correlation between pornography and sex offenses does not itself establish a causal connection between the two. *It may be that some other factor, some sexual or emotional imbalance, for example, might produce both excess use of*

232

pornographic materials as well as a tendency to commit sexual offenses" (emphasis added).

Laboratory tests were not very reliable either, he confessed, because they involved mostly the opinions of college males.

And, finally, the commissioners dipped in and out of data as they pleased, favoring whatever bits of information that suited their disposition. "Each of us has relied on different evidence from among the different categories of evidence," the professor wrote, "and specific studies that some of us have found persuasive have been less persuasive to others of us."

Furthermore, some of the commissioners had a fondness for shaky research, too. *"And in many instances we have relied on certain evidence despite some flaws it may have contained,"* averred the professor candidly, "for it is the case that all of us have reached our conclusions about harms by assimilating and amalgamizing a large amount of evidence" (emphasis added).

This was Professor Schauer's way of saying that he did not vouch strongly for either the record of the commission or its members' grasp of the data. Despite the enormous holes in the case for harms—weak witnesses and narrowly drawn data—the majority was happy to endorse the flying assumptions of Professor Schauer to get pornography.

Violent Pornography: Acquitted By Social Science

"Sexually violent material" (Class I) was the first category condemned as harmful. This category featured "actual or unmistakably simulated or unmistakably threatened violence presented in sexually explicit fashion with a predominant focus on sexually explicit violence." Some examples: sadomasochism, rape scenes with women begging for more, slasher films.

Where is the connection between sexually violent images and sexually violent acts? Professor Schauer named no

233

scientist or study, because no such evidence existed. Instead, he rested his "harmful" claim on a hunch that *some* man *somewhere, somehow, sometime* must have been incited to hurt *somebody* after watching an arm-twisting sexual encounter:

> Finding a link between aggressive behavior towards women and sexual violence, whether lawful or unlawful, requires assumptions not found exclusively in the experimental evidence. We see no reason, however, not to make these assumptions. The assumption that increased aggressive behavior towards women is causally related, for an aggregate population, to increased sexual violence is significantly supported by the clinical evidence, as well as by much of the less scientific evidence. They are also to all of us assumptions that are plainly justified by our own common sense. This is not to say that all people with heightened levels of aggression will commit acts of sexual violence. But it is to say that over a sufficiently large number of cases we are confident in asserting that an increase in aggressive behavior directed at women will cause an increase in the level of sexual violence directed at women.

In addition, Professor Schauer alleged that in lab experiments, violent porn changed men's attitude toward women. Apparently, such thoughts were harmful:

> The evidence also strongly supports the conclusion that substantial exposure to violent sexually explicit material leads to a greater acceptance of the "rape myth" in its broader sense—that women enjoy being coerced into sexual activity, that they enjoy being physically hurt in sexual context, and that as a result a man who forces himself on a woman sexually is in fact

234

merely acceding to the "real" wishes of the woman, regardless of the extent to which she seems to be resisting. The myth is that a woman who says "no" really means "yes," and that men are justified in acting on the assumption that the "no" answer is indeed the "yes" answer. We have little trouble concluding that this attitude is both pervasive and profoundly harmful, and that any stimulus reinforcing or increasing the incidence of this attitude is for that reason alone properly designated as harmful.

The professor's style of argument in the "Harms" chapter is not quite honest. Back in Scottsdale he himself voted for the finding that violent porn showed only "negative effects" in the laboratory. Along with the majority he conceded that no research connected this class with crime. Yet, contradicting the sense of Scottsdale, he dared to forge a link in the Meese report by false and misleading language. Consider the following constructions conveying the idea that social-science data has proven a cause-effect relationship, *which they have not*, between violent sex pictures and sex aggression:

"The research, which is described in much detail in the appendix, shows a *causal relationship* between exposure to material of this type and aggressive behavior to women."

"Although we rely for this conclusion about a causal relationship on *significant empirical evidence* . . . ."

"Sexual violence is not the only negative effect *reported in the research* . . . ."

"*Finding a link* between aggressive behavior towards women and sexual violence, requires assumptions *not found exclusively in the experimental evidence.*"

"Thus we reach our conclusions by combining the *results of research* with highly justifiable assumptions . . . ." (emphasis added)

The average intelligent reader of the above quotations

would probably conclude that the author meant porn caused crime according to the research. Professor Schauer's words allow for no other interpretation (although the reader would be confused by the last remark, which alludes to the hitherto-unrecognized social-science combination of fact-plus-guesses).

Actually, science is absolutely mute on the issue of pornography and real-life behavior. And the weaseling professor, who boasts of intellectual integrity, knows it.

Degrading Pornography: The Big Stretch
Nonviolent material depicting degradation, domination, subordination or humiliation (Class II) was next on the list of the condemned. This second category stretched across the erotic horizon. In the professor's head, degrading porn was almost ubiquitous. "If anything," he wrote, "it constitutes somewhere between the predominant and overwhelming portion of what is currently standard-fare heterosexual pornography and is a significant theme in a broader range of materials not commonly taken to be explicit enough to be pornographic."

Here is his wide, wide definition:

The degradation we refer to is degradation of people, most often women, and here we are referring to material that, although not violent, depicts people, usually women, as existing solely for the sexual satisfaction of others, usually men, or that depicts people, usually women, in decidedly subordinate roles in their sexual relations with others, or that depicts people engaged in sexual practices that would to most people be considered humiliating. To give an admittedly extreme example, we would all consider a photograph of an upright male urinating into the mouth of a kneeling woman to be degrading. There are other examples as well of the types of images that we consider degrading

236

and which we have seen in enormous prevalence in most "adults only" establishments. These would include depictions of a woman lying on the ground while two standing men ejaculate on her; two women engaged in sexual activity with each other while a man looks on and masturbates; a woman non-physically coerced into engaging in sexual activity with a male authority figure, such as a boss, teacher, or priest, and then begs for more; a woman in a role as nurse or secretary portrayed as required by the job to provide sexual satisfaction to a male physician or boss; a woman with legs spread wide open holding her labia open with her fingers; a man shaving the hair from the pubic area of a woman; a woman dressed in a dog costume being penetrated from the rear by a man; and a woman lying on a bed begging for sexual activity with a large number of different men who approach her one after another. Although these examples are extreme, forms of degradation not totally different from those represent the *largely predominant proportion of commercially available pornography.* (emphasis added)

(Professor Schauer's colleagues voted 10-0 to drop all but the urolognic example from the final report while the author vacationed in the world's largest non-pornographic nation—the People's Republic of China.)

There is monstrous bad faith in this passage. In a sexual context, "degrading" usually refers to relatively rare and/or generally shocking acts like incest, necrophilia and bestiality. That is precisely how Canada's commission defined the term in 1984. In Scottsdale, too, degrading porn consisted of a confirmed and kinky genre sold mostly in sleazy sex shops. Specific examples mentioned were golden showers, master-slave scenes and bestiality. As executive director Alan Sears memorably exclaimed about this class, "We had a hard time finding vaginal intercourse."

237

Yet between Scottsdale and Washington, the professor doctored the definition. Now degrading meant practically everything from *Deep Throat* ("standard-fare heterosexual pornography") to Calvin Klein fragrance ads ("materials not commonly taken to be explicit enough to be pornographic"). Any picture that displayed a woman "existing solely for the sexual satisfaction of others" (e.g., centerfolds, high-fashion layouts, Marilyn Monroe calendars) was banished to this lower realm.

How did transubstantiation happen? The professor had adopted Andrea Dworkin's polymorphous understanding of pornography. The rest was easy.

By this sleight of pen, he solved the dilemma that almost collapsed the commission in Scottsdale. Since the "predominant to overwhelming" share of the mainstream porn market was now degrading and therefore harmful, there was no more reason to anguish over the positive effects of the mainstream variety, as the panel did in the desert. Dr. Dietz, Ms. Tilton and Judge Garcia, who originally voted for positive effects with the professor, accepted the professor's shameful word games in Washington. Dr. Becker and Levine did not.

The scientific evidence against the degrading sort was much thinner than the dossier on violence. Almost no studies on this class have appeared. But Professor Schauer would not be denied by the mere invisibility of data. Turning logic upside down, he proceeded insouciantly with his lawyerly attack, clinging to the same assumptive ground as in the "violent" class:

> *The absence of evidence should by no means be taken to deny the existence of the causal link* (emphasis added). But because the causal link is less the subject of experimental studies, we have been required to think more carefully here about the assumptions necessary to causally [sic] connect increased acceptance

of rape myths and other attitudinal changes with increased sexual aggression and sexual violence. And on the basis of all the evidence we have considered, from all sources, and on the basis of our own insights and experiences, we believe we are justified in drawing the following conclusion.

Here comes that big hunch again about somebody out there somewhere abusing women after swallowing too many degrading centerfolds:

Over a large enough sample a population that believes that many women like to be raped, that believes that sexual violence or sexual coercion is often desired or appropriate, and that believes that sex offenders are less responsible for their acts, will commit more acts of sexual violence or sexual coercion than would a population holding these beliefs to a lesser extent.

But how large a sample? And who are these mysterious men who really believe that women crave rape and who rape accordingly? Has the professor any evidence that such deviates were motivated by porn? And should an estimated $8 billion industry, as well as millions of sexually curious consumers, both male and female, be curtailed for the psychotic reactions of unknown madmen? The professor's careful thoughts on these questions are not recorded.

Mainstream Pornography: Narrow and Relatively Harmless

Nonviolent and non-degrading materials (Class III) is a meaningless third class in the final report. After rerouting most of its inventory to the degrading, the professor noted that "this category is in fact quite small in terms of currently available materials."

And no wonder, since his examples mimic Gloria Steinem's pie-in-the-sky ERA erotica. Here are some hot scenes from the professor's WAP-whipped Class III fantasies: "a sexually explicit depiction of a man and a woman meeting and then engaging in consensual and equal vaginal intercourse; a depiction of a couple engaging in oral-genital sexual activity under the conditions of consent and equality; and two couples simultaneously engaging in the same activity."

Common sense told the professor that images of politically correct and non-violent coition/sodomy do not lead to violence, and so this class escaped the hook of "harm."

Despite this huge concession, which several commissioners begrudged but did not ultimately oppose in the final draft session, there was the problem of promiscuity. This category seemed to promote the possibility of sex without love and marriage, and that was bad. "Although there are many members of this society who can and have made affirmative cases for uncommitted sexuality," the professor preached, "none of us believe it to be a good thing."

As a last-resort smear, the professor dragged in the little ones. When children laid their mitts on such porn, it was bound to harm *them*: "For children to be taught by these materials that sex is public, that sex is commercial, and that sex can be divorced from any degree of affection, love commitment, or marriage is for us the wrong message to send at the wrong time."

It seems strange that the professor would suddenly emphasize the coldness of nonviolent and non-degrading scenes when his examples specifically cited the consenting and equal qualities of Class III congress. However, as previously demonstrated, he is not always a straight shooter on the subject.

As for the positive effects of mainstream erotica, which shook the rafters in Scottsdale, he allowed a few niggardly sentences.

There has been other evidence, however, about the
extent to which such material might for some be a way
of revitalizing their sex lives, or, more commonly,
simply constituting a part of a mutually pleasurable
sexual experience for both partners. On this we could
not agree. For reasons relating largely to the question
of publicness in the first sense discussed above, some
saw this kind of use as primarily harmful. Others saw
it as harmless and possibly beneficial in contexts such
as this. Some professional testimony supported this
latter view, but we have little doubt that professional
opinion is also divided on the issue.

Those were the only words in the "Harms" chapter suggesting that some agreeably tame erotica somewhere, somehow, might foster sexual pleasure and health instead of
crime and cruddy attitudes toward women. But even in this
instance the gnat-minded professor felt obliged to speculate
that "professional opinion is also divided on the issue," a
demurrer that he did not allow for Class I and Class II,
where the experts had shown much greater division.

If only Professor Schauer read Woody Allen, he would
not appear so obtuse. When Allen, a knowing critic of erotic life, was asked by his analyst if he thought sex was dirty,
Allen replied, "Only when it's good."

Nudity (Class IV), the fourth and last class of porn, likewise avoided the stigma of "harm," although Father Ritter
blasted nakedness in a dogmatic statement thrown elsewhere into the Meese report.

THE CRUSADER TEST

In the final paragraph of the "Harms" chapter, the professor attempted to clean the commission's skirt of tainted testimony. "We have tended to rely most on evidence provided by those who seem less committed to a particular

point of view beyond their scientific expertise . . . ." he proudly wrote, "Where a researcher has taken on the role as active crusader, one way or another, on the issue of governmental control of pornography, we are forced to question more than we would otherwise have done the way in which this judgment and discretion has been exercised."

Of course, no specific crusading scientists were cited. But the professor's protest cannot be taken at face value given the prominence he bestowed on the teamwork of the Marquis de Zillman and Dr. Jennings Bryant. Their studies were the only ones that permitted Professor Schauer to call the mammoth "degrading" class harmful. For they were the only researchers who found negative effects from dosing their subjects with "nonviolent" pornography. (Dr. Donnerstein, the hero of Class I, reported positive reactions resulting from Class II, but his contribution did not fit into the professor's plans.)

"The materials we have used never featured sexual coercion or even reluctant parties," the Marquis told the commission in Houston. "And at no time did these materials show violence or the infliction of unwanted pain." Despite the tame "Swedish-type" erotica of their experiments, Professor Schauer scandalously extended the Zillman-Bryant results to cover the waterfront, from coprophilia to the White Rock Girl.

Why should the commission have doubted the scientific bona fides of the pair? Were they committed to a viewpoint beyond their professional competence, a circumstance that would have vitiated their credibility in the professor's eyes?

Surely Dr. Bryant's opening remarks to the panel suggested a moral agenda transcending his academic training. "Forget family," he fulminated in Houston. "Forget commitment. Forget love. Forget marriage. Here in this world of ultimate physical hedonism, anything goes. If we take seriously the social-science research literature such as social learning or cultivation effects, we should expect that the heavy consumer of hard-core pornography should acquire some of these values which are so markedly different from those of our mainstream society, especially if the consumer does not have a well-developed value system of his or her own."

Love, hedonism, mainstream society, value system? Are not these topics alien to the "scientific expertise" of the head of the radio and television department of the School of Communications at the University of Houston?

Dr. Bryant's crusading commitment to chastity should have jolted a commissioner alert to special pleading. For example, the radio-and-TV man collaborated with Dr. Zillman, another communications whiz, on a survey of young, nonstudent subjects. After dosing them with consenting erotica as described above, they asked a list of value-laden questions about sex and society. Then the answers of the erotically immersed subjects were compared to those of the control group, which had not watched any erotica. According to Dr. Zillman, "heavy exposure to pornography fosters greater acceptance of pre- and extramarital sex." And that is not good.

But how much greater? A close examination of Dr. Zillman's testimony reveals that approximately *half* the controls, who had not seen the nasty films, endorsed sex outside marriage, compared to approximately 70 percent of the aroused moviegoers.

Clearly the crusading media experts were exaggerating the danger of pornography's polluting effects. Half the controls in their experiment liked the idea of sexual freedom from the start, that is, without the supposedly corrupting influence of pornography! Obviously Drs. Zillman and Bryant were not only operating outside their circle of competence, but they were excoriating the beliefs of the majority of young Americans, who engage in sex outside marriage without fear of tumbling our civilization.

Any fair commission would have discounted the fanaticism of scholars like Zillman-Bryant. Professor Schauer promised that the Meese commission was careful about crusaders. But Zillman-Bryant were all the research he had to execute degrading pornography as harmful. And so he grabbed their questionable studies to support his own misbegotten crusade.

If the degree-of-zealotry test were applied to all the witnesses, the commission would not have had much to make a case for harms. The cops and the prosecutors would be dropped first, because their beat assumes the worst; moralists in and out of cassocks would not count, since they believe sexual sinners are doomed to eternal punishment (in the company of Hitler, Stalin and Alfred Bloomingdale); the microphone-hogs from Women Against Pornography would be dismissed for their unconstitutional civil-rights ordinance; and, of course, the ubiquitous victims, who regard pornography as the root of all evil, would not even be allowed to testify.

Actually, most of the panelists would have to recuse themselves under Professor Schauer's crusader standard. Therefore it can be no surprise that a panel like the attorney general's saw harms where there were none to be seen.

13

THE GOOD OF PORNOGRAPHY

Although the case against pornography as presented by the Meese commission collapses under scrutiny, what about the opposite case? Was there any evidence indicating that porn was normal or beneficial? Could a conscientious panelist have concluded that pornography may be part of the solution instead of the problem? Apparently two of them did. But with what authority?

What were the best arguments in favor of porn? Can common sense, the last refuge of the Meese Majority, truly support the eroticized commotion of Brian de Palma's *Body Double,* the raunchy in-and-out of *Deep Throat,* the naked objects in men's magazines and other controversial manifestations of explicit sex?

Not unless a mind is open to erotic reality. Not without an appreciation of the natural appeal and psychological dynamics of pornography. Dr. John Money of Johns Hopkins, the nation's leading sexologist, brought some fundamentals to the attention of the panel in Houston. He explained that a man's eye for an ankle originated far back in evolution, when vision supplanted smell as the primary sexual turn-on among male primates.

THE BIOLOGY OF EXCITEMENT

"In the human species," Dr. Money observed, "both men and women are able to be erotically turned on by what they see. However, to become erotically attentive, and to take an erotic initiative, men are more dependent on vision than women are, whereas women are more dependent on the skin senses and touch. This difference between the sexes is prevalent throughout the population and is individually resistant to change. It is a basic difference that generates a high degree of misconception on the part of women (and some men) regarding the function of visual erotica in the sexual life of the male—their own husbands and sons included—and hence of the function of the visual image of pornography."

Dr. Money's biological point is crucial to the debate because it accounts for men's almost universal and irrepressible response to reproductions of naked women, from time immemorial. Hard-core erotica did not spring forth full-blown in Scandinavia in the 1960s. It was an element in the ancient cultures of China, Japan, India and Peru and flourished in classical Greece and Rome. The Renaissance, Victorian England and pre-war Paris were also golden ages of erotica. And the gender of the artists and the consumers was constant: men.

Gloria Steinem's knee-jerk feminism would blame the

patriarchy for this apparent imbalance, but there is no evidence anywhere that shows women mimicking men in the desire for thrilling sights. Kinsey documented this gender preference by noting that twice as many men preferred having sex with the lights on than women.

The conscientious commission would probably have no quarrel with accepting a basic pornographic difference between the sexes. *Playgirl* does only a fraction of *Playboy*'s business. But where does violence fit into the picture? What is the purpose of hardball fantasies?

Dr. Money informed the commission that taste for brutal and bizarre sex, which creates a market for brutal and bizarre pornography, originates in a perverted childhood lovemap and cannot be spread from mere exposure. In other words, men cannot catch a paraphilia for passionate crime by watching *Tool Box Murders*. But what about young boys, whose lovemaps may not be as rigid? Could not they be bent by impressively violent depictions?

Dr. Dietz wondered about this possibility, too. "If 1000 boys were to observe a lust-murder training film/R-rated movie the night before their first wet dream or first masturbatory episode," he asked the 65-year-old therapist, "would you expect that the exposure would change the probability that those boys would have some violent component to their lovemaps?"

"No," replied Dr. Money, "because they already had years to incorporate other concepts of sexuality. In order to create a particular paraphilia in a person, one would need an extremely explicit program over a long period of time."

THE SEXUAL PSYCHOLOGY OF PORNOGRAPHY

Even if a conscientious commissioner granted that snuff killers were extremely rare and did not originate directly from porn, what about the carryover effect? One does not have to dive over the cliff with Andrea Dworkin to feel offended, aesthetically and otherwise, by some explicit images on the market and to wish that somehow the problem would disappear.

Dr. C.A. Tripp, a New York sex researcher who filmed humans in the orgasmic state for the Kinsey Institute back in the 1950s, testified in Houston on the essence of pornography's attraction—taboo.

"Pornography always uses a resistance base," he said. "That means the thing that is taboo is the turn-on. In China, admittedly a culture far from ours, the most dirty thing in pornography is any picture of mothers' milk, and copulation. Therefore, the centerfold in dirty Chinese pornography will show a couple in ordinary copulation and a third person, usually a woman, squeezing her breast and shooting a stream of milk. This is the epitome of a taboo idea."

Next Dr. Tripp made an amazing assertion about the role of taboo in America. According to Masters and Johnson, he commented, the sexual fantasies of the healthiest heterosexuals were full of taboo behavior, that is, the basic script of pornography.

The data cited by Dr. Tripp were revealed in Masters and Johnson's *Homosexuality in Perspective* (1979). Thirty men and women from their "sexually functional study subjects" were surveyed on the contents of their "free-floating fantasies." Both sexes seemed to conjure up the same scenes. The top three fantasies were identical: replacement of an established partner, forced sexual encounter and observation of sexual activity. How pornographic can you get?

Masters and Johnson discovered a surprise when they analyzed the details of men's daydreams of sexual aggression—the fellows were on the bottom more often than not:

Forced sexual encounter was the second most frequent

248

fantasy pattern reported by heterosexual men. Many heterosexual men introduced thoughts of rape during free-floating fantasies and even occasionally as a short-term performance stimulant. For heterosexual men the mental imagery of being forced sexually was of just slightly higher incidence than the imagery of using force in a sexual assault. Usually when heterosexual men imagined themselves forced sexually, it was by a group of unidentified women rather than by a single female. When they were forcing the sexual encounter, the fantasy usually involved one woman who generally was identified.

Women, however, thoroughly enjoyed playing rapee when the going got tough:

This type of fantasy was usually free-floating in category, although occasionally being forced sexually was a short-term, "old friend" fantasy pattern. Being raped while helpless to resist was consistently fantasized, while the heterosexual women rarely reported assuming the role of rapist and attacking a helpless male. Although usually fantasizing themselves as restrained from effective resistance to the rape episode, there was little sadism and no masochism reported as fantasy content.

Women also reached for a New Bedford incident when they absolutely needed to:

In the heterosexual woman's fantasies of gang rape, she was predominantly the victim. She usually fantasized herself as powerless to resist, whether physically restrained or socially dominated, and in her daydreaming she was forced sexually time after time. Heterosexual women repeatedly used gang-rape fantasies as

249

a short-term stimulant when masturbating or when responding to cunnilingus.

Dr. Tripp would have expanded on the significance of Masters and Johnson's study, but the chairman cut him off prematurely.

"Pornography is full of positive things," he hurriedly concluded. "Let me quickly mention that every marriage manual tells you this is the way to perk up a marriage. This is the kind of advice that was in Marabel Morgan's *The Total Woman*, which is the only book in North America to outsell the Bible in three consecutive years. She makes such suggestions as greeting your husband at the door dressed only in Saran Wrap or something. What is the wife doing? She is bringing in the mechanisms of pornography—shock, contrast, variation and perk-up. I am sorry I can't continue this a little longer, but I think I better obey the chairman."

A conscientious commissioner might object to the selectivity of Masters and Johnson's sample of highly functional laboratory lovers. After all, how many women volunteer to copulate while having electrodes stuck in their torsos in plain view of technicians?

What then do average American women want in their fantasies? The mutuality, solidarity and punctuality of Steinem's erotica? Not by a long pole. They want the passion of rape and degradation—just what they get in romance paperbacks that comprise more than a third of all paperback sales.

Take Janet Dailey, the best-selling author of bodice-ripping fiction. Her oeuvre rests on the supposedly despised proposition that women say "no" when they mean "Fuck me, fuck me." Such is the behavior of Diana Somers when she is crudely mounted by a roguish rancher named Holt Mallory in Dailey's recent novel titled *The Rogue*:

For an instant, she was pinned by his weight, but she twisted and wiggled, pushing and kicking from beneath him. He still had a hold on her, pulling her back when she tried to crawl away. Her fingers curled into the gravelly earth as Diana tried to claw precious inches, unable to manage a centimeter. Holt's superior strength was turning her onto her back. Her fingers closed around the gravel in her hand. As he succeeded, Diana flung the sandy grains in his face, momentarily blinding him . . . .

All her senses came to life. The bed of hard gravel was rough beneath her, chunks of rock poking into her flesh. Her arms scraped the ground as Holt drew her wrists down even with her shoulders . . . . The sensual possession of her lips shivered through her, exciting and arousing, despite Diana's attempts to block out the pleasure it held . . . .

It had been so long since Diana had known the touch of a man wise in the art of arousing a woman. Not until this moment, when the masterful skill was being practiced by a man who had always been her enemy. But if this was defeat, Diana knew she was going to glory in it as her lips softened in an initial response . . . . At the moment of total possession, her hips lifted to meet his thrust, her nails digging into his flesh, like the flexing claws of a cat in a state of satisfaction. She was drowning in a sea of desire.

Women's pornography is not always pretty but, presumably, it is usually exciting to its audience. Apparently, sexually active persons—whether male or female—naturally feed on the meat of the forbidden. "In a great variety of sexual fantasies, pornography included, an initial put-down is often the first expression of a fiendish fascination—so much so that even the most devoted lover may welcome the sharp edge of rough lust as a guarantee of his or her contin-

251

ued appeal," Dr. Tripp pointed out in Houston.

"Even fundamentalist love manuals with conservative feelings for sex recognize this principle when they recommend that bored but loving Christian couples seek sex at unusual places and times: the classic example is taking one's wife to a motel and treating her like someone new. Moreover, sex is replete with easy reversals in which a strong move South is the way to go North—not unlike throwing a tennis ball hard against the ground to send it highest. And while pornography can be simplistic and crude in various raunchy expressions that may emphasize lust alone, this is not 'all bad' for people who enjoy sex per se."

So far, the conscientious commissioner has not heard any moving violations of reason or logic. So-called violent and degrading pictures, as inelegant as they may appear, do not seem utterly irredeemable viewed in the context of history, biology and sexual psychology.

If pornography is the theory, common sense dictates that fantasy-saturated climax is more likely the practice. And the majority of American lovers, fans of Linda Lovelace as well as of Janet Dailey, are grateful beneficiaries of this extra stimulation-inspiration.

THE CATHARSIS THEORY

Still, the conscientious commissioner might pause. Maybe pornography enhances the responses of normal people, but sex offenders could get the wrong notion, could they not? As Professor Schauer argued, not everyone who plays with erotic fire torches the erogenous zone. The arsonists are the ones the professor was worried about most of all.

Nevertheless, Dr. Gene Abel, professor of psychiatry at Emory University and a respected expert on the treatment of rapists, assured the commission in Houston that pornography was not a big clue to the creation of perversity. Only one percent of his subjects traced their predicaments back to pictures.

His survey of 256 offenders was restricted to their use of erotica, that is, nonviolent or noncoercive materials in magazines like *Playboy, Penthouse* and *Gallery.* (Apparently these were the only kind of explicit pictures that interested them.)

And what did Dr. Abel discover? Not much.

"The major finding was what we didn't find," he commented about his ongoing research. "If erotica is going to have a significant impact, one would expect the crispest way of evaluating that would be to have people who would be most prone to commit sex crimes already. They would be the most vulnerable. If erotica is going to impact on the commission of crimes, it's really going to manifest itself in those individuals who already have been committing these crimes. Well, when you do look for that impact, you really don't see it."

For example, Dr. Abel compared offenders who used erotica with those who did not. He expected the two groups to differ in the numbers of crimes committed, victims abused and level of violence perpetrated. But they did not diverge at all.

Switching to pornography, Dr. Abel went on to revive the provocative catharsis theory, which the panel neglected to explore.

"These fellows are not limited in intelligence," he said of offenders. "They know very well that when they commit sex crimes they run a risk of being arrested. So many times they will use their fantasies in solitude and masturbate to those fantasies rather than go out and commit a sex crime."

In other words, pornography kept convicted rapists, the highest-risk aggressors toward women, out of trouble. These were strong words from a psychiatrist of Dr. Abel's reputation. *Pornography actually reduced the incidence of sex crimes!* The conscientious commissioner would have pricked up his or her ears.

At the Washington hearings a psychotherapist described the porno-catharsis of a patient Peeping Tom who routinely carried *Playboy* and *Penthouse* with him on his nightly rounds.

"He took along the magazine in case he was unsuccessful in finding a woman to watch," said Dr. Dennis Harrison. "He then proceeded to masturbate to relieve his sexual tension. If he did not do this, then he was fearful of acting out his violent fantasies of murder and rape on the woman. The peeping and masturbation was his self-learned way of controlling his violent impulses."

To be honest, the same panelist would have to weigh the downside of catharsis. Masturbating to violent pornography, in Dr. Abel's opinion, also reinforced the original deviance, which is not a good thing in itself.

A short-term gain perhaps portends a long-term risk. The longer a man remains aroused by rape images, the more opportunities he will have for rape, even though some potential acts will be dissolved in pornographic privacy.

However, there is an escape from this dilemma. Rape is a young man's obsession. The average rapist is between the ages of 18 and 24. If the methadone of mere depictions can vent his fantasies for a few years, that is, while the anger decays, this is all to the good.

Of course, there will always be sex offenders, and pictures will always be found at the scene of some crimes. But what types of offenders and what sorts of pictures? And does one have much to do with the other? Consider the following undated profile of sex perversion, from the blotter of the Burbank, California, police department, that dissenting commissioner Charles Keating submitted to the 1970 panel:

Sex Perversion—Suicide—H____Case—D.R. 64-5456. "The body was discovered by the wife of the suspect, who is 24 years old, when she came home from work as a social worker. He attended law school. She found him lying on the bed in a supine position, face down and naked. On top one end of a rope was tied to his ankles, the other end was around his throat. A pair of white sox kept the rope from connection with his skin as did a towel around his throat. She screamed and the neighbor came in and cut the ropes. The Fire Department tried resuscitation and called the police. When the police arrived, his ankles were still trussed but rigor mortis had set in. Just above him on the bed were 5 or 6 nudist magazines (2 were Sun and Sport), all open to female forms. When he was moved, it was found he had a contraceptive on and had an emission on the bed. All windows, doors were locked. The neighbors had seen him enter and he had no visitors until his wife came home.

In the investigation with the Coroner's office and Los Angeles County Sheriff disclosed a type of masochism—in which sexual excitement is reached upon tying oneself up and hanging to almost a point of blackout—substantiated by psychiatry and case histories. Interrogation of suspect's wife revealed that ever since their marriage he was unable to obtain satisfactory intercourse without the use of ropes, being tied up and subjected to this before he could perform satisfactorily. He had received psychiatric help for 8 years. The death was accidental—he did not intend to do it. In Los Angeles County, cases of this type occur about 6 times a year in which the defendant goes too far. He had sox on and a towel on his throat to prevent rope marks."

If nudes from *Sun and Sport* magazine, rather than the deranged sexuality of Mr. H., truly contributed to this auto-erotic asphyxiation, the great pornographic massacre would have engulfed the republic by now.

Just as the brain is our most erogenous zone, so, too, it is the most pornographic. That is why the British report despaired of well-meaning censorship. The conscientious commissioner would heed the logic of his or her peers in England:

"What is also striking is that if one tried to eliminate the stimuli in published material which may have some relation to sexual deviation or the commission of offenses, the net must be cast impossibly wide. As an illustration of this point, Dr. Gallwey mentioned to us a patient who killed himself in the course of his masochistic practices which had started when, as a disturbed child of only 8 or 9 years, he had been excited by coming across a picture of a woman bound to a stake.

"The protection of the young raises special considerations which we shall come to later, but even so it is clearly impossible to suppress pictures of Joan of Arc. A glance at the list of books found in the home of Ian Brady, the Moors murderer, makes the same point. There are people who will gain a perverted satisfaction from reading accounts of Nazi atrocities or of other historical happenings, or even passages in the Bible, but publications cannot be suppressed on that account. All kinds of literature can have a destructive effect. The case of Goethe's *Sorrows of Young Werther*, which was said to have made suicide fashionable, is famous, but equally we heard of a romantic novel linked to the drowning of a teenage girl and of an Agatha Christie story linked to real-life poisoning. There can be no question of suppressing such works. Art galleries cannot be closed to those who find excitement in paintings of barbarous acts or semi-clad women; nor can such people be kept away from beaches or be prevented from reading daily newspapers. For those who are susceptible to them, the stimuli are all around us; but the main point we wish to make from our study of the anecdotal and clinical evidence is that there is very little indication that pornography figures very significantly among these stimuli.''

THE PEOPLE'S CHOICE

Where do the people stand on erotica? It would behoove a conscientious commissioner to check Gallup on the pornographic pulse of the nation before wishing it all away.

A March 1985 Gallup poll published by *Newsweek* showed that most Americans do not want stricter community standards for the sale of sexually explicit materials. The majority (52 percent) of the 1854 people surveyed said that standards should be less strict or kept as they are.

Gallup divided the respondents into subgroups based on gender, race, age, education and party affiliation.

Although *Newsweek* did not publish the breakdowns within the various groups, a close look at the data indicates startling differences. For example, women, whites, the elderly and the less educated are significantly more aroused by censorship than men, minorities, college graduates and people under 30.

In general, men are far more accepting of erotica than women are. Only a third of the men queried want stricter standards for its sale, but half of the women desire to tighten the reins. Nor are men as bothered by the sexual content of television shows, advertisements or movies—there was a spread of more than 20 percent between the sexes on this index of tolerance.

Men are also less likely, by 11 to 15 percent, to ban magazines which show adults having sexual relations, X-rated movies and X-rated videocassettes. Men are also the main purchasers of sexually explicit materials. Half of all the men polled sometimes buy or read magazines like *Playboy,* while only a fourth of the women do. Men also watch more X-rated movies and videos.

It seems unfair for one group—women—to try to restrict or ban materials that another group—men—regularly enjoys. According to Gallup, the majority of men surveyed claimed direct benefits from erotic magazines, books and films; they said that pornography improves sex lives, provides sex information and entertains.

But not to be forgotten is the important fact that 4 out of 10 women stand tall with men on the gains of erotica. Those females who complain about the negative effects of X-rated materials may not be the best witnesses. Half of the women questioned have never read *Playboy* or *Penthouse,* yet about three fourths of them believe that sexually explicit materials lead to a breakdown in morals.

Race, too, is a clear-cut indicator of opinion. Nonwhites had a more lenient and positive attitude toward porn than did whites on every single question asked by Gallup. Nonwhites were far less concerned about the sexual content of novels, television programs, ads and movies. And they were less likely to ban sex magazines (by 12 percent) and X-rated movies (by 16 percent).

Furthermore, the age-group (50 +) that points the finger at pornography is least familiar with it.

Although America's more senior sexual citizens are the most ardent censors (55 percent want stricter controls), many of them have never laid their eyes on the materials they hate. In fact, more than half of all elderly people polled have never read *Playboy* and *Penthouse,* yet two thirds of them would like to see a total ban, and 80 percent of them believe sexually explicit materials lead to immorality, disrespect for women, and rape.

If Americans under 30 had been given a voice on the Meese panel, it is clear how they would have voted. Most of them (58 percent) want community standards to be kept as they are. Apparently, porn serves youthful interests.

There is an educational difference as well. Forty-six percent of all college graduates sometimes buy or read magazines like *Playboy,* as compared to 34 percent of all high-school graduates. And the least educated members of society, those who have not graduated from high school, are also the least likely to buy or read sex magazines—25 percent in this instance.

The notion that Democrats are more tolerant of sexually explicit materials because they are more "liberal" is mistaken. Although the majority of Democrats (51 percent) approve keeping community standards as they are or making them less strict, Republicans oppose erotic repression by an even greater margin (53 percent). Actually, party animals from the GOP buy magazines—*Playboy* and *Penthouse*—at a significantly higher rate (17 percent).

In their campaign against erotica, politicians like Ronald Reagan and Ed Meese are not only in the minority of Americans, but they are also outnumbered by members of their own party.

GOOD SEXUAL POLITICS

The conscientious commissioner has an obligation to probe scenarios that compete with the porno status quo. For it may be that current affairs, as loathsome as they seem to some, make for the most practical sexual politics.

There were only two alternative visions on the panel's agenda—religious and ultra-feminist. The former's idea of total national chastity is unimaginable short of a venereal police state like Iran, China or Russia. The latter approach, on the other hand, demands more inspection.

Although Andrea Dworkin is the earth mother of the model anti-porn civil rights ordinance, she does not oppose hard-core films or pictures per se. Despite appearances, the

Women Against Pornography brigade is not prudish. Like almost everybody else, they can get down on passionate depictions—with one proviso—everything must pass an ultra-feminist purity test.

Ellen Levine had drawn out Dworkin's tolerance for obscenity at the New York hearings.

MRS. LEVINE: Ms. Dworkin, do you make any distinction in your definition between erotica and pornography?

MS. DWORKIN: This is a recently emerged definition within the feminist movement, articulated, for instance, by Gloria Steinem, that says that erotica is sexually explicit material that shows mutuality and reciprocity and equality. I am prepared to accept that definition as something that is not pornography . . . .

MRS. LEVINE: Would there be sexually explicit pictures of intercourse that was mutually agreeable that would therefore not be a civil-rights suit, according to your definition?

MS. DWORKIN: Yes, there would be.

MRS. LEVINE: So in some ways it [WAP's civil rights ordinance] would be broader?

MS. DWORKIN: In some ways it would be broader and in some ways it would be narrower.

So where was Steinem when the Ms.'s of America really needed her? Why did the glamorous 50-year-old feminist-in-excelsis skip the hearings when she could have pitched her distinction between good and bad explicita? Since Steinem has repudiated conventional morality in theory and practice—defending abortion, fornication and watching couples in equal coition—she ought to have taken the occasion to break the ludicrous alliance between pro-choice, pro-erotic women's-rights advocates like herself and the anti-abortion, anti-erotic patriarchal forces behind the commission. Suffering an apparent failure of nerve, Steinem the eroticist ducked the one commission that could do something about the porno-predicament that, in her view, enslaved every woman in America, especially *Ms.* subscribers. Without the benefit of her distinction, the Meese majority condemned almost everything explicit.

Steinem's dogma was unfurled in two *Ms.* essays from 1977 and 1978 and reprinted in her best-selling collection *Outrageous Acts and Everyday Rebellions.*

According to Steinem, there is a world of difference between erotica and pornography. "These two sorts of images are as different as love is from rape, as dignity is from humiliation, as partnership is from slavery, as pleasure is from pain," she explained.

In words and pictures, erotica emphasizes images of mutuality, warmth, shared sensuality, equal nudity, empathy, love, positive choice, yearning for a particular person; in other words, the feminine romantic ideal.

Pornography, in contrast, derives from domination—man over woman, homosexual man over homosexual man, lesbian over lesbian. "Whatever the gender of the participants, all pornography is an imitation of the male-female, conqueror-victim paradigm, and almost all of it actually portrays or implies enslaved woman and master," she declared.

The warts of porn include force, violence, unequal racial, class or sexual power; in other words, Steinem's caricature of the open-fly, unromantic sex drive of men throughout history.

This analysis is hurt by a gap in reality. One of the divi-

261

sions does not exist. The author of the new definition of erotica could not cite a single illustration. "The problem is that there is so little erotica," Steinem admitted.

Why not? Since women cherish the kissy-huggy vibrations of explicit egalitarianism, there should be a huge market for the product. Yet there is none.

Steinem's excuse: "Women have rarely been free enough to pursue erotic pleasure in our own lives, much less to create it in the worlds of films, magazines, art, books, television and popular culture—all the areas of communication we rarely control."

This is a surprisingly supine interpretation of modern herstory by one of its most successful entrepreneurs. Since women have their own cigarettes, banks, tennis tournaments, national organizations and gothic paperback lines, surely they could be sold erotica-Steinem-style—*if* the demand existed.

But it does not. Thus the conscientious commissioner might hesitate to supplant the reign of masculine pornography with an entirely dummy category of no certain appeal to either gender merely at the nod of Dworkin, Steinem and their swooning sisters.

Furthermore, the crude cleavage of arousing materials into beauty (erotica) and beast (pornography) is not only dishonest but also political. Essentially, the ultra-feminist march against men's movies and magazines is an attempt to feminize sex. Dworkin said it herself in her book *Our Blood:* "I think that men will have to give up their precious erections and begin to make love as women do together." This is easy for an avowed lesbian living in an unlicensed open marriage with the homosexual founder of Men Against Pornography to say.

But surely Steinem recognizes the folly of trying to shoehorn one gender's sexuality into the other's. She has fashioned a brilliant career around the right of women to define themselves independently, particularly in the erogenous zone. Steinem rightly resents the imposition, even with good intentions, of male ideals on females. For example, Krafft-Ebing wanted to protect women but patronized them at the same time. "If she [womankind] is normally developed mentally, and well-bred, her sexual desire is small," observed this trailblazing sexist in *Pathologia Sexualis.* "If this were not so, the whole world would become a brothel and marriage and family impossible."

Actually, Steinem has repeated history by pulling a Krafft-Ebing herself when she demands that men get excited her way, or else.

(And even the editor of *Ms.* cannot keep the rules of her parallel anti-porn universe. Although in her magazine she called for a boycott of porn purveyors and compared its collaborators to Nazi sympathizers, she conducts regular business with the enslavers and their supporters: e.g., Steinem recently gave an interview to *Playgirl,* published *Playboy* columnist Cynthia Heimel in *Ms.* and interviewed Shirley MacLaine in *Ms.* shortly after this reincarnated feminist was interrogated in *Playboy.*)

THE PRESIDENTIAL WINK

The conscientious commissioner, sensitive to the demands of social convention, would also realize the folly of sweeping anti-sex crusades. The dragnet of the reverends (e.g., Falwell, Wildmon, Ritter) would catch too many suspects with too much to hide. Winking at departures from conventional morality is the homage virtue pays to the hormonal condition of mankind. America would not happily survive the bonfire of the erotophobes. Even Ronald Reagan, the moral leader of the West, is entangled in the permissive mores of the day.

For instance, Ron, Jr., is a contributing editor of *Playboy* who covered his dad for Hugh Hefner at the Geneva summit. Apparently the president granted the skin magazine exclusive behind-the-scenes access which was denied to other news organizations. Daughter Patti has also indulged in the medium of sex. "It didn't seem possible that Greg could know more about my body than I did, but in a few minutes he brought to life something inside me that would have scared me to death if I'd had the time to think about it," she sizzled in her best-selling autobiographical novel *Homefront*. "A violence roared up from within and screamed from every corner of my body, a thousand high notes shattering a thousand panes of glass. To keep from crying out and to keep from flailing away at Greg's shoulder, I bit at my wrist. Gradually, I came down, feeling like my blood had been drained . . . ."

Both offspring are, in the language of the commission chairman, well-known fornicators. Ron, Jr., lived openly with wife, Doria, before marrying her. And Patti hung out with a member of the Eagles without exchanging vows. The president's oldest daughter, Maureen, has been married three times. Ronald Reagan himself is a divorced man who had numerous liaisons with Hollywood starlets. Even the First Family falls short of the president's professed ideals.

So did the man in charge of the government's anti-porn campaign. Alfred Regnery headed the Justice Department's Office of Juvenile Justice and Delinquency Prevention. Regnery, a former official of the Young Americans for Freedom, used his post to fund controversial studies to nuke pornography.

His plan was outlined in a June 1983 memo prepared by his deputy Robert Heck and calling for $8 million in grants to study the impact of pornography.

"Something is seriously wrong psychosexually between today's men and women," the memo asserted. The solution, it said, hinged on finding evidence that pornography results in attempts to duplicate in real life the sexual fantasies depicted or described therein. A thorough investigation should even uncover the role pornography plays in the divorce rate, homosexuality and battered women.

Regnery approved the proposal and named Heck program director, despite his scant qualifications for the task. Prior to this, Heck supervised canines for the Massachusetts state police bloodhound unit for 12 years and worked for the mayor of Madison as a liaison with other police units that spied on "radicals."

Yet Al Regnery had a secret in his past—his own hard-core collection. Back in October 1976, Regnery was finishing a campaign to become district attorney of Madison, Wisconsin. The candidate's pregnant 28-year-old wife called police three times in the course of the final week to report obscene phone calls and vandalism. On Halloween afternoon she told of a horrible crime: Two men broke into her home and warned her that her husband should drop out of the race. She said that the two cut her with a knife and forced her to have oral sex.

Police investigators recorded her story: "Both men got up, and the [Negro male] grabbed her by the hair and pulled her towards the bathroom. He dragged her to the edge of the tub while he got into the tub behind her. She explained again that the bathroom is extremely small, and that the man had to get into the tub to be anywhere behind her. The [white male] dropped his pants to his knees and raised the lid and seat of the toilet. She stated that he had an erection, and he leaned towards her. The [Negro male] directed her head motions by jerking on her hair and head, and the [Negro male] forced her head a little forward so that she had to take the [white male's] penis into her mouth.

The fellatio took place with her head directly over the toilet. She stated that the penis was in her mouth for no more than ten seconds when the man ejaculated. Some of the sperm ran out of her mouth and down onto her chest, and some of it landed in the water in the toilet. The two men changed positions, 'and the second time it was exactly the same.' She threatened to bite the [Negro male] and he told

265

her that he would cut her again if she did. He then forced his penis into her mouth and ejaculated.''

The Law and Order candidate told reporters that the rape was aimed at getting him to withdraw. But Regnery said he would stand tough. The voters still rejected his candidacy: He was easily beaten on election day.

Cops were suspicious about the affair from the start. Although Christina Regnery had 73 slash marks on her breasts, none was serious.

Mrs. Regnery also said the two assailants left the house through a basement door. However, the police found the basement door blocked by an immovable lamp and by boxes of dusty, empty beer bottles, which showed no signs of having been disturbed for months.

"This door is supposedly the door used by the burglars in the exit,'' the police report stated. "However, this would be impossible . . . .''

Upstairs in the master bedroom, police expected to see signs of a struggle. They found none—nor did they locate any spots of blood in the bedroom where Christina was supposedly tortured. But they did uncover some evidence she had left out of her account.

On the bed, under the telephone book and in drawers in the nightstand, police came across a stash of hard-core magazines and catalogs for sex toys. Curiously, some of the photographs depicted acts strikingly similar to the ones ascribed to the rapists.

"Under the telephone book was a book with numerous color photos of various sexual gratification, including oral sex and the placing of objects into the vagina including bottles, carrots, etc.,'' the police report stated. "Another magazine was in the drawer with color photos of various sex acts. This book was printed in German. The *Penthouse* magazine on the bed also depicted the usual sexual activities.'' The investigators concluded that Mrs. Regnery had fabricated the entire incident.

Nine years later, Regnery was steeped in his anti-porn battle: His office gave Dr. Judith Reisman, the songwriter from "Captain Kangaroo," nearly $800,000 to study the cartoons in men's magazines and doled out $125,000 for the pornography commission's labors. *Penthouse* exposed Regnery's private erotica collection in its December 1985 issue. Though Regnery threatened to sue, he never did.

A few months after the *Penthouse* story was published, *New Republic* assigned a reporter to Regnery's case.

Regnery explained to journalist Murray Waas that he did not feel hypocritical on the pornography issue. At first he claimed that the police discovery of numerous catalogs and magazines was "a fabrication." He said that he only had "one copy of *Playboy* or something like that." Then he conceded, "I think a friend of mine in Germany sent me one magazine and I had it around." When asked about all the items in the police report, he finally surrendered: "I probably had a little [pornography] around the house, like I bet lots of people do." But Regnery denied that he was a consumer of pornography. "I wasn't then and I never have been. I don't use it and I don't enjoy it."

Before the *New Republic* piece entitled "Al Regnery's Secret Life"—guaranteed to be big news in Washington—was printed, he suddenly resigned from office, surprising his staff and supervisors at the Justice Department.

The irony here is obvious. Only under an Administration that declares war on pornography can a copy of *Penthouse* on the nightstand be a career-shattering discovery. In an inevitable twist of fate, Al Regnery became the Administration's most visible victim of pornography.

And, finally, the conscientious commissioner cannot take the president's protests seriously in light of the Alfred Bloomingdale affair.

Bloomingdale and his wife, Betsey, were bi-coastal cronies of the First Couple. Al was a California millionaire, the founder of Diner's Club; the Mrs. attained the platonic ideal of the California millionaire's wife.

The Ethiopian in the fuel supply was Al Bloomingdale's magnificent obsession: S&M. The presidential pal liked to spank and whip bound women and paid out large sums of money to satisfy his urges.

In a confidential memo prepared for J. Edgar Hoover in 1959, the tycoon's passion for hookers was revealed. This document, obtained by the authors under the Freedom of Information Act states: "Al Bloomingdale is a family man, but not the ordinary sort. At about 43 years of age, he lives with his wife and children in an appropriate house in Bel Air. His principal interest is the internationally famous Diner's Club, of which he is president.

"There is another facit [sic] to BLOOMINGDALE. He likes girls. In fact in another circle of society he is known as quite a playboy—ready, willing and able to accept the services of high-priced Hollywood prostitutes. This story is not just fancy—it is substantial information from a man who for many years was connected in the bail-bond business with the notorious IZZY GLASSER, at one time a henchman of Mickey Cohen, and is verified in part by BLOOMING-DALE himself."

Bloomingdale's indiscretions became public knowledge when his longtime mistress, Vicki Morgan, sued him for support as he was dying of cancer in 1982.

Is it possible that Ronald Reagan did not know of his pal's aberrant appetites—through either the Bel Air grapevine or White House security checks? Could the president have looked the other way when he appointed him to the Foreign Intelligence Advisory Board, a group whose duties include overseeing the CIA's covert operations abroad?

In light of Ronald Reagan's professed ideals, this apparent wink was inexplicable. Some of the West's most closely guarded secrets were entrusted to a moral reprobate, a public adulterer and closet sadist who must have been prey to

PLEASURE PERSONAL CLASSIFIEDS

CHERRY POPPER: Personal Polaroids shot at home by swinging "families." Very explicit, daring and dirty. *Mailart, North Hollywood, California*

WET VIDEOS: Photo of female sitting on toilet accompanying ad. Four videos available: "Golden Showers," "Wet Sex Party," "'P' for Pleasure," and "Little Wet Panties." *Video Exchange, Van Nuys, California*

PICTURES OF MY 4 GIRLS: New censorship restrictions on magazine publishers prevent me from telling you how old they are or what my girls are doing in them. *Mr. Hale, Los Angeles, California*

WOMEN WHO FUCK ANYTHING MAGAZINES: Four magazines offered. "Farmgirl Fantasies," "Fucked on All Fours," "Balling in the Barn," and "Susie's Stud Service." A drawing of a female bent over with a dog's snout near her crotch accompanies this ad. *Nuwave Publications, Los Angeles, California*

I'LL MAKE US BOTH COME!!: When I spread it wide open, rub it, finger it and masturbate just for you! I also do . . . home sex with my husband and two girls. *Mrs. Marie Alexander, Van Nuys, California*

(Excerpted from the Final Report of the Attorney General's Commission on Pornography—Government Printing Office, 1986)

269

blackmail threats from pimps and prostitutes for most of his adult life.

Despite Bloomingdale's pornographic lifestyle, he walked with kings and princes and had the ear of the most powerful and popular politician in the world.

It seems that Bloomingdale's sadism was forgiven by an old-boy network that operated on the principle that boys will always be boys and that a deviant double life is no bar to the White House inner circle.

All things considered, Ronald Reagan's campaign to construct an anti-pornographic shield over the entire body politic cannot be sincere.

CONCLUSION

After pondering the arguments in defense of pornography—the male instinct for visual stimulation, historical ambiguity, Dr. Money's lovemap, Dr. Tripp's taboo theory, Masters and Johnson's porno-fantasy statistics, the popularity of rape/romance novels, Dr. Abel's discoveries about sex offenders, and the *Newsweek*/Gallup survey—a conscientious commissioner might have dissented from the harmful verdict of the attorney general's commission.

Two did. What about the nine others? Were they less conscientious about the evidence, or were they rather obeying a Higher Conscience?

14

THE CONSCIENCE OF THE MAJORITY:
PIETY AGAINST PORN

Despite the attorney general's formal mandate to investigate the impact of pornography on society and make recommendations for containment consistent with the Constitution, in truth, the Meese commission was a moral Trojan horse. Mountains of research were culled and 208 witnesses were heard, but a majority ended up exactly where they came in: Pornography is a sin.

On the eve of the final session, Dr. Park Dietz parted the

curtain on the group's hidden moral impulse. He read a two-page statement titled "The Sentiments of the Commission" to his fatigued colleagues and suggested tacking it on at the end of the report.

His sermon attempted to sum up the case against explicit sex:

"We have attempted to provide a reasoned analysis of the permissible and desirable relationship between government and the regulation of sexually explicit materials, including the rights of citizens to take private action. As a government body, we have studiously avoided making judgments on behalf of the government about the morality of particular sexual acts between consenting adults or their depiction in pornography. This avoidance, however, should not be mistaken for the absence of sentiment among the commissioners.

"We have no hesitation in condemning nearly every specimen of pornography that we have examined in the course of our deliberations as indecent, lewd, and in the opinion of this eleven-member community, obscene. We find these same materials offensive and tasteless. According to our values, these materials are themselves immoral, and to the extent that they encourage immoral behavior they exert a corrupting influence on the family and on the moral fabric of society.

"Pornography is both symptomatic and causal of immorality and corruption, but in this it does not stand alone. A world in which pornography was neither desired nor produced would be a better world, but it is not within the power of government or even of a majority of citizens to create such a world. Pornography is but one of its causes. Nonetheless, a great deal of contemporary pornography constitutes an offense against human dignity and decency that should be shunned by the citizens, not because the evils of the world will thereby be eliminated, but because conscience demands it."

OH, MY GOD

The group was stunned. The sun danced in the sky over Washington. Father Ritter, who looked as if he had swallowed a box of Communion wafers, smiled and handed the unordained psychiatrist his Roman collar. "Oh, my God," chuckled Tex Lezar. "That's great," said Diane Cusack, noting that Dietz's "sentiments" would allow the liberation of moral judgments that had been suppressed all along.

Chairman Hudson so loved the sermon that he wanted everyone to sign it. Judge Garcia said to include him in. Dr. Dobson was well pleased. "Given the rather legal and analytical tone of the rest of the document, which I have been complaining about for three days now," he exclaimed, "this statement represents the punctuation that is needed at the end of the report." Among the majority only Professor Schauer held back hosannas; he was a lawyer, not a moralist, or at least he did not lead with a moral jab. Dr. Dietz's prayer was not the amen he wanted at the close of his report-within-the-report.

The emerging minority of two recoiled from Dr. Dietz's revivalism. Dr. Becker winced; Levine said sarcastically that she did not relish seeming immoral if her signature were not appended. Why could not Dr. Dietz keep his document to himself? But the sermon on Mount Venus stayed in the final report, tucked into his personal statement and endorsed by Hudson, Lezar and Judge Garcia. As a last resort, the minority women and their turncoat sister, Deanne Tilton, who went with the boys in the crunch, uncorked their own ethical manifesto in an eloquent *J'accuse* of the sexism of some commissioners and the sexism of some pornography.

They expressed their horror over women held in pornography against their will and horror over the idea that women cannot look out for themselves in the mansion of passion. Their plea for sexual peace, written without tears, shamed

273

the male majority's rally for more sexual war:

We are three women who have, in varied ways, devoted our lives to the welfare of children and families: one as a specialist in the treatment of those who sexually abuse women and children, another as a journalist covering the diverse issues facing contemporary American women and the third as a specialist in the prevention and treatment of child abuse, neglect and molestation.

We share a deep concern about the effects of pornography on American women. Nevertheless, we found these issues troublesome because those women who testified before us were so deeply divided. Many condemned pornography as an ultimate offense against women, others opposed censorship categorically and defended women's rights to consume and perform in pornography.

Although each of us has her own very strong negative, personal reactions to the various pornographic depictions, we believe our acceptance of service on this commission carried with it the responsibility to enter this arena with an open mind, to weigh fairly the evidence presented to us and to set aside our personal biases in order to develop credible and balanced recommendations for the Federal Government regarding this extremely controversial subject.

We have, through the Commission's hearings, witnessed devastating testimony from women victimized in the production or forced consumption of pornography, and we have seen material that is offensive to the most permissive boundaries of our imaginations. Much of this material violates the very fabric of our own ethical and moral standards.

We wish to express our strong personal objections to the offensive and totally inaccurate materials that portray women as eager victims of abuse or as being of less competence or value to society than men. We disapprove equally of media depictions that discriminate unfairly against men, or against specific races, cultures or those with physical or mental disabilities.

After consideration of the evidence presented, we conclude that those who exploit women's vulnerability in the production or consumption of pornography are inflicting harm that profoundly violates the rights of women, damages the integrity of the American family and threatens the quality of life for all men and women.

We abhor the exploitation of vulnerable people and condemn those who profit from it. We respect, however, the rights of all citizens to participate in legal activities if their participation is truly voluntary. We reject any judgmental and condescending efforts to speak on women's behalf as though they were helpless, mindless children.

Our most profound desire is that the women of America be provided an environment that encourages their sense of self-worth, self-respect and their ability to make genuine choices. We consider both the limitation of choice and sexual exploitation to be degrading attacks on the basic value and dignity of women.

PERSONAL STATEMENTS

Despite the cover story of suspended judgment, the Meese commission was decided at the moment of its appointment. The majority, with the possible exception of Deanne Tilton, could not have acted otherwise. The proof of this original suspicion is laid out in the personal statements published in the front of the final report. These confessions reveal pious and timid souls, victims of *La Grande Peur Sexuelle,* who

275

have little business setting the erotic agenda for a nation of people so unlike themselves. *Au profond,* it was the Meese Commission on Fornication, or, from a positive angle, the Commitment Commission.

Henry Hudson:
Chairman from Another Planet

Henry Hudson was never regarded as anything but a square who intended to go federal with his small-time anti-porn mentality. All he ever wished to hear from the witnesses was incriminating evidence: "Could you give us your explanation of what the causal link is between pornography and incest?" he asked a therapist.

"How many adult sex offenders, Sergeant, have you interviewed who have told you that the reading of pornography had a direct relationship to the crime they had committed?" he asked a cop.

"Do you feel that the experience that you had with pornography has substantially affected your ability to engage in normal sex relations today?" he asked a victim.

Despite his constant search for the missing clue, the chairman failed to cite a single instance of cause-and-effect in his personal statement. The professional prosecutor moralized instead. The statement began with a regret that violent and degrading pornography was not condemned "in more forceful language." Then from lofty ground he lashed into Class III, pretending that Professor Schauer had not narrowed its scope in Washington.

For him, consensual-and-equal erotica is still "morally offensive," "conveys the impression that women are fundamentally immoral and hedonistic," distorts "the moral sensitivity of women" and "de-emphasizes the significant and natural bond between sex and affection in their portrayal of adultery, fornication and sodomy."

The last lash—from an Old Testament lexicon—is the

final giveaway. Adultery, fornication and sodomy?

In the night, can a real man fail even to fantasize that extramarital, premarital and oral and anal sex might occur under friendly circumstances? More than moral, this prosecutor is a Conehead in the precincts of passion. All arguments for a more decent nation collapse on the example of Henry Hudson.

James Dobson:
Chaste to the Last Drop

Some husbands like to carry nude snapshots of their wives in their wallets. Others, probably just as rare, brag about wives who have never impaled themselves on the milkman or anybody else since the day of their wedding.

James "I've Only Slept with Shirley" Dobson is among the latter. He worked the chastity routine into a brief speech at the National Religious Broadcasters Association meeting last February. He told the sympathetic audience that being a porn commissioner was rough on the eyeballs. Grossed out by the slide show at the first meeting in Washington, he flew back to Los Angeles in a rush.

"I had a great desire to get out of there . . . to go home," he said. "What a beautiful word 'home' is. I got to Los Angeles about three in the morning, got in my car and drove home, drove into that driveway, to the clean little house, clean little neighborhood, walked up those steps, put the key in the lock, opened the door and I was home. My children were safe from all that misery, molestation, death, in their bedrooms. In the other bedroom Shirley waited for me, being faithful to me, in thought and deed, every minute, every second from the time that we were married, and I to her. Both of us having reserved ourselves for one another, for that moment."

But how many husbands who say such things about their wives also believe that Satan drives a black Porsche? Per-

Dr. James Dobson: *president of Focus on the Family, an organization dedicated to preserving traditional values; licensed marriage counselor; former professor of pediatrics at U.S.C.; pushing 50; has called pornography "a river of smut"; consultant to Army chief of staff; occasional White House visitor; wife Shirley ripped up men's magazines in convenience store; says Satan is plaguing his family because of his porn investigation; favorite quote: "Is it degrading to publish* Pussy Pumping Ass Fuckers?"; *prayed for stern verdict against erotica—voted for it, too.*

---

haps Dr. Dobson is alone in this sample of the American population. While he sat on the panel, both his children, a daughter and a son, reportedly had separate, near-accidental-death experiences with the Devil at the wheel of a black Porsche. "I think the Lord said to me, 'Yes, these things are connected and I did do a miracle on behalf of your children,'" he told the same NRB crowd. "And I would appreciate it if you all would remember to say a prayer, especially as we go to write the final report."

For a religious zealot, Dr. Dobson unexpectedly laid off the heavenly language in his personal statement. Nevertheless, he complained in some detail about the awful exhibitions he had seen all year long. He called for a more pure America where pornography could be kept out of the hands of curious kids.

"At an age when elementary school children should be reading *Tom Sawyer* and viewing traditional entertainment in the spirit of Walt Disney, they are learning perverted facts which neither their minds nor bodies are equipped to handle," he commented. "It is my belief, accordingly, that the behavior of an entire generation of teenagers is being adversely affected by the current emphasis on premarital sexuality and general eroticism seen nightly on television, in the movies, and in the other sources of pornography I have mentioned. It is not surprising that the incidence of unwed pregnancy and abortions has skyrocketed since 1970. Teens are merely doing what they've been taught— that they should get into bed, early and often. And to a large degree, pornography has done this to them."

But Dr. Dobson, the moralist, almost single-handedly blocked the commission from recommending sex education that could alleviate the problems he blames on porn. He exited with a blast at Caesar and a divine entreaty in harmony with his militant theology.

"It is my hope that the effort we invested will provide the basis for a new public policy," he wrote, "but that will occur *only* if American citizens demand action from their government. Nothing short of a public outcry will motivate our slumbering representatives to defend community standards of decency. It is that public statement that the pornographers fear most, and for very good reason. The people possess the power in this wonderful democracy to override apathetic judges, disinterested police chiefs, unmotivated U.S. Attorneys, and unwilling federal officials. I pray that they will do so. If they do not, then we have labored in vain."

For a disciple of juvenile corporal punishment, Dr. Dobson kept his temper well in trying times. By the end he could even joke about his lonely-guy status on the panel. Although some of the press mercilessly ridiculed his gonzo view of the venereal, he was large enough to invite a pair of reporters to dinner on their next visit to Southern California. These journalists admitted respect for the evangelist's consistent extremism in the pursuit of moral cleanliness.

No other commissioner felt Jim Dobson's pain, but no other commissioner, even the one who has never had sex, was so out of it.

279

Judge Edward Garcia and Harold (Tex) Lezar

Matching their contributions to the commission, the two least valuable members passed on a personal statement. But as friends of the moral court, they both concurred with the remarks of Hudson and Dr. Dobson and joined Dr. Dietz's declaration of anti-porn conscience.

Frederick Schauer:
The Thinking Man's Censor

Frederick Schauer is a card-carrying moralist, but he does not flash his credentials unless forced into it. Although he resisted signing Dr. Dietz's world-without-porn oath, he felt required to tout his virtue in his statement.

"Although I consider myself as moral as the next person, and more moral than most, I do not deceive myself into thinking that my appointment to this task was a function either of my own morality or of my ability to identify, to reflect, or to speak for the moral values of others," he wrote.

Rather the professor considered himself the thinking man's commissioner. To be a value-free academic, he argued, is to be almost perfect: "It is to be willing to pursue an inquiry in the most intellectually honest way possible, to be open to new ideas and to challenges, to follow the inquiry where it leads regardless of personal views, to be free to reach conclusions without having to serve an external constituency, to be able to make the best case for the opposing view and then confront that best case rather than the worst case, and to be willing to consider today that what one believed yesterday might be wrong."

Best case? Worst case? Actually, the Schauer report was a basket case of analytic thought hastily fabricated by a former advocate of Deep Throat with a head case about explicit pictures.

280

Diane Cusack:
The Thousand-Year-Old Commissioner

Diane Cusack was not woman enough to vote with her sisters. A Sunbelt Thatcherite, she knelt before the masculine model of censorship erected by the Magnificent Seven. Her brief personal statement broke no new ground.

"We have a phenomenon today, in the pervasive presence of sexually explicit materials, that challenges one of those understandings held by society for thousands of years—that sex is private, to be cherished within the context of love, commitment, and fidelity," she wrote. "We can use this wondrous gift to create or destroy, to rule or be ruled, to honor each other or debase each other."

Apparently, the commissioners were more concerned about immoral behavior than immoral images. Despite the clear wording of her statement, and those of the majority coalition, Mrs. Cusack denied that the panel had condemned illicit conduct like premarital sex. "That's far overreaching," she said in a telephone interview.

"Would you say that your moral opinions are out of the American mainstream?" a reporter inquired.

"I would vehemently disagree with that interpretation," she replied.

"But according to Gallup, 52 percent of Americans approve of premarital sex," the reporter said.

"I can't convince you," she said. "I think this conversation can stop right here."

Deanne Tilton:
A Woman Torn

Deanne Tilton should have been a dissenter. According to her personal statement, she disagreed with the majority on the big issues. First, she denied a provable connection between pornography and crime. ("We cannot scientifically show that exposure to sexually explicit materials affects

281

the behavior of most consumers.'')

Second, she deplored censorship. (''It is also important to acknowledge that we have no business regulating any expression in words or pictures without good cause.'')

Third, she faulted the Justice Department for giving bad commission overall (''The workload has been unmanageable throughout the year. The ultimate task of reviewing over two thousands pages of final draft in three days' time to meet our print deadline was totally unrealistic.'')

But her principal complaint concerned sex education, which her colleagues left twisting in the wind. ''I truly believe that a significant measure in the protection of children and subsequent generations against exploitation lies in the incorporation of family life preparation programs within school systems,'' she wrote.

''A large percentage of children who become involved in pornography and prostitution have run away from violent and exploitive homes. Most reported child molestation is perpetrated by a family member. In other words, if we depend completely on parental guidance, many children will never receive the benefits of information regarding their rights and responsibilities in making personal choices and the requirements of healthy parenting. It seems incredible to me that we are unwilling to focus concern and educational resources on promoting healthy parenting and interpersonal skills at a level commensurate with our commitment to other curriculum which may be of far less importance in the lives of future generations.''

The child advocate even dissented from Dr. Dietz's ''Sentiments'' and signed instead a stinging anti-majority rebuke with her spiritual sisters (Dr. Becker and Ms. Levine).

So how did she wind up in the majority? Only Tilton knows for sure. In personal terms, she lived several blocks from the other eight. She probably even got the joke in *Swept Away* when Mariangela Melato begged Giancarlo

Giannini to *"Sodamita me, sodamita me."*

Perhaps Tilton's statement, which mainly empathized with child victims, should be read as a dissent. If this sensible woman were not the president of the Consortium of California Child Abuse Councils, her quarrels with the majority would have been much louder.

Father Bruce Ritter:
The Beatific Vision of Sex

There are two basic varieties of Catholic priest—Franciscan and Jesuit. The disciples of St. Francis love the lilies of the field and seek salvation with the least of the brethren. Bing Crosby, Burgess Meredith and Spencer Tracy play them in movies. The soldiers of St. Ignatius, in contrast, are terrorists for God who will burn a village in order to save it. Cyril Cusack has a lock on this role.

If there is a heaven, the Franciscan in Father Ritter will be close to the throne owing to missionary work among homeless kids. At the same time, the nasty drill-sergeant Jesuit lurking within his soul will not draw throngs of angels to his side.

The trouble with Commissioner Ritter was that he was all Jesuit. The kinky side-canyons of sex agitated him hardly at all. Nor was he levitated by the groans of Women Against Pornography. For him, violent and degrading depictions were a priori anti-Christ and so beyond reasonable debate. "When all is said and done," he wrote in his personal statement, "do the careful conclusions of the Commission with regard to violent and degrading pornography surprise anyone, or does any rational man or woman seriously question the legitimacy of these conclusions—quite apart from any 'evidence' thought to establish such harms?"

What then did Father Ritter want? Nothing less than a holocaust for *all* erotica (with the possible exception of validly married nude couples in joy-of-Catholic-sex textbooks, and only if read with feet in holy water). Harking back to the great celibate theologians of church history, he really believes that coitus without incense and "Ave Maria" on the stereo is somehow beastly.

"To me the greatest harm of pornography is not that some people are susceptible to or even directly harmed by the violent and degrading and radically misleading images portrayed all too graphically by mainstream pornography," he decreed, echoing the 1970 dissenters. "Rather pornography's greatest harm is caused by its ability—and its intention—to attack the very dignity and sacredness of sex itself, reducing human sexual behavior to the level of its animal components."

That is why he hated easing up on Class III. Worse than the blood of *Tool Box Murders* and the degradation of *Biker Slave Girls* were the temptations of middle-of-the-road make-outs in contemporary mass media. "I think it is fair to say that by its refusal to take an ethical or moral position on pre-marital or extra-marital sex, either heterosexual or homosexual, the Commission literally ran for the hills." Apparently Father Ritter took the mandate as a license to impose his catechism on everybody else's private parts.

The seamless web of Catholic sexual morality—"All sins against chastity are mortal"—allows no loopholes. In the eyes of Father Ritter's God, a single, unconfessed impure thought or deed wipes out a lifetime of good works. This is no caricature of credo. When the priest's loyal assistant, a lawyer by the name of Greg Loken, was asked whether Christa McAuliffe would be in hell today if she had masturbated the night before the Challenger tragedy, he replied, "Yes, if she did it in defiance of God."

What makes Father Ritter's imperative so lame is that most Catholics today disobey the Church's teachings on sex. And the friar's own choir is bare and ruined, in part, because of this great rejection.

Dr. Park Dietz:
The Sherlock Holmes of Schmutz

Among the majority, Dr. Park Dietz was the most admirable and honest character. Fastened neither to the mast of religion nor to that of politics, he roamed around the pornographic zone in the whites of a forsenic humanitarian.

Violence was his devil. *"Tool Box Murders* is of greater concern to me than *Taxi Driver,* which is of greater concern than *Debbie Does Dallas,"* he said during the deliberations. But he was unsuccessful in turning his colleagues' gaze from the peep show. Nor did he try very hard, since he had plenty to chew on in Classes I and II.

Composed in tears, Dr. Dietz's personal statement reflected both his humanism and his inheritance from Krafft-Ebing, the original sex detective, who prowled the streets of Vienna in the 1890s. When these two elements are mixed together, the result is *pathologia sexualis*, where mythical victims are given erotic sovereignty, not of the asylum but of the world beyond.

"Pornography is a medical and public health problem because so much of it teaches false, misleading and even dangerous information about human sexuality," he wrote in a sublimely perverted vision of sex on earth. "A person who learned about human sexuality in the 'adults only' pornography outlets of America would be a person who had never conceived of a man and a woman marrying or even falling in love before having intercourse, who had never conceived of two people making love in privacy without guilt or fear of discovery, who had never conceived of tender foreplay, who had never conceived of vaginal intercourse with ejaculation during intromission, and who had never conceived of procreation as a purpose of sexual union.

"Instead, such a person would be one who had learned that sex at home meant sex with one's children, stepchildren, parents, stepparents, siblings, cousins, nephews,

285

nieces, aunts, uncles, and pets, and with neighbors, milk-men, plumbers, salesmen, burglars, and peepers, who had learned that people take off their clothes and have sex with-in the first five minutes of meeting one another, who had learned to misjudge the percentage of women who prepare for sex by shaving their pubic hair, having their breasts, buttocks or legs tattooed, having their nipples or labia pierced, or donning leather, latex, rubber, or childlike cos-tumes, who had learned to misjudge the proportion of men who prepare for sex by having their genitals or nipples pierced, wearing women's clothing, or growing breasts, who had learned that about one out of every five sexual encounters involves spanking, whipping, fighting, wres-tling, tying, chaining, gagging or torture, who had learned that more than one in ten sexual acts involves a party of more than two, who had learned that the purpose of ejacu-lation is that of soiling mouths, faces, breasts, abdomens, backs, and food at which it is always aimed, who had learned that body cavities were designed for the insertion of foreign objects, who had learned that the anus was a genital to be licked and penetrated, who had learned that urine and excrement are erotic materials, who had learned that the instruments of sex are chemicals, handcuffs, gags, hoods, restraints, harnesses, police badges, knives, guns, whips, paddles, toilets, diapers, enema bags, inflatable rubber women, and disembodied vaginas, breasts, and penises, and who had learned that except with the children, where secrecy was required, photographers and cameras were sup-posed to be present to capture the action so that it could be spread abroad.

"If these were the only adverse health consequences of pornography, the most straightforward remedy would be to provide factually accurate information on human sexuality to people before they are exposed to pornography, if only we could agree on what [that] information is, on who should provide it to the many children whose parents are incapable of doing so, and on effective and acceptable means by which to ensure that exposure not precede education. In the absence of such a remedy, the probable health consequences in this area alone are sufficient to support recommendations that would reduce the dissemination of that pornography which teaches false, misleading, or dangerous information about human sexuality."

A sensitivity so finely tuned to the causalities was not immune to feelings of porno-pacifism. And so he concluded his statement with a kind of emancipation proclamation titled "Pornography and Freedom":

"When Andrea Dworkin challenged us to find the courage to 'go and cut that woman down and untie her hands and take the gag out of her mouth, and to do something, to risk something, for her freedom,' I cried. And I still cry at that image, even as I write, because if we do not act with compassion and conviction and courage for the hostages and victims of the pornographers we do not deserve the freedoms that our founding fathers bequeathed us. It has been nearly two centuries since Phillipe Pinel struck the chains from the mentally ill and more than a century since Abraham Lincoln struck the chains from America's black slaves. With this statement I ask you, America, to strike the chains from America's women and children, to free them from the bonds of pornography, to free them from the bonds of sexual slavery, to free them from the bonds of sexual abuse, to free them from the bonds of inner torment that entrap the second-class citizen in an otherwise free nation."

A hard saying, but Dr. Dietz meant it. His moral *"Sentiments,"* introduced to the commission in Washington and reproduced in his personal statement, argued that a world without desire or production of pornography would be a far better place because such materials "encourage immoral behavior."

But in the polymorphous mind of Dr. Dietz, everything is not as it seems. For example, he does not regard the man who reads *Playboy* as immoral, although the Meese report clearly put it in the degrading class of pornography that was linked to sex crimes.

"*Playboy* is not a moral issue," he frankly averred in a midnight telephone interview during the final conclave in Washington. "Even though the magazine supposedly degrades women?" enquired the reporter.

"I don't think *Playboy* centerfolds are degrading," he replied. "They're artful nudity and they stimulate erections. Maybe they affect the economic status of women, but it's wild to claim that *Playboy* causes rape."

What gives? Dr. Dietz had just voted in favor of Professor Schauer's "Harms" chapter, which labeled mainstream pornography degrading when it shows women as sex objects "existing solely for the sexual satisfaction of others." Surely the Playmate of the Month fits this description exactly. Andrea Dworkin thinks so. Obviously, the professor thinks so. But Dr. Dietz, on the other hand, thinks centerfolds are dandy.

Dr. Dietz's fervent prayer for a world without porn is another puzzle. When the reporter reminded him that there has never been such a world and so nobody could say that it would be better, he conceded that his prediction was not supportable.

And he admitted that men would always covet naked images because the desire was in their brains.

As his cry of conscience collapsed, Dr. Deitz sought refuge in mere social convenience. "Come on," he said, "don't you agree that the world would work better if men were fulfilled at home?"

In the end, the Meese commission came down to this Liberty Federation send-up of sex without fantasy, mystery or adventure.

The Twelfth Commissioner:
A Baptist Mole

Alan Sears, a right fielder in the game of life, was the twelfth commissioner. But nobody knew that he was also a fundamentalist Southern Baptist mole. Not just an ordinary devout layman, Sears was practically a papal knight of America's largest Protestant denomination. In June of 1986, as chairman of the Resolutions Committee of the annual meeting of the Southern Baptist Convention, Sears performed the supreme act of auto-congratulation by getting his church to commend the Meese commission while reproaching secular sex education. But apartheid escaped official wrath, as Sears explained to the convention, because he did not want to bring up divisive issues. The devout Kentuckian even got his flock to endorse the shocking notion that "pornographers lure or kidnap many women and children annually for the purpose of being forced into a life of prostitution and sexual abuse." This disturbing proposition was never debated seriously by the commissioners. But Sears was fond of the hysterical touch.

A few commissioners said they were surprised that Sears led a double life. One of the female panelists said that she felt his interest in the sexually bizarre seemed obsessive. "I couldn't figure out why he was so taken by that 42nd Street stuff," she reflected. "But now it makes sense . . . ."

The Taxi Driver:
A Baptist of a Different Color

An old black taxi driver picked up two reporters outside a Justice Department building last April and drove them to National Airport. En route, the passengers noticed a copy of the Bible on the dashboard and were led to inquire about the driver's views on pornography, having themselves just quit a roomful of sanctimonious commissioners.

Actually, the old man was fond of erotic images. They

PEEP-SHOW LOOP

A white female (represented to be known porno star Marlene Willoughby) [is shown] inserting one finger in the vagina of another female (represented to be known porno star Vanessa Del Rio). Then Willoughby inserts two fingers in Del Rio's vagina. One finger has a large ring. A close-up is shown of the insertion. Then Willoughby uses her left hand and inserts one finger in Del Rio's vagina; then two fingers are inserted; then three fingers are inserted. Then she inserts her fist in Del Rio's vagina, twisting it around.

The next segment shows Willoughby removing her fist from Del Rio's vagina, then inserting it again. Del Rio holds Willoughby's wrist as she continues to fist her vagina. Willoughby is wearing a gold-colored bracelet on her left wrist. A close-up is shown of the insertion, with Willoughby twisting her fist around in Del Rio's vagina. Then Willoughby removes her fist from Del Rio's vagina and reinserts one finger from her right hand in Del Rio's vagina and performs cunnilingus on her at the same time.

A close-up is shown of Willoughby performing cunnilingus on Del Rio, spreading her labia and inserting her tongue. The next segment shows Del Rio inserting a finger in Willoughby's vagina as Willoughby fondles her own breasts. Then Del Rio inserts one end of a two-headed dildo in Willoughby's vagina.

(Excerpted from the Final Report of the Attorney General's Commission on Pornography—Government Printing Office, 1986)

aroused him. But did not such feelings incite promiscuity?

No problem, said the taxi driver; he had a lot of girlfriends, approximately 11, in his life despite his happy marriage of 42 years. As he told it, all the deacons on his church board, including the minister himself, kept an ungodly eye on the ladies.

But was not adultery a sin worthy of the fires of hell?

The old man smiled and responded, "Not everything that's a sin is wrong."

15

DISSENTING SISTERS

D
r. Judith Becker detests a lot of pornography, especially the brutal variety. She treats victims of rape and does not like to be reminded of the terrible things that some violent men do to women. When the psychologist was approached for the job of commissioner, she did not hide her feelings. Personally, Dr. Becker told the Justice Department's interviewer, she found much of the material horribly offensive. As for social science, she was not so sure where the literature led, but she was willing to review the evidence.

Her specialty in victims of rape and the recommendation of the genial G-man psychiatrist—fellow panelist Park

Dietz—made Dr. Becker a natural for the commission. She would provide professional backup and sympathy for the parade of pornoplegics at the hearings. A congenial single woman of 42 who graduated from Spokane's Gonzaga University, Dr. Becker was not expected to make waves. She was living in the trenches, bandaging the wounds of the war between the sexes. If any commissioner understood the real physical and psychological degradation of women, it was this bleeding-heart therapist with the pleasant smile and sturdy character of an Irish nun.

DR. BECKER'S LAMENT

Yet Dr. Becker had pondered resignation after the Houston hearings last September and wound up repudiating the final report in a biting dissent (see page 00).

"The idea that 11 individuals studying in their spare time could complete a comprehensive report on so complex a matter in so constricted a time frame is simply unrealistic," she protested with co-dissenter Ellen Levine.

"No self-respecting investigator would accept conclusions based on such a study, and unfortunately the document produced reflects these inadequacies."

How did Dr. Becker arrive at this level of contempt for the Meese commission? In a long conversation in her upper-Manhattan office overlooking the George Washington Bridge, she explained her grand disillusionment. She noticed the odor of a Justice Department fix in the initial business meeting in Washington, when the panelists talked together for the first time. She wanted to get the definition of pornography on the table. As a scientist she was taught to begin an experiment by defining the concept under study. But Chairman Hudson was in no hurry; a definition would evolve as the hearings unfolded. Dr. Becker bit her tongue at this odd modus operandi.

What almost moved her to quit in midstream was the cavalier attitude her colleagues had toward the social science data which was the theme of the Houston stop. "John Money and Richard Green are eminent and respected sexologists," she remarked. "I heard them say in Houston that a person's sexual preference pattern is established very early on in childhood, at an age when children are not exposed to explicit material. Thus perversions are not caused by pornography. And then at the business meeting, I heard the majority say that we can't depend on social science. I guess I felt upset. If we couldn't depend on hard data for our judgments about pornography, what were we going to rely on? Religion? Common sense? That made me very uncomfortable as a scientist."

Despite her good manners, she grew to distrust some of the commissioners and their motives. The chairman's objectivity was especially doubtful. "Here is a person who spent a good part of his career wiping out pornography because he believes it's dangerous. And he was chosen to lead the inquiry. What does that say about the people who put the commission together?"

Father Ritter was another thorn in her side. She bristled at his mini-sermons laced with Catholic condemnations of sexual pleasures and fantasies.

"Listening to him, I felt as if I were back in theology class at Gonzaga. Actually, I have the same God as he does, but mine is not as punitive."

While other commissioners publicly beat their breasts with private prejudices, Dr. Becker was silent about her own therapeutic use of porn. Nine years ago, on a government grant, she treated pedophiles, who were not at all aroused by adult women, with exciting depictions of grown-up sex. The idea behind the experiment was to build up a taste for nondeviant activities. However, she purposely failed to mention her own peaceful applications of porn because she was afraid it would hurt her image. "I was considered a liberal when I'm actually a moderate," she said. "To cite my own work with explicit materials would not have added to my objectivity."

Although many sex and marriage counselors prescribe porn for their inhibited patients, not one ventured to defend their methods before the Commission. "It is difficult for professionals to speak out on the topic—even to say that the literature hasn't shown such and such—because they would open themselves up to ridicule," she noted. "I've gotten lots of hate mail since Ellen's and my statement appeared in the *Times*. These conservatives are really mean. They damn you in the first sentence. I knew our statement would raise a lot of flak, but my conscience would not allow me to remain silent any longer."

Dr. Becker regards the failure to examine the other side of the pornographic coin a major flaw. "The fact is that millions of Americans use this material," she said. "But I wonder what government agency would ever make monies available to a researcher to discover what customers get from it. On a number of occasions I requested that we hear from people who consider pornography sexually beneficial. But the issue was too charged. I mean, can you imagine people coming forth, even behind a screen, and relating their positive experiences? That's not the way to reach them."

Instead, Dr. Becker listened to an endless caravan of so-called victims of pornography. She had the impression that their testimony was tailored for the commission, but she dared not press her reservations at the hearings. "Clearly, these witnesses were victims of sex crimes and pornography was somehow brought into the picture," she said. "I wish that I could have posed direct questions about the connection. But I was very mindful that challenging their belief system could be detrimental [to them]. That's why I didn't take an active role in questioning them."

In contrast, the majority was willing to identify pornography as the smoking gun. "Most of the commissioners saw it as a disease, but I think it's reflective of something else. We have seen over 800 sexual offenders at the Institute and I still do not know why people commit sexual crimes. Believe me, if they consistently said imagery alone made them do it, I would publish that. Then I'd be able to say that we discovered the cause of sex crimes. But that's not what offenders tell me. There is no universally agreed-upon theory to explain why men rape.''

This gap in the evidence did not stop Professor Schauer. The link was not perfectly envisioned in the professor's maze-like mind. He could not honestly argue that pornography *caused* sex crimes but rather that porn's vast proliferation was bound to increase the incidence of mayhem among those at risk—presumably the unstable.

Dr. Becker recoils from the professor's mad logic of creating social policy based on the weakest citizens. "According to Fred's view, neither cigarettes nor alcohol should be allowed,'' she commented. "Cars would be forbidden, too, because some people are bad drivers. If restrictions depend on how the most vulnerable deal with their problems, what happens to the rights of the rest of us?

"This is not to say that I accept the casualty count. We can educate men and women about healthy and functional behaviors and we can provide treatment for victims and offenders. To do more is to limit the freedom of the majority.

"For instance, when the rape rate went up in Israel several years ago, some Israelis suggested a curfew for women: Men were raping, so they thought by restricting women, rape would be reduced. In a sense, that's the logic of some commissioners.''

Such was her alienation from the process that she permitted Professor Schauer to play with the social-science evidence. During the final deliberations, instead of vying with his contention that pornography led to sexual violence, she saved her dissent for her personal statement.

297

If Dr. Becker acquits pictures from sparking erotic fire storms between man and woman, what is the cause of rape? What are the real motivating factors which turn a penis into a dangerous weapon? "For some men, it's prior victimization," she said. "Forty percent of the adult men that we have seen had been sexually victimized themselves when they were children. On some level these rapists need to attain a mastery over their own past. I'm speculating now— though I am trying to get the data—but I think that some men gain mastery by changing it around in their fantasies. For example, when they reach adolescence, they fantasize abusing somebody else and thereby feel in control. Then they masturbate to these deviant fantasies. They may seek out material about which they have already imagined or were already exposed to. And some will find an opportunity to rape and do it. So the dynamics are very complex.

"If you take away all the sexually explicit material in our society, I am not naive enough to suppose that prohibition is going to stop people from committing sex crimes."

But would a ban reduce the body count?

"I don't even know that," she said.

Would a less eroticized environment at least reduce sex harassment?

"No," she said. "Look back in history. Men were raping women and molesting children long before videos or color centerfolds."

Violence is Dr. Becker's greatest worry—in the media and society. The research of Donnerstein and Malamuth has persuaded her that the combination of sex *and* violence rather than sex alone is far more problematic. "Everybody says that violence is the big issue in our society, and yet Congress has just voted to liberalize gun control."

Apart from the intellectual aberrations of her peers, Dr. Becker was appalled by the manipulations of Henry Hudson and Alan Sears. Items the commissioners had dismissed kept surfacing at business meetings. Recommendations

298

which were never discussed or voted on would mysteriously appear in a draft. But what upset her the most was the deference Hudson paid to Sears at the final session in Washington. It was a humiliating scene. Sears lost much face when the majority decided to dump his embarrassing draft in favor of the more sophisticated Schauer report. Yet Hudson continually invited Sears' opinion on conflicts between the Schauer report and the staff document. Dr. Becker resented the apparent elevation of the boy prosecutor to commissioner status. She almost expressed her objections out loud to the chairman but once again held back.

To Dr. Becker's disappointment and the commission's lasting shame, her colleagues in porn dismissed the best antidote to the perceived poison of explicit images—sex education. She pointed out that Donnerstein and Malamuth both endorsed education as a means to alter negative attitudes about women. They "debrief" their test subjects after dosing them with *Tool Box Murders* and recommend similar detoxification efforts instead of censorship.

But their advice was ignored. Over the objections of Deanne Tilton, Ellen Levine and Dr. Becker herself, the commission voted to keep quiet on sex education. Dr. Becker recalled the colloquy in Scottsdale when family advocate James Dobson led the charge against the enlightenment of little ones. "Dobson said, 'What would happen if a child stood up in a first-grade classroom after hearing a good touch/bad touch lecture and said, "My uncle molested me last week"? What would that mean?'

"And I said, 'Jim, it would mean that the teacher had done an effective job of teaching about sexual use and sexual abuse.'

"And Diane Cusack said, 'Well, I think we ought to be giving sex education to parents and teachers instead.'

" 'And who do you think is doing the abusing?' I replied.

"I was appalled," she remarked. "I remember coming

back to the Institute and saying to the people here, you are not going to believe what happened to sex education in Scottsdale.''

Among the Meese commissioners, Dr. Becker was probably the most sensitive to the anguish of sex victims and the most knowledgeable on the pathology of sex offenders. And yet, all but Levine were deaf to pleas to tell the truth about pornography and crime.

ELLEN LEVINE: NOT LA PASIONARIA

Ellen Levine was a worm in the bud, but she did not burrow swiftly or deeply. Despite her stand in Scottsdale and her joint dissent with Dr. Becker, she feels that she let her side down. As the sole media person on the panel, she carried the hopes of the liberal intelligentsia, who reflexively disdain the sexual politics of Meese country. Although she suspected that a new commission would probably lean away from the 1970 panel, she was encouraged to sign up by colleagues at CBS and a close friend at Harvard's Kennedy School of Government. But the role of La Pasionaria of porn did not suit her temperamentally or professionally. Instead she satisfied herself with loyal opposition until it was too late.

Just before the final deliberations in Washington, one of her liberal critics wrote her a Class II note along the same line:

It is a pity that the prison Henry and boys built before your very eyes, with a lot of help from cops and victims, may withstand the huffs and puffs of the dissenters. The good guys (almost all girls) waited too long. While Henry was assiduous in foreplay, you were protecting your intellectual virtue by holding back the big prize. And now that Henry has ejaculated prematurely, you got to lie on the wet spot.

300

Ellen Levine: *best-dressed;* Cosmo *girl in 1970s, now editor of* Woman's Day *and V.P. of CBS Magazines; Helmut Newton fan; close to Senator Bill Bradley; lives with physician husband; early 40s; strongly dissented from majority but collaborated with killjoy agenda.*

Apparently Levine agreed with these sentiments.

"I have to say that I hold myself personally accountable for some of the lack of progress," she said during a conversation in her Times Square office. "I should have come to some of my conclusions sooner rather than later. On the other hand, the formats of the hearings—what evidence would be heard, where and when—were carved out very early. Not until later did I understand what we were missing. I made several attempts to redirect the inquiry, but I was not successful. I should have been a lot noisier."

What disappointed Levine the most was the abysmal intellectual level of the investigation. Compared to the 1970 effort, whose seriousness she admires, Henry Hudson's sequel was mickey-mouse. "If you're going to discuss the connection between pornography and antisocial behavior, you must begin by defining both terms," she said. "Let's assume that antisocial behavior means criminal behavior. Then you have to ask: 1) What makes a criminal, and 2) What are the crime statistics? You have to start from the bottom, not from the middle or top. We had no cinder blocks, that's what bothered me."

301

On the other hand, Levine is convinced that the attempt to define antisocial acts would have foundered on the personal morality and aesthetics of the commissioners. "If you believe that premarital sex is antisocial behavior, your position on pornography will be different from somebody who considers rape antisocial."

Levine was likewise exasperated by the neglect of fundamental questions about the appeal of pornography. Why do people find pictures of sex so enjoyable? "The commission did not pursue this avenue at all," she said. "It was a major fault, a major fault. There was no discussion of the genesis of sexual arousal, whether it is different in men and women, whether women are aroused by this material, whether they feel guilty about it, whether there's any difference between reading Anaïs Nin and *Penthouse*. We didn't talk about these issues at all, but we should have."

Levine was surely the most relaxed commissioner in the pornographic zone, the most likely to possess a private collection of erotica. Although she was repulsed by the violent specimens viewed at the hearings and advocates prosecution of bloody obscenity, her eyes do not automatically close when private parts are splashed on page and screen.

The wailing of Andrea Dworkin, which drove Dr. Dietz to tears, did not move her greatly. Nor did she accept Professor Schauer's incredible expansion of degrading pornography from scatology to high-fashion advertising. "I don't find those ads degrading," she said. "I know some women do, but I don't."

Putting razor to delta was not irredeemable either. "There were some things on Fred's list that I could imagine not being degrading at all. For example, a man shaving a woman's pubic hair."

Levine is not unaware of the irony that all the male commissioners hung tight on porn while the females split down the middle. The Magnificent Seven bonded together to save women from the marauding erotomaniacs of their sex.

302

"There's nothing unusual in that," she kidded. "They try to save us from working too hard as well. Didn't Torval try to save Nora?"

Levine will not say that her association with the commission was a complete mistake. "I wish that I had had a more fruitful year," she allowed. "You learn from everything you do."

As for the report, she wished it instant oblivion. "I think nothing's going to happen, absolutely nothing. My feeling is that the Justice Department is going to dissociate itself from the report. And the first step in that direction is releasing it on July 3rd. Short of Christmas Eve, I can't think of a less auspicious day to release a report." (The report, which follows, was eventually released on July 19, 1986.)

THE BECKER-LEVINE REPORT

In accepting appointments to the Attorney General's Commission on Pornography, we both believed that stimulation of a national dialogue and debate on this very controversial subject was well within the purview of the government and in the best interests of the country. To this challenging commitment we bring very different personal and professional expertise. Dr. Judith Becker is a behavioral scientist whose career has been devoted to evaluating and treating victims and perpetrators of sexual crimes. Ms. Ellen Levine is a journalist and editor who has focused on women's news. Although our backgrounds are different, we have found throughout the hearings and Commission meetings that we share similar views about the nature of the testimony presented and alternative ways in which the issue of obscenity might be approached. We have, therefore, decided to submit this joint statement.

I. The Process
During its public hearings, the Commission has accomplished much, garnered some press attention, and, as antic-

ipated, created a certain amount of controversy. Our hope is that the past year's work will not end with the publication of this report, but will begin a process of discovery and disciplined study of the complicated problems associated with this subject.

We would be remiss, however, if we did not point out the limitations inherent in the investigative process we have just finished, because in some serious ways, the Commission's methods themselves have hindered the adequate pursuit of information.

A. THE LIMITATION OF THE PUBLIC FORUM: All meetings and hearings have been held as public forums, according to law, and although we do not suggest that it should have been otherwise, we must emphasize that such an open forum naturally inhibits a frank and full discussion of a subject as personal, private and emotionally volatile as the consumption of pornography. In collecting the testimony of victims, it was difficult enough to find witnesses willing to speak out about their intimate negative experiences with pornography. To find people willing to acknowledge their personal consumption of erotic and pornographic materials and comment favorably in public about their use has been nearly impossible. Since such material is selling to millions of apparently satisfied consumers, it seems obvious that the data gathered is not well balanced.

B. THE CONSTRAINTS OF TIME AND MONEY: A number of factors directly affecting the Commission complicated its work and strained its abilities to work as thoroughly and effectively as it might have. Both the time and the money needed to work through these complications was lacking and hence they were largely unsolved.

1. The very word pornography, with its negative connotation, imposes impediments to an open-minded and objective investigation. Every member of the group brought suitcases full of prior bias, including previous personal exposure, religious, ethical, social, and even professional

beliefs. To some a discussion of pornography raises concerns of sincerely and deeply felt moral imperatives; to others it is a feminist issue of violence against women; and to still others, it is a lightning rod attracting debates about First Amendment guarantees with the threat of censorship seen as the overriding danger. Full airing of the differences of the members of the Commission and establishment of a wide and firm common ground was not possible in the time and with the funds allotted.

2. The issue of pornography has confounded people for centuries and has long been a subject of sincere disagreement among decent people. Pornography has religious, ethical, social, psychological and legal ramifications. The idea that eleven individuals studying in their spare time could complete a comprehensive report on so complex a matter in so constricted a time frame is simply unrealistic. No self-respecting investigator would accept conclusions based on such a study, and unfortunately the document produced reflects these inadequacies.

3. The variety of pornography, in its forms, qualities, and intensities of expression is vast. The Commission concentrated almost exclusively on formulating recommendations aimed at law enforcement. While that fulfills the Commission's mandate, we believe that the core issues involving pornography and its prevalence are more usefully viewed as health and welfare concerns. As such, they would properly be matters for research by committees established by the National Institute of Mental Health.

Given the varied backgrounds of the commissioners, the depth and complications of the subject historically, and the variety of the materials available today, the Commission's most severe limitation was imposed by a lack of time and money to complete a thorough study. Because it has been sixteen years since the last Commission on this topic met and it is likely to be years before another government group tangles with these questions, we believe it would have been reasonable to grant the group, if not more money, at least more time, as requested.

II. The Mandate

A. The first element of the Commission's mandate was the assessment of the problem's dimensions. While there is little doubt about the proliferation of pornography since 1970, no serious effort has been made to quantify the increase, either in general or specifically as to the various types of pornography sold. We do not even know whether or not what the Commission viewed during the course of the year reflected the nature of most of the pornographic and obscene material in the market; nor do we know if the materials shown us mirror the taste of the majority of consumers of pornography. The visuals, both print and video, were skewed to the very violent and extremely degrading. While one does not deny the existence of this material, the fact that it dominated the materials presented at our hearings may have distorted the Commission's judgment about the proportion of such violent material in relation to the total pornography material in distribution.

The Commission's investigations did reveal that technological innovations have created a new delivery system for the consumption of pornographic and erotic material (notably via home video and cable). Since the home video industry is still young, it is reasonable to assume that the supply and public demand for pornographic materials may increase. Some recent industry figures actually show video purchases and rentals of pornography on the increase. There is, however, a significant corresponding decrease in both the number of adult theaters in this country and the circulation figures of the so-called skin magazines. This may indicate that although there is a change in the way in which pornography is purchased, there is actually a stable (non-growth) market for it. We simply do not know.

Because of the stunning change in the way in which people now receive erotic stimuli (a shift from print to video), we suggest that research be conducted to discover whether and to what extent video makes a greater or stronger impression on the vulnerable users, particularly children and adolescents, than does print.

B. One critical concern of this Commission was to measure and assess pornography's role in causing antisocial behavior; but although the Commission struggled mightily to agree on definitions of such basic terms as pornography and erotica, it never did so. This failure to establish definitions acceptable to all members severely limited our ability to come to grips with the question of impact. Only the term "obscenity," which has a legal meaning, became a category we all understood. In fact, the commission failed to carve out a mutually satisfactory definition of antisocial behavior. In this statement, it should be noted, therefore, we use the phrase "antisocial behavior" to describe forced sexual acts: acts involving coercion of any kind or lack of consent. We do not include (as certain commissioners desired) such private sexual practices as masturbation, homosexuality between consenting adults or premarital sex, practices that are not the province of government to regulate.

C. The final responsibility of the Commission was to recommend to the Attorney General specific measures to limit the spread of pornography. While much of the Commission's time was spent on these proposals, only the child pornography recommendations received thorough discussion. Accordingly we strongly endorse those proposals.

We reiterate our strong belief that the paucity of certain types of testimony, including dissenting expert opinion and the haste and absence of significant debate with which other recommendations and their supporting arguments were prepared did not leave adequate time for full and fair discussions of many of the more restrictive and controversial proposals. Consequently, while we endorse many of these rec-

307

ommendations, we dissent on some, for reasons of critical policy differences, lack of clarity and more importantly, because evidence essential to a considered evaluation of the proposals was not presented.

For example, the concept of mandatory sentencing supported in several recommendations is a theory hotly debated by both law enforcement personnel and experts specializing in penal reform. Little testimony was heard on the merits or liabilities of this concept with the exception of pleas from understandably frustrated prosecutors discouraged by light sentencing. Without reasoned assessment of this problem, we cannot support the proposal for mandatory sentencing. Other specific recommendations with which we disagree will follow here.

CONGRESS SHOULD ENACT A FORFEITURE STATUTE TO REACH THE PROCEEDS AND INSTRUMENTS OF ANY OFFENSE COMMITTED IN VIOLATION OF THE FEDERAL OBSCENITY LAWS.

CONGRESS SHOULD AMEND THE FEDERAL OBSCENITY LAWS TO ELIMINATE THE NECESSITY OF PROVING TRANSPORTATION IN INTERSTATE COMMERCE. THE LAWS SHOULD BE ENACTED TO ONLY REQUIRE PROOF THAT THE DISTRIBUTION OF THE OBSCENE MATERIAL "AFFECTS" INTERSTATE COMMERCE.

CONGRESS SHOULD ENACT LEGISLATION MAKING IT AN UNFAIR BUSINESS PRACTICE AND AN UNFAIR LABOR PRACTICE FOR ANY EMPLOYER TO HIRE INDIVIDUALS TO PARTICIPATE IN COMMERCIAL SEXUAL PERFORMANCES.

STATE LEGISLATURES SHOULD AMEND, IF NECESSARY, OBSCENITY STATUTES TO ELIMINATE MIS-

DEMEANOR STATUS FOR SECOND OFFENSES AND MAKE ANY SECOND OFFENSE PUNISHABLE AS A FELONY.

STATE LEGISLATURES SHOULD ENACT, IF NECESSARY, FORFEITURE PROVISIONS AS PART OF THE STATE OBSCENITY LAWS.

THE PRESIDENT'S COMMISSION ON UNIFORM SENTENCING SHOULD CONSIDER A PROVISION FOR A MINIMUM OF ONE YEAR IMPRISONMENT FOR ANY SECOND OR SUBSEQUENT VIOLATION OF FEDERAL LAW INVOLVING OBSCENE MATERIAL THAT DEPICTS ADULTS.

LEGISLATURES SHOULD CONDUCT HEARINGS AND CONSIDER LEGISLATION RECOGNIZING A CIVIL REMEDY FOR HARMS ATTRIBUTABLE TO PORNOGRAPHY.

ANY FORM OF INDECENT ACT BY OR AMONG "ADULTS ONLY" PORNOGRAPHIC OUTLET PATRONS SHOULD BE UNLAWFUL.

III. Testimony on Social Science Data

We have limited our comments here to the relatively bias-free testimony and social-science data.

Our interpretation of the material presented is, consequently, somewhat different from that of other commission members. It has lead us to a different emphasis in priorities and recommendations.

The Commission sought to break down pornography into the various types of sexually explicit material available in our society. Unfortunately, social science research to date has not uniformly followed any such categorization (although we certainly suggest that future researchers consider

309

this option), and the attempt to force the available social science data to fit the Commission's categories is fruitless. That is why in this statement the conclusions and interpretations of what the social science data *says* and *does not say* follow the research, not the Commission, categories.

First, it is essential to state that the social science research has not been designed to evaluate the relationship between exposure to pornography and the commission of sexual crimes; therefore efforts to tease the current data into proof of a causal link between these acts simply cannot be accepted. Furthermore, social science does not speak to harm, on which this Commission report focuses. Social science research speaks of a relationship among variables or effects that can be positive or negative.

Research has evaluated adults rather than children, and it is the latter who are most likely to be influenced by pornography. Studies have relied almost exclusively on male college student volunteers, which means that the "generalizability" of this data is extremely limited. The only other category studied in depth is sex offenders. Information from the sex-offender population must be interpreted with care because it may be self-serving. The research conducted to date has been correlational and experimental. Despite these limitations, the research data can be interpreted to indicate the following:

A. In a laboratory setting, exposure to sexually violent stimuli has a negative effect on research subjects as measured by acceptance of rape myth and aggression and callousness toward women. We do not know, however, how long this attitudinal change is sustained without further stimulation; more importantly, we do not know whether and why such an attitudinal change might transfer into a behavioral change. There is reason for concern about these findings because we do know that experience with sex offenders indicates they harbor belief systems and attitudes consistent with deviant sexual practices (e.g. "women enjoy being raped'' or ''sexual acts with a child are a way of showing love and affection to that child''). We know further that such attitudes appear to be a precursor and maintainer of actual deviant behavior in an offender population. Although we believe the potential exists for attitudinal changes to translate into behavioral changes in some circumstances, this possibility needs considerable additional investigation.

B. Very little social-science research has been conducted evaluating the impact of non-violent degrading material on the average adult. Furthermore, there is a problem of definition about what constitutes ''degrading material.'' We strongly encourage further research to define and evaluate the impact of such material.

C. Although research findings are far from conclusive, the preponderance of existing data indicates that non-violent and non-degrading sexually explicit material does not have a negative effect on adults.

D. In documents attached to the main report mention has been made of a possible relationship between circulation rates of pornographic magazines and sex crime rates. One of the authors of the study on which the Commission has based its conclusion, Murray Straus, has written to explain his own research, which he suggested was being misinterpreted. ''I do not believe that this research demonstrates that pornography causes rape . . . . In general the scientific evidence clearly indicates that if one is concerned with the effects of media on rape, the problem lies in the prevalence of violence in the media, not on sex in the media.''

E. To date there is no single comprehensive theory that is agreed upon to explain the development of paraphilic behavior. Human behavior is complex and multi-causal. To say that exposure to pornography in and of itself causes an individual to commit a sexual crime is simplistic, not supported by the social science data, and overlooks many of the other variables that may be contributing causes. Research

311

must be conducted on the development of sexual interest patterns if we are to understand and control paraphilic behavior.

F. Unfortunately, little is known about the impact of sexually explicit material on children. Ethically and morally one could not and would not conduct experiments to examine such a relationship. We do know that adolescents and young adults are large consumers of these materials, and little is yet known about its impact on this population. We underscore the statement made in the main body of the Commission's report regarding social science research: "In many respects, research is still at a fairly rudimentary stage, and with few attempts to standardize categories of analysis, self-reporting questionnaires, types of stimulus materials, description of stimulus materials, measurement of effects and related problems. We recommend that moneys be made available to fund further research on this topic."

IV. Enforcement Priorities

We have been encouraged by testimony from federal, state, and local officials that those involved in the heinous crime of child pornography are being prosecuted vigorously and that this effort is a national priority. We applaud that action and believe that this prosecution should continue to be a number one priority in law enforcement resource allotments.

On the other hand, we have heard frequently that there is virtually no enforcement of adult obscenity laws. Our analysis of the data leads us to believe that the sexually violent material that is unquestionably obscene and described in the main report is of sufficient concern to warrant intensified prosecution. We are concerned about such material because the violence and the eroticization of that violence may indeed be a potentially explosive mix. Even in this category, however, social science research does not claim a causal link.

The social science data, however, provides even less basis for the claim of a causal link between non-violent degrading and humiliating pornography and sexual violence. One might assume that this material may teach offensive, though not necessarily criminal, behavior to certain vulnerable consumers.

Accordingly, in communities where standards so dictate, prosecution of non-violent degrading obscene materials may assume a lesser priority. It is in this area of non-violent degrading and humiliating pornographic images that the most controversy may arise. What is seen as degrading by one viewer may in fact not be so seen by another, much in the same way that one person's erotica is another's pornography. But this is one of the categories about which much needs to be learned. Perhaps there is a distinct difference between what men see as degrading to women and what women consider to be degrading.

As vital as this category of non-violent degrading material may be to the ultimate understanding of the effects of pornographic material in society, we caution against an overinclusive interpretation of it. The Report suggests that most of the pornographic material in circulation now belongs in this category. We have not been able to draw this conclusion based on evidence presented. As stated earlier, attempts to quantify the materials in circulation and the particular character of the content of that material remain only "guesstimates."

V. What of Our Children?

The most disturbing issue facing the panel this year was the concern about children and their exposure to child and adult pornography. Adolescents are acknowledged as an enormous market for pornographic materials, and despite legislative efforts to restrict access, this material remains easily available to youngsters.

In fact, from an early age American children are bombarded by very stimulating sexual messages, most of which are not pornographic but certainly are frightening. This year, for example, the AIDS epidemic has prompted health officials to broadcast urgent radio and television warnings against homosexual anal intercourse and group sex and pleas for the use of condoms.

Because children may have trouble with these very public messages, and because too many young people get too much of their sex education from pornographic magazines and films, we strongly support relevant school sex education programs. Appropriate and accurate information about loving sexual experiences can help inoculate children against the potential damage from early exposure to negative images. Furthermore, we urge parents to monitor carefully their own children's exposure to these materials.

There cannot be enough done to protect our children—both from people who would abuse and seduce them into the abhorrent world of child pornography and from the unwelcome intrusion of too many sexual messages. And we urge that child pornography prosecutions be given priority over all other forms of obscenity violations.

VI. Conclusion

Why does pornography thrive and proliferate today? Is the demand for pornography a mirror or a beacon? Why do consumers support a multi-million dollar market for such a variety of products? Is lack of vigorous law enforcement to blame? Is society more tolerant of pornography than ever before? Is society's perception of what constitutes pornography changing? Do the production and increasing sophistication of sexually explicit materials in themselves stimulate more interest in pornographic magazines, films and videos? Or vice-versa? Or are other social forces chiefly to blame?

The most knowledgeable observers suggest that these are complex and difficult questions, ones that cannot be easily answered and which in our opinions this Commission did not adequately address.

Consider what has occurred during the past two decades. The birth control pill has become widely used, with an associated increase in sexual activity. The mobility of the population continues to increase, with a subsequent breakdown in community attachments for more and more people. The divorce rate has skyrocketed. We have a national drug abuse problem. The Vietnam war has taken its toll on the national psyche. Twenty-five million additional women have joined the work force. The so-called Sexual Revolution has come and gone. (*Time* magazine on April 9, 1984 announced its demise). Has not each of these factors and others had a role to play in the growth of pornography?

After a year of forums and deliberations, it is tempting to join in offering simple solutions to complex problems, in the form of the Commission's Recommendations. But we are not persuaded to do so. We believe it would be seriously misleading to read this report and see a green light for prosecuting all pornographers. We still know too little about why many men and some women use and enjoy pornography; if and why women's and men's sexual arousal response patterns to pornography differ. We still have more questions than answers, and we stress the need for both non-governmental solutions and tolerance for the views of others.

The commission of sexual crimes, the degradation of women, and the abuse and mistreatment of children are terrible and pressing problems that concern us urgently. As we face up to the extensive public consumption even of certain types of extreme pornographic materials, a need for massive public re-education about potential problems associated with them seems strongly indicated. We cannot tolerate messages of sexual humiliation directed to any group. But to make all pornography the scapegoat is not constructive. In the absence of significant social sanctions against pornography, the possibility of halting its use seems as slim as was the chance of halting the sales of liquor during Prohibition. In conclusion we repeat that we face a complex social and legal problem that requires extensive study before realistic remedies can be recommended.

16

THANKS FOR THE MEMORIES

The attorney general's commissioners hacked their way through America's sexual underbrush for a year. They discovered a few things along the way that startled, amazed and puzzled them. And this is not surprising. For the most part, the prudish majority was seeing fresh stimuli. But old hands in obscenity, like Alan Sears, bore the burden well.

"I had some pretty strong foundational beliefs about sex before I ever got involved in this," Sears told the *Washington Post*.

"This is a terrible analogy, maybe, but just because you're in a car wreck, does that change your attitude about cars? No, it doesn't change your attitude about cars."

Herewith, a few of the more memorable moments of the Meese commission:

C'mon, Everybody Does It

Of the 208 witnesses who went before the commission, only one said that he used pornography to help him masturbate and was glad he did. Dennis Sobin, the president of the First Amendment Consumer and Trade Society, let it all hang out.

"I first became interested in erotic materials when, as a typical teenager, my sexual curiosity and frustration was at its peak. The materials . . . proved to be a valuable masturbation aid which helped me relieve tension and frustration, enabling me to concentrate on my studies, which I excelled in—the studies, not the masturbation, by the way."

Sobin fondly remembered 1968—the year he saw his first porn film. "It featured sexual activities which were normal for me at the time, except for one scene that I thought was very bizarre. I told my wife [of three years] about it and she laughed and called me a jerk, saying that she wished I would try that scene on her. The scene showed a woman having an orgasm, something that I did not know was possible before seeing that film, and something my own wife was too embarrassed to tell me."

The compulsively honest witness went on to make a serious allegation. "The great majority of us—I dare say the president and the First Lady included, enjoy sex and have erotic fantasies."

The White House did not issue a denial.

Got a Light?

Miami vice cop Mike Berish told commissioners that his

line of work keeps him on his toes. The detective spends lots of time in peep-show booths watching eight-millimeter films. The clientele of many of these establishments is "primarily a homosexual-type crowd," he testified. "They not only go there to watch the movie, but it's a cheap place for sex, and they usually have two of the guys who get in the booths and they will perform sexual acts there.

"It's extremely difficult to work these places sometimes," complained Sergeant Berish, "because I'm not there to bust people for lewd and lascivious conduct. I am there to make cases against the films.

"Now, I have to sit there with a tape recorder and I have to watch the entire film.

"I am pretty occupied, and it becomes a little bit of a hindrance when you have these homosexuals reaching through the sides of the booths trying to perform sexual acts on you."

What does Sergeant Berish do to ward off these unwanted advances? He reaches for a Don Diego. "I smoke cigars so that whenever they reach through the booth, I just hit them on the edge of their hand with a cigar.

"This way," he said, "I am able to maintain my train of thought."

Gee, Brooke, What's That Stubble on Your Chin?

Alan Sears was talking about the peep shows in Houston when he got into his homosexuality rap.

"We were told, I believe, that there was a significant amount of homosexual activity [at these establishments] but also a lot of heterosexuals who engaged in acts which were between two males, and would, I suppose, be classified as homosexual activities, but they were not homosexuals engaged in those acts. It was anonymous sex."

Ellen Levine thought Sears' wires were crossed.

"What's the definition of 'homosexual,' then, Alan?"

she asked gingerly.

"A person," said Sears, "who wanted as a preferred partner a member of the same sex." So far so good.

The folks in the peep shows, he explained, "don't prefer a same-sex member but are simply seeking a sexual release through a hole in the wall. They are not homosexual if there happens to be a male at the other end."

Just their rotten luck, we suppose.

Dr. Dietz's Greatest Lines (Part One)

Degrading porn was the topic. Did people see fisting movies and then run out and stick their arms God knows where? Dr. Dietz said that only certain depicted activities were a matter of concern.

"In other words, this is only a problem if one thinks that it's a bad thing to encourage those behaviors that were construed as degrading; and that's an issue on which there would not be much societal consensus."

"Would you give us an example?" Ellen Levine asked.

"Sure," said Dr. Dietz. "I think more people would agree it's bad to encourage rape than it's bad to encourage ejaculation in the face."

"One's a felony," said the chairman.

"Maybe both should be," said Diane Cusack.

Dr. Dietz's Greatest Lines (Part Two)

At the public hearings in Los Angeles, Dr. Dietz questioned Jack Valenti, the chief executive officer of the Motion Picture Association of America. He wanted to know how violent a film had to be before an X was slapped on. Or as the inimitable criminologist phrased it:

Could Valenti "confirm my impression that the quantity of blood it takes to fill a penis, and therefore earn an X

320

rating on sexual grounds, is considerably smaller than the quantity of blood that needs to be splattered for a film to be X-rated on violence grounds''?

Valenti admitted that the doctor was correct.

Honey, Are You Going to Be in There All Night?

Alan Sears relished reporting on the most outrageous discoveries of his intrepid six-city adult-bookstore tour. At a very late-night business session in Scottsdale, the boyish Kentuckian insisted that the federal panel had to do something about the ''literature of enemas.''

Say what?

Sears had an example ready: ''One close-up photograph of a Caucasian female with a douche bag inserted in her nose, extending through her legs to her anus.''

As commissioners pondered the width and breadth of this troubling subgenre, Sears had a few more deviations to share.

''A photograph of a Caucasian female wearing a full head and constrictive mask, supporting a black dildo between her labia . . . .''

Chairman Hudson said, Whoa. ''I think there's enough there to warrant further discussion. Let's do it first thing tomorrow morning,'' he said to Sears.

A few commissioners slept fitfully in Arizona that night. Eventually they tossed the enemas into Class II and condemned them.

And Improperly, It's Still Pretty Good!

Father Ritter did not want the commission to be a total downer. In the midst of debate over Class IV—nudity—the Franciscan boomed: ''It's high time we said that sex is beautiful, it's glorious, and nudity is absolutely marvelous in its proper perspective and should and must be celebrated."

"Love it," chuckled Dr. Dobson.

"It can become the motto of the nudist colonies," grinned Dr. Dietz.

Wife Swapping and the New York Review of Books

"Our next topic involves 'swinger magazines,' " a weary Henry Hudson told commissioners at a late hour in Scottsdale. He asked for comments.

Dr. Dietz, his nose close to the forensic grindstone, piped up that there were "well-documented instances in which people have been victimized through these publications." He specifically mentioned a book from the 50s entitled *The Lonely Heart Murders* and the sordid case of a Canadian couple who ran swingers' clubs and murdered a customer as well as a member of the Royal Canadian Mounted Police.

Tex Lezar remembered real-life swinging casualties. "We did hear women who testified that their husbands got the idea that wife-swapping would be fun from these magazines and told them they were going to be swapped as well."

Father Ritter did not consider the topic a major concern but noted for the hell of it that swinging represented a "formal attack upon the institution of marriage."

Dr. Dietz wondered where you drew the line. "I mean, the *New York Review of Books* has ads in the back saying 'Jewish sensuous female desires romance at lunch hour with sensuous opera lover.' "

Chairman Hudson was sorry he ever brought up the topic and moved the discussion on.

No one argued.

Back in the Late 20s, the Mob Pushed All the James Joyce It Could

The lengths to which the commission went to link pornography to organized crime were extraordinary. One of the panel's star witnesses, retired FBI agent William Kelly, had no doubts about the porn-underworld connection.

"Where else but from organized crime could a retailer obtain sexually explicit materials to sell to customers?

"I am talking about the hard-core stuff, where a producer or distributor of hard-core materials possesses an office, toll-free telephone numbers, a warehouse a half a block or a block in size, a raft of traveling salesmen and possibly even a fleet of his own trucks.

"I call that highly organized business interests, and when it's dealing in legally obscene materials, I call it organized crime."

Thanks for the Adulteries

Father Ritter and the staff put together the religious-witness list for the New York hearings. Whoever selected Mrs. June Griffin, an officer of the Cumberland Missionary Society, was playing with fire.

The cannibal-converter from Evansville, Tennessee, came on like Sissy Spacek's mom in *Carrie*: "I would say to this panel that in America since the reign of Hollywood and Madison Avenue and its system of temple virgins, thousands of brides have experienced spiritual death, along with their husbands. The designers who have hated what God created—a man and woman who are dependent upon Him for their help—these carpenters have taken their lines and planes and compasses and designed what they decide the ideal man or woman is. These designers and distributors have destroyed marriages of those who follow their pornographic system of gods."

The righteous Mrs. Griffin even went after Old Ski Nose

for promoting promiscuity: "Bob Hope, with his adulterous troops, has promoted the soldier image as one whose wife waits patiently for him while he takes a break at the USO clubs."

Hope Enterprises' spokesman Frank Liberman said he was "stunned" at the "preposterous" charge, adding "I won't dignify that with further comment."

No Virginia, Not in Virginia

Hudson was not a wild and crazy fellow. In an interview with Robert Scheer of the L.A. *Times,* the commonwealth's attorney took a hard line against a lot of enjoyable sex acts. For example, Scheer asked him for a definition of pornography. "It's any portrayal which is designed to be sexually arousing, which depicts sodomy, sexual degradation, humiliation or violence," Hudson answered.

Why sodomy? he was asked.

"Sodomy," Hudson responded, "is any unnatural act. Bestiality, cunnilingus, fellatio—these are violations of common law, which are still unlawful in most states. In fact, they are felonies in Virginia." (So much for the state tourist board's "Virginia is for Lovers" theme.)

Even within the privacy of marriage?

"Right; I don't make the laws, I enforce them," said the Eichmann of the erotic police.

17

THE SHADOW COMMISSION

O f course, not all thinking Americans agree with the narrow views of the Meese commission. We solicited the opinions of 11 other citizens—feminists, journalists, sex therapists, civil libertarians—who have considered the Attorney General's report.

Like the panel Meese selected, ours is composed of seven men and four women. Unlike the government investigators, this body abhors censorship and is willing to consider erotica dispassionately and without bias. Herewith the report of our Shadow Commission.

BETTY FRIEDAN

A Feminist Diversion

I generally take a dim view of censorship attempts on pornography. I don't like them. It's a dangerous diversion of feminism. Some pornography is disgusting, some is just plain boring, yet some people may find it titillating. That's not the point. And some of it degrades not only women but sex and man altogether. It's a dehumanization of sex, defining sex as dirty, which isn't good for sex—or for life. All this is simply beside the point. Porn doesn't really hurt anybody.

But what is truly dangerous and harmful is any attempt to undermine the basic constitutional protections of freedom of speech in this country. The far Right and the church want to suppress that freedom. In subtle and overt ways, they want to suppress the absolutely basic and essential American right of dissent, without which we would never have had, for instance, the women's movement.

The danger to feminism, and to women as people, as Americans, is this threat to suppress free speech. In that respect, no matter how repulsive anybody might find any part of pornography, it is simply dangerous to join those right-wing forces who are using pornography to undermine civil liberties, and who, if they had their way, would, for instance, outlaw textbooks that show women in nontraditional roles. In fact, they would outlaw women's very basic right to choose when and whether and how many times to bear a child.

Another fear I have, as far as feminism is concerned, is that attacking pornography is a very dangerous diversion of energy. It is a very difficult job just now to preserve and defend our basic rights of empowerment and the laws protecting equality of opportunity in employment, education and the like. The Reagan administration is trying to gut these laws. Further, attacking pornography diverts energy that should be directed toward what I call the second-stage questions. By this I mean going beyond the male model of equality and obtaining maternity and paternity leave and good child care—in short, the right to give birth to children.

These basic rights of life, if you will, are what the women's movement should be concentrating on. The drive to suppress pornography is at best irrelevant to the empowerment of women, and at worst dangerous.

I am worried about this diversion of feminist energy because it has an historical precedent. After the hundred-year battle to win the vote earlier in this century, the women's movement in effect petered out. Instead of tackling basic economic issues and various realities of life where the vote is not particularly effective, it got diverted by notions of sexual purity and campaigns like Prohibition. It should have gone on to tackle the concrete and complex questions of empowerment and economic opportunity. The energies of the women's movement in the 1920s were vitiated to the point where, after a while, the very notion of women's rights became a dirty word. Equality was just too painful to dream about when women could not live it.

Most women continued to marry and have children. They worked a few years before marriage or in a national or domestic emergency, and a few exceptional women had to forego marriage and children in order to move into professions. Feminism and women's rights were suppressed until people like me came along in the 1960s to invent the wheel all over again.

It will have to be invented yet again if the women's movement, in the face of the current backlash, diverts its energies. The right wing would be delighted to see this happen. It prefers to blacken the issue of pornography instead of moving on to basic priorities like economic empower-

ment and the restructuring of women's role in the workplace
and at home.

Betty Friedan is a feminist activist and the author of The
Feminine Mystique

BARRY LYNN

Fathers Who Know Best

I spent much of the last year stalking the pornography commission, commenting regularly on their inadequacies and
criticizing the civil liberties dangers posed by many of their
proposals. The zaniness of the pornography commission
was, of course, so inspired that it will provide the grist for a
lifetime of my censorship lectures. Who can forget the FBI
agent detailing the photographs he seized in his career,
including the terrifying one of a "woman surrounded by a
vagina"? How about the commissioner discussing a recently viewed bestiality slide of a man and a chicken and who
queried, after noting it was but a "small point," whose
penis was in whom (or what)? When the laughter ends,
though, the real tragedy of the commission starts to become visible.

This body was not encumbered with the need to accept
Supreme Court-articulated limitations on the availability of
sexual material. They were writing on a clean slate and
could have chosen to repudiate, as did their predecessor
commission, the archaic constraints of "obscenity" law
and let consenting adults see what they choose, regardless
of whether their neighbors would be offended by it.

Instead, they tried to breathe new life into "obscenity"
regulation. They applauded the most dangerous reasoning
of all to suppress speech—that it generates bad "attitudes."
I'm convinced that much pornography does generate bad
attitudes, along with much in cartoon shows, floor-wax
advertising and network sitcoms. But when in this battle
against "bad attitudes" we abandon what we view as
affirmative alternative speech and turn instead to use of
governmental censorship or moral mob rule, we are all the
losers.

The commission could not really discover much more
than a smidgen of science to bolster the claims of real-life

sexual violence caused by pornography. No matter. They simply filled in the gaps of science with the legion of their own preconceptions and intuitions buttressed with some Gestalt derived from the sometimes plaintive, sometimes pathetic, voices of alleged "victims" of pornography.

Many of their "victims" were obsessed "addicts," one of whom claimed to have seen a deck of pornographic playing cards and then became obsessed with stealing *Playboy* and, finally, took to sexually abusing the family dogs; and the rapists who sought to explain away their crime and guilt by scapegoating a medium more contemporary than comic books and more plausible than the Twinkies which drove Dan White to murder. The "victims" also included women so mired in abusive relationships steeped in pathology, substance abuse and family crisis that any claimed causality from pornography was so tangential as to be nearly an invisible afterthought.

They could have endorsed things which would have made a difference to real "victims" of the rampant abuses of a still sexist culture—strengthening sexual harassment laws; removing spousal immunity in sexual-assault cases; providing real help to those actually coerced into pornography. And then to prevent the creation of future "victims," they could wholeheartedly have embraced a serious sex-education program in our schools. Instead, they launched a national crusade against dirty pictures, as if they had some magical powers to corrupt the young, obliterate the values taught by the other institutions in our culture and preserve a dying patriarchy. I am underwhelmed by pornography's power to do any of these.

They were, on balance, quintessential censors, sharing all the arrogance of censors throughout the world and throughout our history. They truly believed that they knew best what all should see about sex—and most even knew how all should "behave" sexually as well. Moreover, although they have wallowed in the worst of pornographic muck for a year and been apparently unaffected, they remain convinced that the average American would be led down the path to criminality or deviance by his or her chosen encounters with the same material.

Here is a group that says it would be "socially harmful" if people picketed the bookseller hawking *Ulysses*—a book nearly as unreadable as the turgid prose of the commission's report—but embraces with all their hearts the boycotters of stores which hustle *Penthouse* from behind the counter. Let the elite read; keep the masses from even looking. Historically, there was no "obscenity" law before the printing press finally gave average people a chance to see the sexually explicit material previously available only to the wealthy and powerful, who undoubtedly thought only they could handle it.

The 1,000-page report they wrote was so predictable, it could have been drafted the day after the commission convened and saved the taxpayers a good $500,000. But the particular way it was styled is clever to a fault, slippery enough to be cast outside if it becomes too much of a personal or professional embarrassment. It sometimes reads like a scientific discourse and occasionally like a legal treatise. Mostly, though, it crows like some elephantine moral tract passed out at the bus station.

Commissioner James Dobson told the *Washington Post* that I had "neutralized" the commission with my incessant attacks. I don't believe most of what he says elsewhere, and there is little reason to begin now. I believe it was the commission which ultimately neutralized itself—its methods for gathering evidence, evaluating it and finally reporting it were so intellectually indefensible that it sank from its own irrelevance and irresponsibility.

Barry Lynn is the legislative counsel for the American Civil Liberties Union

BARBARA EHRENREICH

Discrimination Is the Real Obscenity

I am a feminist, and my concern is primarily with the effect of pornography—or the restriction of pornography—on women and their status in society. While this was not the Meese commission's only concern, it was certainly a major one, and is reflected in the commission's conclusion that "substantial exposure to materials of this type [violent or "coercive"] bears some causal relationship to the incidence of various non-violent forms of discrimination against or subordination of women in our society." This statement, offered without evidence as a "necessarily incorporated conclusion," calls for some reflection on the actual causes of women's subordination and the likely impact on women of restricting or outlawing pornography.

First, it is worth recalling that both violence against women and nonviolent discrimination predate the emergence of the pornography industry by many centuries, perhaps millennia. There is no question that ideas degrading to women—expressed as images and text—have played a major role in reinforcing women's subordination throughout history. But in Western culture the most influential sources of sexist ideas have also been the most highly respected sources of social wisdom in general—religion and, the last century, science. Here I would mention just two of the more dangerous notions propagated by these sources: One, the biblical injunction that women "submit" to their husbands in all matters, a rule which implicitly condones various kinds of abuse, sexual and otherwise. And, two, the psychoanalytic notion, presented as a "scientific" finding, that women are inherently masochistic, and hence, presumably, willing victims of sexual violence and other forms of subordination.

Offensive as these ideas are, I would be opposed to banning material containing them or prosecuting the purveyors of such material. Even ideas that are threatening to women—and indirectly threatening to our physical safety—have a right to be heard. But the Meese commission was negligent in totally omitting from its consideration the vast amount of readily available, if not inescapable, literature—including the Bible and dozens of medical texts—that is degrading to women in a manner that many women find both dangerous and often prurient.

Second, we need to bear in mind that the single most clear-cut cause of women's victimization in the hands of individual men does not lie in the realm of ideas or images at all, but in the realm of economics. The average American woman, working full-time, year-round, earns only $13,000 a year—or 60 percent of what a man earns, hour for hour. In fact, the most common way in which women are objectified and degraded in this society is not in porn films, but as cheap labor in our factories and offices. Beyond that, it is well known that economic necessity is a major factor in women's vulnerability to sexual harassment on the job and abuse from husbands. No doubt, also, it is the lack of well-paying alternatives that drives women to work as models, prostitutes, etc., in the sex industry. (This consideration applies to children also: One out of five American children is growing up in poverty, hence with heightened vulnerability to recruitment by the child-pornography industry.)

While I realize that economic considerations may seem far afield from the purview of the commission, they have been negligent in failing to address the economic vulnerability that is the cause of so much sexual victimization. This is especially true given that the report was commissioned by the attorney general, who is responsible for enforcing labor and antidiscrimination laws, and who, in addition, represents an administration that has been relentlessly brutal in its attacks on social programs benefitting women and their dependent children.

Because the real causes of women's subordination do not

lie in pornography, restricting or eliminating it will do nothing to improve women's status. On the contrary, if pornography is defined as the commission defines it—that is, not at all—we could once again be forced into ignorance of our bodies and our sexual and reproductive functions. In its discussion of the Comstock laws, the commission's report fails to mention that the laws' most notorious application was in the harassment of early-twentieth-century birth-control reformers. Similarly, one of the chief targets of contemporary censors has been the feminist health book *Our Bodies, Ourselves*.

Finally, I wish to say that I share the commission's revulsion against violent pornography. The problem, however, is not that it is sexual, but that it is violent. Popular culture assaults us continually with images of violence, most of them, unfortunately, not even redeemed by a hint of eroticism. Beyond the imagery is the reality of a violent and belligerent foreign and military policy that terrorizes us all with the possibility of nuclear annihilation.

I cannot help but conclude that both the addictive violence of our culture and the growth of the pornography industry may in part reflect the same problem—the widespread denial of genuine erotic opportunity. The prevalence of violent imagery, in pornography and elsewhere, should lead us to reflect, above all, on the punitive and repressive attitudes our society still harbors toward sexuality and, ultimately, toward the human body itself.

Barbara Ehrenreich is a journalist and the author of For Her Own Good

HENDRIK HERTZBERG

A Political Loser

If everything had gone the way the attorney general had planned, then the report of the Meese commission would have touched off a gigantic national crusade, fronted by Right-thinking political leaders, against demon porn. For the fact that this has not happened we can thank the people of Maine.

On Tuesday, June 10, 1986, the voters of that rocky, laconic state were asked to approve or disapprove a new, four-and-a-half-page statute that for ballot purposes had been boiled down to a one-liner: "Do you want to make it a crime to make, sell, give for value or otherwise promote obscene material in Maine?" Coming shortly before the Meese release, a "yes" vote would have provided a timely fanfare. And a "yes" vote was a perfectly reasonable expectation: Maine is among the most conservative states of the Northeast. It is remote from the sophistications of urban life and possesses a noisy and powerful movement of politically active evangelicals.

The turnout was high, the vote decisive: 3-to-1 against. However much these good people may dislike smut, they plainly dislike censorship (and the busybodies who promote it) even more.

Among the politicians, true believers like Jeremiah Denton and Pat Robertson will continue to denounce porn and call for its suppression. The more opportunistic and less principled right-wingers, however, will understand that "as Maine goes, so goes the nation." Posturing against porn may not yet be quite the political equivalent of herpes, but we will see rather less of it from now on. As for the president, he may be expected to make a dutiful speech or two in order to please his friend Meese and to placate the constituency Meese represents. But the old trouper—who has a history of tolerance of sexual deviation among his Holly-

335

wood cronies, his staffers and his wife's social circle, who has a son working for a magazine built on the bare breasts and labia of the girl next door and a daughter whose novel includes the normal quota of steamy sex scenes, and who himself divorced one actress and then married another after remarking that he was tired of not knowing the name of whatever starlet he happened to wake up next to—will probably refrain from expending much of his popularity on an uncongenial issue that is now a proven political loser as well.

Still, even if the report fails to accomplish its sponsors' most ambitious aims, personal liberty may be degraded in small but tangible ways. Most of the fuss over dirty books occurs at the local level, in small cities and towns, where ad hoc groups of self-righteous citizens try to impose their own narrow preferences on the rest of the community and particularly on its schools, libraries and convenience stores.

Experience shows that these vigilante actions are almost never aimed at violent or even "hard-core" pornography. The targets are usually books that treat sex realistically or, in the case of convenience stores, magazines that publish both erotica and what might be called politica—magazines like *Penthouse* and *Playboy*. The Meese report gives local vigilantes plenty of encouragement. One doesn't need to exaggerate their likely impact to understand that it will be real enough for the schoolteachers and librarians forced to choose between their consciences and their jobs.

The commission's conclusion, as well as I can make it out through the fog of qualifications and internal contradictions, is that certain kinds of very violent pornography seem to cause "harm" (though not as much harm, they note in a moment of lucidity, as kung fu magazines or slasher movies), and that therefore the police powers of the state should be mobilized to suppress those kinds of pornography, and maybe other kinds as well.

The process by which this conclusion is reached relies on

336

a highly tenuous chain of causation. Certain college students were shown certain movies—exactly which movies, the body of the report does not say—and then were taken to mock rape trials. When questioned after the trials, they seemed to show less sympathy toward the complainants than college students who had not been shown the movies. From this it is concluded that pornography causes—well, maybe not sex crimes, exactly, maybe not even "unlawful" sexual aggressiveness, but *something*.

This is as intellectually rigorous as the commissioners get where the question of "harm" is concerned. Mostly they turn with relief to more capacious definitions. "An environment, physical, cultural, moral, or aesthetic, can be harmed," they write, "and so can a community, organization, or group be harmed independent of identifiable harms to members of that community." Broad enough? Apparently not, for in the very next sentence they add that "the idea of harm is broader than that."

Despite its many assertions to the contrary, the commission has simply failed to demonstrate that pornography is harmful. But even if some such showing could be made, it would not follow that freedom of speech and of the press ought therefore to be abridged. The First Amendment contains no requirement that the speech it protects be harmless. On the contrary, speech that somebody thinks is harmful is the only kind that needs protecting.

The commission's report will be widely read because even a government book about sex is irresistible, especially if it's as fat, as obsessed with kinky practices and as full of inadvertent humor as this one. A small but apposite example of the last: After a long section on the problem of "underprosecution," the commissioners conclude:

"We urge that many of the specific recommendations we suggest be taken seriously."

How wonderfully lame. The logically required corollary, of course, would be this:

"We urge that *some* of the recommendations we suggest *not* be taken seriously."
Though insufficiently inclusive, this seems wise.

Hendrik Hertzberg, the former editor of the New Republic, *is working on plans for a new national journal of opinion*

DR. JOHN MONEY

A Conspiracy Against Women

The Meese commission report purports to be a modern-day Saint George, slaying the evil dragon of pornography to protect women from its violent and degrading effects. But the real intent of the report is not to protect women, but to exploit them. By adopting the militant-feminist rhetoric of Catharine MacKinnon and Andrea Dworkin, the Meese commission affirms that women have no right to be sexual. They are obliged only to be loving wives committed to their men, whom they must treat not as sex, but as status and success, objects.

The Meese report turns out to be a conspiracy against women—the most furtively sexist and antifeminist document of our time. It declares that women are so morally delicate that they may not partake with men of the explicit depiction of the frankly erotic. Can you believe it? Even the sexual normalcy of the naked human body and of healthy, happy people having joyful sexual intercourse must be suppressed, lest it lead the viewer downward on the ladder of degeneracy to the warped and pathological sex of violence and degradation.

With women excluded, men will not, of course, relinquish pornography, for by nature's decree they are dependent on their eyes more than women are to get turned on sexually. As they did with alcohol under Prohibition, men will simply take pornography back to where it used to be, distributed commercially by bootleggers on the nontaxable underground market and seen in locker rooms and at stag parties restricted to men only. Women once again will be divided into Madonnas and whores, lust belonging only to the whores, not to the sexually neutered Madonnas. The deceptive purpose of the Meese report is to deny women's equality with men; and to put women back in their traditional place, unliberated, dependent on men and under men's patriarchal protection.

It is not surprising that the commission split, 9-2, and that the two dissenting voices are those of two of the four women commissioners. Ellen Levine and Judith Becker had the wit to perceive the overall effect of the report in subjugating women, and the wisdom to recognize that it is just plain foolish to attribute all the injustices of women's inequality in society to dirty pictures.

That does not mean that the two dissenting voices condone the kind of pornography which the report classifies as violent and degrading and which medicine and science classify as paraphilic and pathological. This kind of pornography is erotically useless to people who do not have the particular paraphilia that it depicts. The report singles out for special mention urophilia, the paraphilia in which a man or a woman is turned on and climaxes sexually not in the usual way, but by being urinated upon and drinking urine. People who are not urophiliacs could be locked in a viewing room and forced to watch 50 hours—or 500 hours—of urophilic movies, but they would not be turned into urophiliacs as a result of the experience. If you don't believe that statement, then try the experiment.

Paraphilias are not contagious. They are not caught from books, films or videotapes. The contagion theory is as old as the theory of witchcraft. Less than three centuries ago, people, mostly women, were being burned at the stake because of it. Today they are imprisoned—at exorbitant taxpayer expense, one should be reminded. The commission was given expert testimony on the falsity of the contagion theory, but it elected to disregard the evidence of its own experience. If the contagion theory were correct, then the commissioners should by now all be imprisoned as sex criminals, for they have been exposed to large quantities of all varieties of pornography, violent, degrading and otherwise.

By clinging to the ancient falsehood of the contagion theory, the report evades what should have been its major responsibility, namely, finding out how to prevent the development of paraphilias, especially those that it classified as violent or degrading, in the generation of children now growing up. A boy does not need to look at pornography to know what turns him on sexually. Nature presents him with his own personal pornography in his wet dreams. Developmentally, the sequence is from wet dreams and masturbation fantasies to homemade pornography that copies the dream content and possibly, as he grows older, to commercial pornography—but only if he finds the type of commercial pornography that matches his own wet-dream and masturbation fantasies. Any other type, no matter how much it may stimulate someone else, will leave him cold.

Girls at puberty do not have the same dramatic experience of seeing pornography vividly and visually as the accompaniment of a wet dream. Only a few girls have explicit sexual dreams, with orgasm, at the time of puberty. This is one reason, and a very powerful one, why females, by and large, do not understand the male's interest in and arousal by visually explicit pornography. Women's pornography is different. It is more verbal, more romantic and centered more on cuddling, hugging, kissing and the sense of touch.

Children who grow up sexually healthy develop a healthy, usually heterosexual, mental "lovemap" in their brains (see J. Money, *Lovemaps*, New York, Irvington, 1986). They become the future purchasers of normal, healthy pornography. Children, especially boys, who fail to develop a healthy lovemap are those who are sexually traumatized while growing up. The greatest single source of traumatization is the brutal punishment and humiliation of children who are discovered playing with their own genitals or engaging in normal sexual rehearsal play with playmates. Traumatic punishment of children for obeying nature's way of preparing for healthy sexuality in maturity vandalizes the

341

lovemap and either destroys it or turns it into a paraphilic one. Not unexpectedly, brutal punishment of childhood sexual rehearsal play introduces brutality and violence into the lovemap, thus creating a person who will grow up to be dependent on violence for sexual arousal and climax. This is the person who becomes a patron of violent pornography.

Because the commission does not address the issue of the origins of pornographic imagery, and because it advocates an escalation of punishment related to pornography, its report will prove to be self-defeating. Instead of protecting women, the report will have the long-range effect of actually producing an ever-expanding epidemic of violence and degradation presently evident not only in pornography, but also in reality. The next generation, and the next, will hold us all accountable.

Dr. John Money is a professor of medical psychology and pediatrics at the Johns Hopkins University and Hospital

MARCIA PALLY

Ban Sexism, Not Sex

The Meese commission's recommendations hang on the belief that pornography is the source of violence against women and children. While I am grateful for this sudden, unexpected federal concern, it seems pertinent to ask if the porn-causes-harm theory is correct: Is porn a significant factor in rape, battery and incest? Will getting rid of porn diminish violence against women and children? Or is it merely a progressive patina on old-fashioned sin-and-morality finger-wagging? After all, the porn-causes-harm argument makes the banning of books, magazines, rock and roll and video seem reasonable to millions of Americans who would laugh at threats of brimstone and hellfire. Is it a mirage, a "quick fix" that kids us into thinking the solution to abuse is just a matter of banning dirty pictures? Is it a distraction that turns our attention away from the real causes of harm and prevents us from finding solutions?

The mass-market porn industry took off only after World War II. Prior to the twentieth century, few people save the wealthy elite saw any porn whatsoever. Yet violence and sexism have been flourishing for thousands of years, and nobody needed porn to show him how to do it. Most of history's rapists, misogynists and child-abusers read nothing at all. And if we look at societies where no porn is permitted, like Saudi Arabia or Iran, we don't see societies with strong women's rights records. We find instead a great deal of violence against women. So it seems unlikely to me that sexism and rape are directly linked to sexually explicit pictures. It seems unlikely that porn initiates violence or lousy pay.

It seems more reasonable that violence against women begins with economic discrimination, so that men learn to consider women burdens and pains in the ass, and with the infantilization of women—either as fragile figurines or hormonal hurricanes—so that men hold women in contempt. It seems more reasonable that violence against women begins with "boy training," which makes aggression a daily project of masculinity, and with child-rearing arrangements that leave Mom as the prime—often only—caretaker.

It's on Mom that all one's infantile expectations are foisted and all one's earliest disappointments are blamed. Dad comes into the picture only later, as a firm but reasonable force. So we act out our desire for Mom's attention and our rage that she's not always there on all women for the rest of our lives. Though we all were raised more by Mom than by Dad in infancy, there is an edge of ire men feel about women that women don't feel because, after all, women are "us."

All this shows up in pornography, just as it does in high art, advertising and fashion. And because pornography is a genre of extremes—schematic, repetitive, ritualistic, fantastic—it exaggerates and distills our psychosexual blueprints. It blows up and illuminates our discomfort with the goo and nakedness of sex, our panic at our arousal and loss of control, and men's lust for and anger at the female figure.

But pornography didn't start any of this. And getting rid of porn won't end it. Porn may be sexist, as much of it is; it may be racist or violent, as some of it is. But it's silly to call it a cause of sexism, racism or violence. It's silly to think banning it will halt the mayhem. The anti-porn brouhaha of the last few years is a red herring. It lures us away from the sources of sexism and its solutions.

Many believers in the porn-causes-harm doctrine rely on a number of laboratory studies which suggest pornographic images affect attitudes about violence against women. But *attitudes,* as even the scientists doing this research will tell you, are notoriously poor predictors of behavior. People just don't accomplish with any statistical reliability what they say they will. And no matter what people do in an experimental setup, they know it's an experiment, make-believe. No one is really going to get hurt.

Anti-porners also cite statistics showing that convicted rapists are guilty of acts pictured in pornography. But so is the missionary position. And certainly gruesome things have been done to women for centuries without *Hustler*'s help. Still other data demonstrate that communities with more porn report more rapes. Yet higher incidences of rape are also found in areas with strong sales of any men's magazines, such as *Field & Stream*.

But what about the anecdotal evidence the commission finds so convincing? Women say their boyfriends or husbands get ideas from porn and force them to do what the photos depict. I wonder if the Meese commission would object if a man forced a woman to make lasagna. I would. The problem is not Italian cuisine or kama sutra positions. The problem is *force*—economic, psychological and physical. It is not only profligate to tell women that their problems at home begin with porn, it's dangerous. It deludes and misleads women and leaves them farther from improving the conditions of their lives. I can think of few greater treacheries.

What about the rapists and wife-batterers who say that they learned their stuff from porn? It's a clever ploy. Just look at who gets off the hook. First it was the devil that made them do it, now it's Miss Jones. And something is not quite right about the proposition that men rape because they learned—from porn—that it's okay or that women like it.

One thing feminism accomplished was the redefinition of rape from a sexual act to a violent one. But I suspect it was always clear to the rapist facing his terrified victim that she didn't "want it." Men rape because it hurts, and they do it to hurt us. If we want to deal with rape, we ought to deal with why. What's going on in "real life" that makes men want to inflict so much pain?

There is still a question nagging: Why does the anti-porn

345

argument feel so right? Why is it persuasive to so many men and women? To begin with, it offers the appeal of activism. Participants in the anti-porn crusade feel they're doing something to better women's lot, and we all need to feel effective. Psychologist Paula Webster suggests that something else is going on. She believes the anti-porn argument feels right because it carries "the voice of Mom." And she may have something here. Most of us have grown up with the idea that sex is icky; most women have grown up with the assurance that men are dangerous. We heard it indirectly or we heard it point-blank, but we heard it all our lives.

As adults, most of us manage to get our own. But the old lessons remain embedded in our imaginations and at the core of our emotions. So when we're told that pornography is icky and makes men dangerous, it "clicks." When we hear—in adult language and political terminology—things we absorbed when we were little, it sounds infallible. Already suspicious of sex, we are ready to call it culprit.

Now, there is a great deal of violence done to women— the FBI reports that a woman is beaten every 18 seconds and raped every few minutes. But rage and violence are the core of the problem, not sexually explicit images. And we must get at the core, spending our time and resources shrewdly.

The government that funded the Meese commission stopped allocations earmarked for battered-women's shelters because they were "anti-family" and ostensibly promoted lesbianism. No one is going to convince me that an administration that has rolled back affirmative action, fought against comparable worth and stripped hundreds of programs that benefit women and children opposes pornography because it's dangerous to those very same women and children.

We can't afford to be duped—either by a duplicitous government or by what "feels right." If we go after pornography when rape, battery and discrimination thrived for so long without it, we'll still be left with rape, battery and discrimination. Would that the solution to women's problems—or even to just rape—were just a matter of eliminating porn. Would that it were so single-issue, or so easy.

Marcia Pally is a member of the Feminist Anti-Censorship Taskforce.

DR. BERNIE ZILBERGELD

Porn As Therapy

Pornography has one great value that is often overlooked—
its use in enhancing marital sex. Pornography can help to
strengthen not only individual marriages, but perhaps the
very institution of marriage itself. The importance of satisfaction in a good marriage is supported by scientific
research and is recognized by many Christian ministers.
Millions of ordinary married Americans benefit from erotica and will suffer if it is taken away from them.

Why do so many people refuse to admit that keeping sex
interesting, exciting and satisfying in a long relationship is
not easy? Couples have to work at it, using whatever aids
they can find. Vacations without children, sharing fantasies
and open communication are reliable ways to rejuvenate a
marriage. Equally valuable is the sharing of erotic materials. It would be tragic if this loving opportunity were
denied them.

Dr. June Reinisch, director of the Kinsey Institute, frequently gets letters like this: "My wife and I belong to the
church, have three children and do everything right. But
once a week we like to spice up our private lives with an
erotic video. Why are people trying to take them away from
us?" I hear similar things all the time from clients and others who talk to me about sex.

Many people in traditional marriages have turned to erotic films, books and magazines to enhance their sex lives.
These people recognize that it is no easy matter to keep
ennui at bay over a long period. Before turning to erotica,
these spouses made love infrequently, found it either boring
or unexciting and realized that much of their sexual desire
was directed at people other than their partner. But they did
not want to have affairs. Rather they preferred to rekindle
passion for their own spouse.

Such couples often report that watching an erotic film,

usually on a VCR in their own bedrooms, or reading sexual letters and articles in magazines like *Penthouse* or *Playboy*, leads to more frequent and more intense sex.

Obviously, erotic materials are not for everybody. Some people are turned off by them rather than on. I simply want to emphasize the popularity of erotica among many traditional couples.

Other benefits of pornography include learning specific sexual techniques and getting ideas about how and where to have sex with their partners.

Exposure to sexually explicit materials also leads to more open communication about sex. "I've always wanted to try that," or "Have you ever fantasized anything like this?" are common reactions to viewing pornography. Such honest conversations usually lead to increased closeness and better sex. I have found that exposure to erotica is one of the best ways to improve sexual communication between a man and a woman. Even if a person's initial reaction is "I could never imagine doing that," a useful dialogue often results. It's a scientifically proven fact that talking about sex plays an important part in a good sex life.

Most of what I have learned about the benefits of erotica comes from middle-aged churchgoers who believe strongly in monogamy and family. Some acknowledge that they would be tempted to have affairs if they failed to put some zest into their marital sex. Contrary to what the critics of erotica maintain, these people are using pornography to strengthen their marriages. But all the negative publicity about pornography causes them to be apologetic or embarrassed about discussing it. Even though they know its value in their own lives, they still feel that perhaps it indicates a defect in their personalities or in their love for one another.

Therapists who work with couples' sex problems are also familiar with the benefits of erotica. It's probable that more than half of all sex therapists recommend explicit sexual materials to their clients. A fair amount of research indicates that exposure to sexual materials increases both a couple's tolerance of the sexual behavior of others and desire for one another.

Many people in the media have a strange attitude toward pornography. A television executive planning a documentary on the subject became upset when I mentioned how married couples use it to enhance their sex lives. "You don't have to say any more about that," she said. "I get it from my married friends all the time.

"A few weeks ago I visited a couple in their late fifties, good friends of mine for many years, and they started in on this. They even showed me their collection of films, books and pictures. They claim it has done great things for them, but I think it's disgusting. I don't want a man to want me because he got turned on by somebody else on the VCR. I don't want him thinking about her when he's having sex with me. I want him to think only of me."

I replied that the kind of purity she desired is hard to come by in couples who have been together more than two months. Her response: "I know, but that means the relationship is over."

It's frightening to me that someone with such a rigid and unrealistic point of view should be in charge of making documentaries on the subject of erotica.

Maybe this executive's attitude explains why the media gives its attention primarily to pornography's alleged negative effects. I have yet to hear any media discussion of the positive and marriage-affirming benefits described above.

Personally I find the vast bulk of erotica to be poorly presented and boring. But I cannot deny the rewards it has brought to many American couples. It is sad to think that this gift may be taken away.

Dr. Bernie Zilbergeld is a psychologist and the author of Male Sexuality

DR. LARRY BARON AND
DR. MURRAY A. STRAUS

Two False Principles

In 1970 the President's Commission on Obscenity and Pornography concluded that there was no evidence demonstrating that sexually explicit materials caused sex crimes. In the intervening years, those who wanted to limit pornography claimed that sex magazines and movies had become increasingly explicit and violent and that new research has invalidated the finding of.the 1970 president's report. On the basis of this assumption, Attorney General Meese mandated his 11-member commission to study a wide variety of pornographic materials, document adverse effects and devise new strategies to curb its proliferation. True to its assignment, the Meese commission concluded that pornography is harmful and urged law-enforcement agencies to crack down on those engaged in the production and sale of obscene materials.

Ironically, the new and more sophisticated research reviewed by the commission makes a causal connection between sexually explicit materials and rape even *less* plausible than it was when the 1970 commission was examining this issue. How then could the Meese commission come to this conclusion? The answer is fairly clear. It is based on two principles.

The first principle is that explicit depiction of sex is offensive and harmful in and of itself. Based on this principle, there is no way of coming to any other conclusion than that pornography should be forbidden. Although the two commissioners (Judith Becker and Ellen Levine) who dissented from the final report lamented that the commission was not granted sufficient time and money with which to properly assess the testimony and reports made available to them, in light of the principle that sexually explicit materials are inherently offensive, more time and money would

351

not have made much of a difference.

The second principle underlying the commission's conclusions and its recommendations to vigorously prosecute those who produce and sell obscene materials is to base conclusions on the "totality of evidence." This is a code phrase which means that the commission gave as much credence to the testimony of fundamentalist preachers, police officers, antipornography zealots and putative victims of pornography as it did to the results of carefully conducted social research. The "totality of evidence" also gave the commission an escape hatch to disregard the warnings and interpretations of researchers whenever they suggested that the findings do not support a causal connection between pornography and rape. In fact, that was the fate of our own research at the hands of the Meese commission.

We found that rape rates are higher in states with a large readership of sexually explicit magazines. That impressed the commissioners. However, they were not impressed by our explanation that this correlation was most likely the result of a common factor which underlies both sex-magazine-readership rates and rape, nor by our recent demonstration that when appropriate statistical controls are introduced, the correlation between sex-magazine-readership rates and rape rates no longer holds.

There are many such "spurious" (i.e., noncausal) correlations. For example, there is a very high correlation between the reading ability of children and their shoe size. but having big feet does not cause children to read better. The underlying factor is the child's age—older children read better and also have bigger feet. If age is statistically controlled, then the correlation between shoe size and reading ability does not hold. Similarly, we pointed out that there are underlying social and demographic factors which cause both high rape rates and high sex-magazine readership. How does the commission report deal with such information? By ignoring our warnings and arguing that: "The absence of evidence should by no means be taken to deny the existence of the causal link." The commission is so bent on showing harmful effects that when the research shows none, they argue that harm simply has not yet been uncovered.

Our view of the totality of the *scientific* evidence is that it shows no causal relationship between pornography and rape. Indeed, Donnerstein's experimental studies show a *reduction* in aggression following exposure to pornography without violent content; and Berle Kutchinsky's recent studies of nations that have removed restrictions on pornography shows either no increase in the rape rate for the years after the legalization of pornography, or a decrease in the rape rate. Of course, there are aggressive and violent people who use sex as a means of expressing aggression, but images of sex do not cause such violence.

The commission probably began its inquiry assuming that the research conducted since the 1970 pornography report would support its belief in the harmfulness of pornography. Instead it was confronted by evidence which shows that the roots of violence are to be found in violence, not in sex, no matter how explicit or "offensive" it may be. The commission ignored or distorted that evidence because, in our opinion, it was more concerned with censoring sexual depictions than with eliminating violence against women.

Dr. Larry Baron is a lecturer of sociology at Yale University. Dr. Murray Straus is a professor of sociology and the chair of the Family Research Laboratory at the University of New Hampshire

JOSEPH H. COOPER

The New McCarthyism

By summer, thousands of food, drug and convenience stores will have stopped selling certain magazines. It's not that these retailers dislike the magazines, or that they were unprofitable, and it's not because these magazines advocated the violent overthrow of our government. These retailers were threatened—blackmailed, in a way—not by gangsters or competitors, but by the United States Department of Justice.

In letters dated February 11, 1986, companies that owned, operated or franchised these stores were advised that the Attorney General's Commission on Pornography has "received [in October of 1985] testimony alleging that your company is involved in the sale or distribution of pornography."

The companies were given "an opportunity to respond to the allegations prior to [the commission's] drafting its final report section on identified distributors" and were to "advise the commission on or before March 3, 1986, if you disagree with the statements enclosed." The letter warned, "Failure to respond will necessarily be accepted as an indication of no objection."

The "relevant testimony" that accompanied these letters was titled "Pornography in the Family Marketplace" but was not signed by anyone or attributed to anyone. The unnamed author was the Reverend Donald E. Wildmon, executive director of the National Federation for Decency. The pornography commission's executive director, attorney Alan E. Sears, attached this "testimony" to his Justice Department letter and had the package and its message delivered at taxpayers' expense.

In effect, convenience-store operators, food and drug-store chains and companies such as CBS, RCA, Coca-Cola and Time, Inc. (with their cable TV, film and videocassette interests) were given less than three weeks to respond to vague yet ominous (given the use of Justice Department stationery) charges about the kind of business they were cultivating and its presumed antisocial effects, and, presumably, criminal consequences.

CBS, RCA, Coca-Cola and Time rebutted the allegations, showing them to be inaccurate and seriously misleading. But any company that failed to refute the condemning testimony to the commission's satisfaction risked being labeled "an identified distributor of pornography."

The Southland Corporation's 7-Eleven chain was a primary target of Wildmon. He testified, "Few people realize that 7-Eleven is perhaps the most important key to successful marketing of pornography in the family marketplace . . . . In my opinion, should 7-Eleven discontinue the sale of porn magazines, both *Playboy* and *Penthouse* would be seriously crippled financially." In April, Southland announced that it would discontinue the sale of *Playboy* and *Penthouse* at its company-operated 7-Eleven stores and would recommend that its U.S. licensees and franchisees do likewise. Some other chains seem inclined to follow this example.

Playboy and *Penthouse* have been judged to be constitutionally protected by a number of federal courts which recognize that not all "pornography" is "obscene," i.e., legally bannable. How could one letter from a porn commission undo all that judicial wisdom?

Sears claims his February porn commission letters and the accompanying "testimony" were intended as alerts, offering companies the right to reply. While the intent may have been honorable, the means and terms of the offer sent another message. Many store owners and franchisees were intimidated and decided that being branded pornographers by the Justice Department would be a stigma too detrimental to suffer. When the attorney general's office speaks, even the purveyors of *Playboy* and *Penthouse* listen,

355

What's next? *Cosmopolitan, Vogue, GQ? Sports Illustrated's* swimsuit issue? Any magazine that runs Calvin Klein or other provocative ads? (Each of these received the porn commission's attention.) What about magazine subscriptions—will the Postal Service be made a part of Wildmon's crusade? And what happened to getting government out of the business of meddling in business? What happened to free enterprise, let alone freedom of expression and freedom of choice?

In the first week of June, the Federal District Court in Washington, D.C., began hearing requests for preliminary injunctions from *Playboy, Penthouse,* the American Booksellers Association, the Council for Periodical Distributors and the Magazine Publishers Association, which had filed lawsuits against the attorney general and his commission, claiming harassment, intimidation, coercion, suppression and censorship.

It shouldn't take a lawsuit for the attorney general to concede that it is most unbecoming for a commission working under the auspices of the Justice Department to abet a self-righteous, church-related lobby in promoting what amounts to blacklisting—and to do so with a blatantly biased bill of particulars that shows so little regard for the Bill of Rights. Misfeasance, like pornography, is hard to define, but you know it when you see it. And you don't have to be a fan of pornography to be a foe of this kind of obscenity.

Joseph H. Cooper is the editorial counsel for the New Yorker

KAREN DeCROW

The Trend Toward Thought Control

The Ohio Periodical Distributors Association has retained me to work on a campaign as American as Mom and apple pie. I am in Cleveland to deal with the Lawson Milk Company and free speech.

There are strange bedfellows indeed on the "other side." Anthony M. Pilla, leader of the Cleveland Roman Catholic diocese, has joined the largely fundamentalist crusade, the Coalition for Decency, which urged a boycott of Lawson convenience stores until so-called pornographic magazines were removed from the shelves.

Lawson's has removed *Penthouse* and *Playboy*, and since May 21 has been conducting a vote among its customers. Buy a carton of milk and vote on whether the magazines should be returned to the shelves or kept out.

Unlike the U.S. Supreme Court, the Coalition for Decency has no trouble defining "pornographic." Says TV evangelist Jimmy Swaggart: "Anything that causes sexual arousal is pornographic."

The Distributors Association is worried about just that. The officers escort me through the enormous plant: literally thousands of titles, magazines and paperback books, are received here, packaged and sent out to retailers throughout the region. *Cosmopolitan* is a big seller in the Middle West. They show me the current issue. It is filled with sex, cover to cover. They show me *Ms.* It contains articles about sex. The same for today's shipment of *TV Guide* and *People* and *Reader's Digest*.

During a television debate I am told that a six-year-old girl allegedly testified that her father had sex with her and that he reads *Playboy*. I ask about the number of fathers who read *Playboy* and do not have sex with their daughters.

We break for a live commercial. An attractive young

blond woman is advertising pillows and mattresses. We wonder whether, in the post-Meese commission era, the commercial will be censored.

Bishop Pilla mailed a letter to the 253 parishes in the Cleveland Catholic Diocese asking the nearly 1,000,000 Catholics to go to Lawson's and vote to keep out the magazines. "We are confident that, with your full participation, we can make it possible for Lawson's to raise the level of decency in its store so that our community can once again feel comfortable shopping there."

Lawson's has almost 1000 stores and sells a large volume of bread, milk, cold cuts and magazines. Since the Coalition for Decency of the Northeastern Ohio Roundtable requested removal of the magazines last year, Gray Drug, Inc., with headquarters in Cleveland, has discontinued their sale in 443 stores, and Revco, based in Ohio, discontinued sale of the magazines in its 2010 discount drugstores nationwide.

On a radio call-in program, the host is, like me, a First Amendment junkie. He tells the audience to go out to buy a copy of *Penthouse* or *Playboy*—to preserve America. One caller says he sends his children to a Christian school but that he likes to watch "Three's Company." Do we think that is obscene, he asks?

The Meese commission—its mandate, its organization, its procedures and its report—represents an all-out war on free speech and expression and should be abhorred by every literate American. It was designed to create a climate hospitable to government repression of ideas.

Those invited to testify were carefully selected so that the vast majority of the testimony would emerge in favor of censorship. Even using "mushy" science, or no science at all, the commission could find no link between sexually explicit materials and crime—so it invented one.

Should we make federal policy based upon the testimony of such "victims" of pornography as a man who blames his compulsive bestiality and urinary-tract infections on his childhood perusal of pornographic playing cards? Can our national attitude toward free speech be formulated by a commissioner who suggests: "Why not teach kids that sex is bad?"

Should we laugh or should we cry at the behavior of a so-called civil-rights attorney, a mentor of the commission, who, during one of her speeches, responded to a lesbian in the audience who said she enjoys pornography: "If pornography is part of your sexuality, then you have no right to your sexuality"? Do we wish to dignify the fascist views of those who want to "clean out" the art museums, by removing among others, Titian, Cranach, Manet, Balthus, Igres and Courbet?

The Justice Department, which cares so little for the rights of women, has created a paternalistic commission (it must be noted that the two dissenters from the commission report are both female) to save women from sex.

The "intellectual" on the commission, Professor Frederick Schauer, wanted to show a crime connection in his "Harms" chapter: "The absence of evidence should by no means be taken to deny the existence of the causal link." Schauer, attempting to sound philosophic, includes allusions to John Stuart Mill and H.L.A. Hart in his chapter. But he cannot cover over puerile ideas.

"With respect to claims that some sexually explicit material causes promiscuity, encourages homosexuality, or legitimizes sexual practices other than vaginal intercourse, there is serious societal debate about whether the consequences themselves are harmful," he writes.

Dr. Judith Becker and Ellen Levine, in an emphatic 20-page dissent, charge that the commission failed to make its case and manipulated the evidence to fit the conclusion it was seeking. Who is to draw the line between art and pornography? Do we want the job done by the federal government? Do we want the job done by Diane Cusack, a commission member, who is a longtime foe of sex education? Cusack writes: "These materials, whose message is clearly that sexual pleasure and self-gratification are paramount, have the ability to seriously undermine our social fabric."

The most important independence-and-freedom event of early July may not be the celebration at the Statue of Liberty. The Meese commission is releasing its final report the first week of July.

The *New York Times* is filled with bra ads. One hopes that they don't have an arousing effect on Jimmy Swaggart.

I also wonder about all those sports events. Good-looking men in tight clothing, hugging, bending over, passing the ball . . . .

Today the government censors sex. Tomorrow it may well be football.

Karen DeCrow is an attorney and the coauthor of Women Who Marry Houses

DR. ROBERT STAPLES

The Black Response

As the black member of the "shadow commission," I am indebted to the opponents of sexual fascism for giving me a chance to express the black view on pornography—an opportunity denied by the government-formed commission. Although we represent 35 million American citizens or one in nine inhabitants of this country, the attorney general did not see fit to include one of us among his carefully selected commission. This is hardly surprising considering that Ed Meese is a known adversary of the black community. Perhaps he thought blacks were too perverse to ever agree that porn debased women, destroyed the family and caused violent rapes and sexual promiscuity. More likely he realized that it would be difficult to find a black representative of his/her community who viewed porn as a major issue. In one sense, we were relieved that Meese's attention was diverted from restoring us to our nineteenth-century status and that instead he had decided to concentrate on regulating what all Americans can do in the privacy of their own homes. To that extent, he has become an equal-opportunity enforcer of the denial of human rights to all members of this society.

Most blacks would agree with Dr. Morris Lipton, one of the experts on the 1970 presidential report on pornography, that "given the major issues of the day, pornography is a trivial issue." Blacks would add to that analysis the caveat that porn is a white man's problem—a particular kind of white man's problem. The presidential commission Dr. Lipton served on found that the typical consumer of porn was a white male and that blacks were underrepresented among the purveyors of erotica. However, blacks were not total abstainers from porn consumerism. Nor did they harbor any particular antipathy toward it. Indeed, many today do buy sex videocassettes, purchase *Penthouse* and enjoy risqué jokes, cartoons, etc. But as a group that earns only 56 percent of the income whites do, they often do not have the discretionary income with which to purchase erotica.

As for the black position on porn, it would certainly differ from that arrived at by the Meese commission. Meese and his minions reflect a particular white worldview that there is something inherently damaging and sinful about sexual activity and interest outside the marital bedroom, and that any participation in other kinds of sexual behavior should produce enormous amounts of guilt in the errant individual. Blacks have traditionally had a more naturalistic attitude toward human sexuality, seeing it as the normal expression of sexual attraction between men and women. Even in African societies, sexual conduct was not the result of some divine guidance by God or other deities. It was secularly regulated and encompassed the tolerance of a wide range of sexual attitudes and behaviors. Sexual deviance, where so defined, was not an act against God's will but a violation of community standards.

Rather than seeing the depiction of heterosexual intercourse or nudity as an inherent debasement of women, as a fringe group of feminists claims, the black community would see women as having equal rights to the enjoyment of sexual stimuli. It is nothing more than a continuation of the white male's traditional double standard and paternalism to regard erotica as existing only for male pleasure and women only as sexual objects. Since that double standard has never attracted many American blacks, the claim that women are exploited by exhibiting their nude bodies or engaging in heterosexual intercourse lacks credibility. After all, it was the white missionaries in fourteenth century Africa who forced African women to regard their quasi-nude bodies as sinful and placed them in clothes. This probably accounts for the rather conspicuous absence of black women in the feminist fight against porn. Certainly black men were unlikely to join with the likes of lunatic feminists such as

Catharine MacKinnon and Andrea Dworkin, who treat pornography as discrimination against women. They belong to the same genre of feminists as Susan Brownmiller, whose book *Against Our Will* implied that black men deserve some kind of punishment for even thinking about the sexual possession of white women. She even suggests that Emmett Till, the murdered victim of white men in Mississippi, was engaging in more than innocent flirtation when he whistled at a white woman. In her view, lust in a male's heart translates into the mental rape of women.

The black community represents organic evidence against some of the assumptions of the Meese commission on pornography. If porn is alleged to lead to male sexual aggression, that is, rape, why are the lowest consumers of porn (blacks) so overrepresented among those arrested for and convicted of rape? A porn commission without a political axe to grind might have concluded that when other expressions of manhood such as gainful employment and economic success are blocked, those men will express their frustration and masculinity against women. In other words, it is the denial of economic rights, not porn, that is in large part responsible for rape in this country. Such a conclusion would not go down well with the Reagan administration, whose policies have led to the burgeoning number of unemployed black males.

As for the Meese commission view that porn is related to sexual promiscuity, it is almost a laughable finding in the black community. One man's sexual promiscuity is another man's definition of sexual freedom. In most cases it refers to keeping women in their sexual straitjackets so that sexual pleasure remains a male domain. The black community has exhibited a lusty sexual appetite while obeying certain rules of common sense and propriety in its sexual conduct. The kinds of kinky sex favored by a small minority of whites is almost unknown among the black population. Group sex, and sexual crimes other than rape, were and are rare among us. And a recent survey commissioned by the National Institutes of Health found that sexually active black women were more likely to be involved in long-term "serious" relationships than were sexually active white women, and that their serious relationships lasted longer than the relationships of white women.

Still, it is one of the ironies of American life that the one racial group in the U.S. whose image is so strongly linked to sexuality in the public mind should be excluded from a commission dealing with the sexual aspects of human behavior. Ranging from the thousands of lynchings of black men for the dubious sin of lusting after white women to the segregation of races in the South to prevent interracial sexual contact, we now have the more recent variation on the theme of black immorality.

While there may be cause for concern over the high rate of out-of-wedlock births occurring among black women in their teenage years, the Meese commission refused to endorse the best weapon against teenage pregnancy—sex education. The same National Institutes of Health survey discovered that twice as many single black women as white women are having sex through their 20s without contraceptives. Nationally, a majority of all out-of-wedlock births occur among black women. Ultimately, blacks suffer more and are the chief victims of white sexual guilt. They are denied sex education in the public schools because a white-controlled bureaucracy either denies it to the school system or forces it to contain a largely moral content. However, in those few public schools that have decided to provide contraceptive services to their students, only schools with a predominantly black student body have chosen to do so. Using black high-school students as the first guinea pigs in these experiments is akin to the same kind of white colonialism that tested birth-control products on Puerto Rican women to see if they would be safe for white women.

Teenage pregnancy is a problem in the black community

because the unwed mothers keep their children and many become dependent on public assistance. The N.I.H. survey found that half of the white women surveyed and only one-tenth of the black women aborted their first pregnancies. Young black women seldom resort to shotgun weddings, because their pool of potential husbands largely consists of young and unemployed black males. Were they to be provided a sound sex education or safe contraceptives, many would never face this dilemma.

The kinds of morals that Ed Meese and Ronald Reagan understand are related to nineteenth-century notions of sin. Blacks would prefer to see their morality expressed in the provision of jobs for the unemployed, shelter for the homeless and food for the hungry.

Finally, a most important reason why pornography is not a burning issue in the black community is that the morals of Ronald Reagan, Ed Meese and Jerry Falwell are not the morals of the kinds of people with which blacks desire to be associated. Their past record is one of supporting racial segregation and black deprivation. Therefore blacks can only hope they will cease to interfere with the private lives of American citizens and adopt a real moral posture toward the conditions of poverty, nuclear disarmament and the conduct of government. Permitting poverty to exist and escalating the nuclear-arms race are the real sins and major issues of today.

Dr. Robert Staples is professor of sociology at the University of California, San Francisco

EPILOGUE

Dr. Park Dietz was too fair and too smart to applaud the rickety science shoring up the Meese report. And so he quipped in his personal statement that the Founding Fathers managed to muddle through the constitutional convention without a cadre of professors to advise them.

"When the First Congress proposed the first amendment in 1789 and when it was ratified by the states in 1791 and made a part of the Constitution, the empirical social sciences had not yet been conceived," he retorted to those who valued facts over feelings.

Dr. Dietz implied that Jefferson and his friends would have found compatible company in the majority of the Meese commissioners, who, after all, acted with enlightened common sense.

For example, a prominent male member of that majority, a man who dearly sympathized with women, gave some gallant counsel to a perplexed female commissioner. The scene occurred in the corridor of a federal courthouse somewhere along the trail. The two panelists had just emerged from the screening of a very bloody sex film, and the woman wondered out loud how men could be aroused by such awfulness.

The male commissioner had an answer. He said that men would lose interest in violent pornography "if women learned how to give better blowjobs."

Sounds Jeffersonian to us.

ACKNOWLEDGMENTS

This book is a collaboration. We are indebted to many colleagues and friends: Jack Heidenry, our sainted co-worker at *Forum* who engineered the project almost from the beginning; Gwenhwyfar Gowen, associate editor of *Forum,* who only asked for time to run (that's all we gave her); Mary Heidenry, who lit up our labors with her splendid college try; Bettina Moss for moonlighting in our zone; and our former editorial and traveling companion, Dawn Stover, who helped in the preparation of portions of this book.

We are grateful to *Forum*'s Managing Editor Penelope Weiss and Assistant Managing Editor Kiki Grossman for treating our manuscript with monkish care. Thanks to *Penthouse* Senior Vice President and Graphics Director Frank DeVino for his creative assistance, and to Art Director John Arocho for making the text look good.

Special appreciation is extended to *Penthouse*'s Vice President and Director of Newsstand Circulation Marcia Orovitz; Circulation Marketing Manager Maureen Sharkey; Production Director Hal Halpner; Vice President, Director of Public Relations Leslie Jay; and Senior Publicist Deborah L. Bronstein. *Penthouse* attorney Laurence Sutter's legal counsel was learned and wise.

We also render homage to attorney Steven Berko of Grutman Miller Greenspoon & Hendler.

David Myerson, Chief Operating Officer of Penthouse International, encouraged the book from its inception.

Our research was aided immensely by the expertise of Dr. C.A. Tripp and Larry Jones.

Although the boys on the press bus were few, we enjoyed our dealings with Robert Scheer of the *Los Angeles Times;* Patrick Owens of *Newsday;* Carol Vance of F.A.C.T.; syndicated columnist Michael McManus; Lisa Duggan of the *Village Voice;* and Barry Lynn of the ACLU, our kind of sex educator.

We also thank *Penthouse* Executive Editor Peter Bloch and former Managing Editor Claudia Valentino for extreme grace under extreme deadline pressure. We profited greatly from suggestions made by *Penthouse* Managing Editor Robert Sabat.

And finally, we thank Bob Guccione.

Philip Nobile, editorial director of *Forum,* was born in Cambridge, Massachusetts. He studied for the Catholic priesthood and has graduate degrees from Boston University and the Higher Institute of Philosophy at Louvain, Belgium. He is the author of *Intellectual Skywriting* and a former contributing editor of *Esquire* and *New York.* Still married to his college sweetheart, he lives in Scarsdale, N.Y., with teenage daughters Megan, Caitlin and Maeve and a golden retriever named Governor. Mr. Nobile placed 12,655 in the 1985 New York City marathon.

Eric Nadler, a senior editor of *Forum,* is a journalist whose work has appeared in many national publications, including *Harper's, The Nation* and *Mother Jones.* He lives in New York with his wife Elisa Rivlin and their daughter Emily Claire.

PLACE
STAMP
HERE

THE PRESIDENT
C/O PERIODICAL AND
BOOK ASSOCIATION OF AMERICA
P.O. BOX 2018
J.A.F. STATION
NEW YORK, NY 10116

STAND UP
FOR YOUR RIGHTS!

FILL IN THE ATTACHED CARD AND SEND IT IN, TODAY!

Dear Mr. President:

As a loyal and patriotic American, I am frightened by the growing threat to my First Amendment rights. Self-appointed censors are creating a climate of fear and repression across the country. Taking their lead from the Attorney General's Commission on Pornography, moral vigilantes are harassing local libraries, schools and the owners of bookstores and other retail stores. Mr. President, I urge you to publicly renounce those in and out of government who are threatening our precious freedoms.

Sincerely,

_____

NAME

_____

ADDRESS

_____

CITY, STATE, ZIP